The Modern Employment Function

DONALD H. SWEET *Celanese Corporation, New York, New York*

ADDISON-WESLEY PUBLISHING COMPANY
Reading, Massachusetts · Menlo Park, California
London · Amsterdam · Don Mills, Ontario · Sydney

 Printed in the United States of America. Published simultaneously in Canada. Library of Congress Catalog Card No. 73-33.

ISBN 0-201-07388-9
BCDEFGHIJK-MA-79876

Preface

This book is about the employment of professional people and the practical ways to accomplish it more efficiently and economically. Because of the tremendous demand for technological and managerial skills, the professional employment function has become more and more critical to many organizations over the past decade. However, this critical function has not matured as the problems of business have become more complex. Most organizations would never allow as costly a decision as hiring a new professional to be made haphazardly, as it is in so many cases, if they were really aware of the risks in terms of dollars. The direct costs of interview expenses, employment fees, relocation, etc., are compounded if the new employee fails to perform as anticipated. In addition, a series of other factors has impacted on the employment process in recent years: antidiscrimination legislation, technological change, and the changing attitudes and motivation of the work force. All of these things require that organizations become more adept at all phases of human relations, particularly their employment practices.

The ten chapters that follow do not attempt to answer all the questions that could be raised by organizations of various sizes. Hopefully, however, this book will provide the employment function with a point of departure and a greater understanding of the responsibilities of everyone involved in any employment process. A primary aim of the book is to suggest approaches and concepts that will increase the chances of success for any employment function, whether it be a full-fledged corporate employment department or one responsibility in the spectrum of an individual personnel manager. These concepts should also be applicable to line managers, who by this definition include all those people with employment responsibilities outside of the personnel function. Finally, this book should be of value to any student of the subject who wants an overview of the total employment process.

Innumerable books have been written on the general subject of employment, but many times they either speak to only one facet of the total process or deal extensively with what has happened in the past. This book is a practical discourse that attempts to explain ways to make employment a more successful process by elaborating on the point that the key to an organization's success is how well it goes about attracting the right people. If the organization is successful in this effort, it will be more likely to be able to retain the people it wants and to move out those it doesn't.

After having spent some 20 years in the employment function, it would be an impossible task for me to indicate all of the sources on which I have drawn. I am indebted to those individuals and organizations that allowed me to quote or refer to their material. A particular debt of gratitude is owed to Messrs. Edmond J. Corry, Corry-Howe Assoc.; William Gallagher, ICI America; Douglas Sheeran, Celanese Corporation; John Williams, Hublein Inc.; Glen Smyth, General Electric Co.; Richard Clarke, Richard Clarke Assoc.; and Benjamin Sands, Celanese Corporation, all of whom provided a particular critical expertise. A special note of appreciation to my employer, the Celanese Corporation, for their support through the long months of writing and to my secretary, Ms. Dorothy Barker, who contributed much of her own time. In the final analysis, this book has to be dedicated to my wife, Mary, and to my three daughters, who suffered in silence through many, long, nonattentive months.

New York, New York D.H.S.
May 1973

Contents

Introduction

As business has become more and more complex in our technological society, the complexity of people problems has magnified. The professional technical employment function (recruitment, selection, placement), as well as all of the functions in the personnel spectrum, have assumed an increasingly important role in the operations of most organizations. However, the employment process, which is quite costly and generally inefficient, has not kept pace with technological development and the increasing mobility and flexibility of the professional/technical work force. This mobility and flexibility encompasses both geography and career, and it will become more and more of a factor in the coming decades. Unfortunately, to add to the complexity, most companies are generally less innovative in their employment practices than in their other personnel practices. These factors, when compounded by a real need for manpower, can make the employment function an extremely critical part of the success or failure in the achieving of an organization's objectives. Companies can no longer afford to allow the employment function to be only the finder of people; rather, they must ensure that it provides the expertise to select and match the skills of those selected to the organization's needs and to be the motivating force in staying alert to all of the factors in government and in our rapidly changing economy that affect the work force.

Few managers would argue about the importance of getting the best man for the job, yet hiring decisions are often made with so little understanding and thought that if other business decisions were made in the same manner, many managers would be fired for incompetence. The hiring of professional/technical employees has always been an extremely costly process, not only in terms of direct costs, but even more so in terms of the total investment in the employee until he starts paying his way. Cost-per-hire figures rarely include anything but obvious expenditures, and yet they may be the minor costs in the final analysis. The problem of cost will continue to intensify as competition becomes greater for the outstanding man. Now is the time, therefore, for companies to take stock of their present employment techniques and procedures. Inefficiencies are costly today—they may be disastrous tomorrow.

Like other functions in an organization, employment is a full-fledged management function that transcends all aspects of a business. As with all parts of a business, there is an increasing pressure to find more efficient and economical ways to get the job done. The fact that employment is a risky business, primarily because you buy something before you *really* know how well it will work, requires that the organization's best thinking and analysis be brought to bear on this problem. Employment cannot be looked at as simply a "Personnel Department" problem, but rather as one that requires the utmost in cooperation and communication throughout the organization. There is a need for an increased understanding by line management as to what their role is in the employment process. It is their job to assess the candidate's specific capabilities for doing the job and making *the* hiring decision. Unfortunately, management in most organizations has yet to think of employment as other than a temporary function. It is not an isolated activity; it impacts on productivity, turnover, future growth, etc. Yet so many times the responsibility and accountability for the employment function are too far down the line to be effective. There are new things going on in employment, and with better understanding and continuing acceptance of new ideas and approaches, the efficiencies and economies that can result will be hard to believe. As is true for so many other business problems, these economies result from common sense and proper planning.

When you begin to really consider the foregoing points and realize that so many variables are at work in our society today that will affect our ways of doing business and that business will be conducted under different rules and circumstances than most of us have known in the past, it becomes obvious that there will be unique and challenging problems facing us in professional/technical employment. Organization as we know it will change; jobs will become more meaningful and will change to accommodate the person; the planning cycle—particularly manpower planning—will shorten; corporate citizenship will become a reality; and equal employment opportunity will become a fact, not just because of government pressure, but because it makes both economic and moral sense. All of this will put increased pressure on the employment function, because quality of hires will really become more important than quantity, and credentials for *doing* the job will really become more important than credentials for *getting* the job. These changes will result from a new awareness of people and their needs, motivations, and desires.

There are five factors that will have a tremendous impact on employment in the next decade or so:

1. technology
2. antidiscrimination legislation
3. the age of the work force
4. minority groups
5. women.[1]

These points, alone, will begin to bring into perspective the dramatic need for changed approaches to the employment process that will be necessary to compete effectively for one's share of the labor market. According to United States government sources, there will be a 36% growth in white-collar jobs between now and 1980, and this makes it further apparent that the time for lip service is past. Despite the high unemployment of the first two years of the 1970s, the rest of this decade will be characterized by fewer entry-level professional/technical candidates, a smaller 35-45 age group, and increased competition from government and other nonbusiness organizations. This difficult employment climate suggests that we will not be able to continue to approach employment problems in the classical way. We can no longer let recruiting be turned on and off like a faucet; companies with continuity to their employment programs and which maintain meaningful relationships with academia and other sources will be way ahead in the manpower race.

Management must both support the development of long-range programs and ensure that new techniques and procedures are developed

---

[1]Speech by Dr. Seymour L. Wolfbein, Dean, School of Business, Temple University, at WCPA Conference, Portland, Oregon, 1970.

and implemented. They must see that "incompetence" is eliminated from the employment function if they are to meet their goals and objectives.

This book has been written to provide some practical understanding of the various aspects of the employment process as it relates to professional/technical people in both domestic and international operations. The principles of employment as outlined are applicable to international organizations because in reality, there is not that much difference in getting the job done, but there is a lack of understanding and historical bias that will be discussed. This book cannot answer all the questions about employment, because the whole subject is too complex and individualized. Minimizing philosophy and theoretical approaches, the book focuses on how to get the job done more efficiently and economically. There are practical explanations of the steps involved in getting the individual on the payroll and the tools needed in making your employment function and your organization more successful. The text will prove to be of value not only for the "employment specialist," but also for anyone involved in the employment process—from the corporate director of employment to the plant interviewer, from the line executive to the supervisor in a plant, or to anyone who shares in the responsibility and wonders how best to handle it. By understanding the long-range implications of this material, you will be able to organize or modify and adapt your employment function in a more efficient and economical way. As a result, you will be able to get the job done better than your competition.

1
The changing work force

It seems appropriate to devote the first chapter of a book on the modern employment function to a discussion of the "changing professional/technical work force." The 1970s have brought industry face to face with some new and very basic problems that will have tremendous effect on employment: first, technology, which has developed so dramatically in the years since World War II; second, and possibly the foremost development affecting employment, is the requirement to avoid discrimination; third, the rapidly changing average age of the population, which will bring many new concepts into the business world and will upset many classical ones; fourth, the reality of minority employment; and fifth, the emergence of the female professional in a significant way on the business scene.

Before we look at each of those five factors that are changing the professional/technical work force in a multitude of ways, let us make a basic assumption: the impact of "white-collar unemployment," which has affected the overall economic condition of the country and the thinking and motivation of many people to a degree not seen since the depression of the 1930s, has been positive in a way which, although not immediately apparent, will become more so as this decade progresses. White-collar unemployment has made organizations *think about their people* in a different way and with a great deal more emphasis on human relations. Add to this the fact that many manpower and economic experts predict a manpower shortage in the 1970s. For example, the Department of Labor has projected a 40% rise in the United States' need for engineering graduates through 1980. Yet there are strong indicators on many campuses that engineering enrollments are off by almost the same percentage. The traditional areas of technology will be competing for talent with new growth areas such as environmental and medical engineering, the reversing of urban decay, and the remodeling of transportation systems. If these trends continue, it becomes apparent that the employment function must be a full-fledged member of the management team and that everyone involved in the employment process will have to understand the changes that are taking place if their organization is to compete successfully for its share of manpower.

1.1 TECHNOLOGY

The last 25 years have seen more technological change in the world than in the prior history of man. The mobility and flexibility of the professional/technical work force are in a great sense attributable to this technological revolution, which has created more jobs; has allowed us to increase output per man hour in the United States 100% in 25 years; has upgraded our standard of living; and has developed communication and transportation systems that allow companies to build and control widespread industrial complexes to take advantage of climate, specific market conditions, tax incentives, and more productive labor.

Such mobility and flexibility become key factors in those organizations with international overtones. There is a real need for such organizations to reorient their thinking by having a truly international management team which will thereby remove national boundaries when thinking about people. A good manager in France should be a good manager in Ohio. We are moving into a world-wide manpower market because we are in a shrinking world.

Technology has its impact on every facet of business, and as the business picture changes dramatically, so, too, do the problems of employment. Business is changing because the economics of it are tougher, e.g., there is a new alertness to staffing and staffing costs. The motivation of the professional has changed. He has reordered his priorities, i.e., the job and company do *not* necessarily come first. In *Future Shock*, Alvin Toffler refers to "the modular man who is geographically mobile and quite likely to be occupationally mobile as well. Whether upward, downward or sideways, the future holds more, not less, turnover in jobs."[1] "You move to improve" in terms of not only income, but also professional

[1]Alvin Toffler, *Future Shock*, New York: Random House, p. 113.

growth. This mobility also makes it easy to take advantage of one's increased standard of living and increased leisure time. We all know someone who relocated to Florida so he could sail and fish all year long. This is not a brand new phenomenon, but more and more organizations will find that the individual will consider his own needs over and above theirs.

"Technological companies are at the center of social change and therefore have a social responsibility." This comment by Joseph Wilson, the late chairman of the Xerox Corporation, is in itself revolutionary in terms of corporate philosophy. Technology is bringing about an awareness of corporate responsibility, particularly toward the community and the environment. However, technology is way ahead of our understanding of human relations, and we will indeed need to reorder some of our priorities. Within that context, technological change will pose a number of specific problems for the employment process.

1. Not only will you have to hire the best people to stay technologically competitive, but you will also have to update them on new technology.
2. There will be an increased need to rethink "campus recruiting" programs to ensure more relevancy to our schools and to avoid further isolation of academia by thinking more in terms of "university relations" and all that that implies (see Chapter 6).
3. Job specifications will have to become realistic to allow for the fullest utilization of the work force, e.g., movement across functional and industry lines based on skills to do jobs.
4. Employment will have to be a process that *includes all* potential workers rather than *excluding some* based on historical generalizations.

1.2 DISCRIMINATION

Legislation directed toward eliminating discrimination in employment will really have its impact in the 1970s not only because of government pressure, but also because of downright necessity in terms of manpower needs. Specifically, we are talking about laws and executive orders that directly affect employment (see Chapter 5 also). Title VII of the Civil Rights Act of 1964, for example, which prohibits discrimination based on race, color, religion, sex, and national origin is the key legislative act in this area. A second is the Age Discrimination in Employment Act of 1967, which prohibits discrimination in employment of persons 40-65 years of age. Third, presidential executive orders, e.g., Executive Order 11246—Affirmative Action Programs, prohibit all government contractors or subcontractors from discriminating on the basis of race, color, religion, sex, age, or national origin. There are also more specific orders, such as Executive Order 11598—Listing of Job Vacancies with the Federal-State Employment Service System, which speak to a more immediate problem, the hiring of Vietnam-era veterans. We also have the equal pay for equal work statute, which requires that women be paid the same as men for comparable work. Additionally, the Fair Credit Reporting Act affects the utilization of information gathered during reference checks.

These and other legislation, both pending and proposed, pose many new and unique problems for the employment function, not the least of which are record keeping and reporting. These concerns will involve more and more of management's time and will force them to rethink many of the classical concepts (or misconceptions) of employment, e.g., you can't hire black salesmen because of the customer reaction; women are too emotional and can't make decisions, so they can't manage; you don't hire anyone over 50 because benefits cost too much; *ad-infinitum*. If you condone any practices like these, you had best examine your employment practices now, because the legislation pending before Congress will expand the role of the government. Several landmark cases have already been decided by the Supreme Court, e.g., *Phillips* v. *Martin Marietta Company*. Mrs. Ida Phillips, a mother of seven, was working as a waitress when she responded to an ad for assembly jobs at the local Martin-Marietta plant. When she applied, she was told she could not be considered because she had a child of preschool age, and she was rejected on that basis—the assumption being that as a woman, her primary responsibility was to her preschool-age child. She filed a complaint with the Equal Employment Opportunity Commission (EEOC), which ruled in her favor, and she finally won her case. Federal, state, and local agencies are becoming more active in declaring unlawful such employment practices as: establishing different retirement ages for men and women; hiring through existing employee referrals; disqualifying women on the basis of child-care responsibilities; requiring women to take maternity leave after a specified month of pregnancy; using general-aptitude tests as a condition of employment; stipulating that for their "protection," women may not lift anything over 30 pounds.

Most organizations have varying degrees of knowledge about equal employment opportunity (EEO) legislation. However, enforcement is complex and will become more so because federal, state, and local legislation is increasing. For the federal government, for example, organizations need to have specific knowledge of Title VII, Equal Pay Act, Age Discrimination Act, plus a knowledge of the Equal Employment Opportunity Commission, Office of Federal Contract Compliance, and the United States Department of Labor. Having a cursory knowledge is not enough when dealing with such a complex and subtle set of problems. You must develop within your organization the specific guidelines that will allow you to comply with these rules and regulations in the most meaningful way. This legislation obviously now has, and will continue to have, tremendous impact in terms of several other important ingredients that make up this "changing work force," namely, age, minority employment, and women. So let's move on to each of them.

1.3 AGE OF THE WORK FORCE

The major factor in the changing age of the work force is the downward trend of average age. We have always had young people in the work force, but never to the degree that will occur in this decade. A majority of people in this country at a point in the 1970s will be under 30 years of age (in 1970, one out of every three people wasn't even born in 1955), and this trend is going to have great impact on business in general and the employment function in particular. The critical impact will be on attitude and values. The young of today are, on the average, better educated, are more independent, and take affluence for granted. Even though they will join business and industry, they generally view it as the "Establishment" and consequently something that they cannot readily relate with. They have formed some generalizations: your personality may be more important than your ability to do the job; your color or religion may be more important than your performance; how you dress or wear your hair is more important than how creative you are. These young people put more emphasis on the quality of life and tend to feel that priorities are out of line, e.g., we can land men on the moon, but we can't breathe the air or drink the water. Rightly or wrongly, they generally think of business as having exhibited little social conscience over the years and having had only one motive—profit. What all this means to us is that we, at least, have to try to understand what they feel. They will be running things in a few years, and their values and motivations are different from ours. They are impatient and want "real" jobs. They are brighter and more mature. They are dissatisfied and nonconforming and will tend to shy away from some of the classical professions, such as engineering.

To really understand "them," let us consider some of their thinking. They have different attitudes and motivations and will not accept the status quo, i.e., this is the way it's done because it's the way it's always been done. They want jobs to be enjoyable and not dull ("If you put the thought into making jobs meaningful, you wouldn't be concerned about making them more attractive with four-day weeks"). They don't want the type of work life "we" have. Roy H. Walters, a management consultant in job enrichment and related fields, has said that "youth these days will never lead the working lives my generation did. They are going to consider what management allows them to do in terms of more challenging work—rather than the plaint of our fathers' generation: 'what they did to me today!' ... which leads youth to say of their fathers, 'I don't know what he does for a living, but I don't want any part of it.' "[2] They want new incentives to measure them against more than profits. They want to see true social responsibility in business. They want a chance to implement ideas and assume responsibility. They want jobs to *fit them*. They feel that much of business has become outmoded by changing customs. Industrial psychologists have warned that once people achieve job security and sufficient pay, they will begin to desire self-fulfillment. The puritan work ethic of past generations has been replaced by the three-martini lunch; although a little tongue in cheek, that not unrealistic view by the young is brought about by their boredom on the job. Above all they don't want to be categorized; they want to know the reasons "why." They want to be respected and they want responsibility.

Generally speaking, these are realistic points and will begin to provide individuals the satisfaction of accomplishing something other than sustaining themselves. These are some of the things that organizations must understand if they hope to get the job done; obviously, the young have an obligation to provide solutions as well as to ask questions, and given the opportunity (which they will have because their numbers dictate that they will be running things in a few years), they will be successful.

---

[2]From a speech by Roy H. Walters, President of Roy H. Walters Assoc., at the Employment Management Association meeting in New York City, April 1972.

Daniel Yankelovich, in an article entitled "The Real Meaning of the Student Revolution," talks about a desire for new career rewards; four out of five students believe that a meaningful career is important, but students rank "the opportunity to make a contribution," "job challenge," "the ability to find self-expression," and "free time for outside interests" as the most important influences on their career choices.[3] Probably because of the recent recession, money and security have increased slightly in importance in this past year. But job prestige continues to rank at the very bottom.

There is also a new attitude toward work. Some 69% of all students no longer believe "hard work will pay off." Indeed, a majority do not even regard work as very important, ranking it well behind love, friendship, education, self-expression, family, and privacy in their hierarchy of values. It is worth noting, however, that there is no visible evidence that students intend to avoid hard work. They have simply ceased to believe that hard work is the royal road to success in our society. And they see their attitude toward authority as a major obstacle to obtaining desirable employment. No other obstacle, including political views, dress styles, or unwillingness to conform, even comes close.

The things that need to be done in employment to answer these types of questions are not really too earth-shaking, but they do require genuine understanding and commitment. We have to be honest and straightforward in our interviews. We have to face up to some hard facts, e.g., "everyone" goes to school (50% of college-age young people in the United States go to college); and four out of every ten graduates will have a history of drug use. (How do we handle this last item when most organizations have not yet faced up to the alcohol problem?) We must build a closer alliance with schools. We must communicate better to the schools what we are doing. We need to develop a real sense of social awareness, particularly in middle management, a critical group in the employment process. We have to get over our "hardening of the categories" (all of the generalizations about people who may be of a different race, sex, religion, or color from us). We need to reshape our policies to develop an environment which will allow us to institute these changes and still make a profit five to ten years from now.

---

[3] D. Yankelovich, "The Real Meaning of the Student Revolution," *Conference Board Record*, March 1972, p. 9.

All of the preceding points emphasize that we live in a youth-oriented society, but we must not forget that there are two other age groups that are also factors in this changing work force—older workers (45-65) and middle-age workers (35-45). (This latter category comprises the smallest segment of the work force.) This combination of factors gives us an "hourglass profile" of our manpower picture during the 1970s. Three things will happen: (1) The older workers will become more important if only in terms of part-time and temporary work (which will be a bigger and bigger item in most businesses in terms of both economics and the need for skilled hands); (2) the demand will be greatest for workers 35-45 years old; and (3) both of these points will ensure acceleration of the careers of the young. So there is no time for any organization to waste in understanding the young and their life style.

1.4 MINORITY EMPLOYMENT

The minorities, a broad term that encompasses such things as geography, religion, and race, is here related primarily to the black professional. Legislation is beginning to make minority employment a fact of life, whether organizations are committed to it or not. The emphasis is beginning to shift to providing real jobs rather than mere "window dressing." Window dressing, or showcase, jobs are not acceptable to either compliance agencies or to the black professional, who has also become very pragmatic about himself in relation to business. If he doesn't get "real" work, he will leave. Again, this whole subject becomes an economic issue rather than a moral one. If there is a need for all the talent we can get in the next decade or so, it just doesn't make sense to have employment functions that still exclude certain groups from consideration, particularly in the face of some statistics. According to the Bureau of Labor Statistics, for example, college enrollments of blacks were up more than 20% in the last couple of years, whereas white enrollments rose by only 5.7%. One out of seven new workers in the work force is black. Pure and simple, the cost of discrimination will be too high.

To have any success in developing solutions to this part of the employment problem, we must have some understanding of what the minorities are saying. In addition, we should not overlook the fact that being "on the outside looking in" *has* made them more perceptive about the business world. Therefore, it is doubtful that the phrase "Equal

Opportunity Employer" on your ad will really impress them. They will believe what they see, but they will have to be convinced about what you say. Slick public-relations efforts will turn them off, and until you prove differently, they will believe that you are more interested in strategic deployment than in equal employment, i.e., a black receptionist is great, but we cannot hire a black salesman; if a black applicant is aggressive, you will call him "pushy," but the aggressive white applicant has "drive and pizzazz." They will be more interested in the level and movement of minority group members in your organization than in the number you may have on your payroll. They do not look at your EEO efforts as granting any "special considerations" because you have always said that your organization prides itself on understanding and being responsive to the individual needs and desires of the employees. They want to be judged on their ability to do the job and will expect that unrealistic standards—the cultural or social criteria for getting the job—will be dropped. They will want to know what your "social or corporate responsibility" *is doing.*

To put it in very simple terms, equal employment opportunity will not be a reality until we remove all the barriers so that an individual can exhibit his skills and abilities for what they are. Logic says you can, conscience says you should, and the government will ask why you haven't.

1.5 THE EMERGING FEMALE PROFESSIONAL

Women are going to become a major factor in the work force, and in all probability this will require more attention and effort by the employment function than any of the other points discussed so far. Most of the problems, as is true about the young and the minorities, are based on generalizations. We all have heard and used a lot of them, so there is no point in belaboring them here. To begin this discussion, let's consider a very important fact: women, as opposed to, say, blacks, have not been denied equal education (almost half of our college graduates each year are women), but they have been denied the opportunity to put their education to work. The problems from the women's standpoint are many, but a primary one is that they know that what happens in business is up to men, and men are always in charge, and those in charge rarely give up their power without a struggle. Yet women really want only one basic thing, to be treated on an equal basis to get and do the job.

Women have developed a much greater freedom in the past decade. The pill, for example, has given them more freedom. Many women work out of economic necessity; others work because they want to be more than a career housewife. Women don't buy the argument that men have families to support and they don't—organizations pay people for the value of the work they perform rather than the number of dependents they claim on their income tax. Women take a great offense at such questions as "Do you take the pill?" or "Are you really serious about a career?" United States government studies have disproved some of the generalizations about women. In fact, absenteeism is almost equal between men and women, as is turnover. Like men, women change jobs for one primary reason—boredom. Women know that equal pay for equal work is a myth; United States Department of Commerce statistics show that across the board in offices and factories, women earn $3000 a year less than do men for the same work. Women managers earn 54% of what their male counterparts earn. So we perpetuate the white-only, men-only, syndrome, and as long as it continues it will inspire insecurity and alienation among workers.

There are hard facts to back up this thinking. For example, a survey conducted by the American Society for Personnel Administration and the Bureau of National Affairs showed that:

1. Only 30% of companies that recruit on campus go to predominantly women's schools.

2. Women historically have been directed to certain fields (as blacks have gone to the so-called safe professions), e.g., clerical, teaching, nursing, etc. Women comprise only 7% of all doctors, 2% of all dentists, 3% of all lawyers, and 9% of all scientists.

3. One hundred fifty executives surveyed indicated that less than 5% of their female employees were classified as professional-technical. Eighty-seven percent of those surveyed had 5% or fewer women in management levels above first-line supervisor.

4. The question of why women are paid less emerged as resting on pretty ridiculous logic, i.e., women have not developed the skills to compete; they choose fields that pay less; they seek short-term employment rather than a career-oriented job; they don't have job mobility.

Whether right or wrong, these "facts" tend to be accepted as truths by most businessmen.[4]

All of this has a familiar ring—just ask one of your black employees! Take it one step further, and we find that unless the woman is exceptional and overqualified, the same "exclusion" from the employment process exists for women as it does for blacks. Again, the cost of discrimination is too great to continue.

1.6 GETTING THE JOB DONE

What does this "changing work force" mean in terms of getting the employment job done? Even if you feel your house is in reasonable order, your continued success in dealing with it will be predicated to a great extent on how flexible and realistic your employment process is. This will pose many problems because the employment process is negative—it is a screening-out process. If you continue to begin on the negative side, it is hard to be objective when interviewing long-haired candidates or aggressive women or someone whose color is different from yours. The proof of your ability to cope with the changing work force may be measured by your objectivity in terms of hiring on the basis of skills to *do* the job and not on the basis of the peripheral things to *get* the job.

Most companies, as stated before, pride themselves on being responsive to the individual needs and desires of their employees. This can be accomplished only through understanding, and that is what we need in employment—understanding, which really is a willingness to change one's values, to accept new ways or approaches to getting the job done, and to be responsive to peoples' needs.

Organizations must learn to face up to all of these "changes" and to factor them into the business. Unfortunately, many of these problems are handled today on a crisis basis, and that only causes waste of both time and money. Nothing is really solved until each of these points is approached in a realistic and businesslike way and becomes part of your *modus-operandi*. Accept the fact that things will never be what they once were in the labor market, and adapt to the changes in people and their desires

---

[4]"ASPA—BNA Survey: Employment of Women," *Bulletin to Management*, No. 1047, Part 2, March 5, 1970, pp. 1-8.

as you do to other facets of the business—new markets, technological breakthroughs, etc.

Let's try to be realistic about all people-related problems, at least until we know what impact they may have. Most organizations, for example, have taken a very strong, no-compromise attitude about drugs, but pay very little attention to alcohol, which has been a problem for years. We have to face up to this type of decision. Would you hire a reformed drug user? Would you hire a reformed drinker? Why one and not the other?

1.7 A SUMMARY

All of those who have employment responsibility will face these problems, so let's summarize some specific things that can be done to improve your chances of hiring good people, retaining them, and keeping them up-to-date technologically.

1. Review hiring standards to ensure that your hiring practices cover the complete range of potential job candidates, i.e., ways to *include all* rather than *exclude some*.
2. Ensure further breaking down of national, racial, and educational barriers through total commitment of the organization.
3. Encourage more females to join the work force.
4. Continue to work at restructuring jobs to make them more meaningful. This can have real impact on retaining people within the organization.
5. Ensure more corporate-campus interchange to help prevent further polarization of academia and business.
6. Develop realistic job specifications to help avoid underemployment and exclusion of certain types of people and training.
7. Develop continuity to employment programs and help it avoid being the "reaction" function.
8. Help develop a total environment whereby credentials for *getting* the job become less important than credentials for *doing* the job (where the man can exhibit his skills and abilities for what they are rather than what he is).

Dramatic changes will continue to take place in our society and will be accepted because, as we are learning, long hair, women in slacks, and skin color really don't affect the ability and skills of the person. We cannot continue to discriminate against any minority, against females, against the worker over 50. No new law or slogan will solve this problem, but we, as employers, will have to, and we will because it is good business and will prove to be cheaper in the long run than discriminating. If we don't accept change, we will have a difficult time meeting our manpower goals and needs.

Companies will have to learn to adapt their organization to derive the fullest contribution from this "different" work force. If they don't, they will not have that cadre of good managers five to ten years from now. Competition for your share of the work force will be fierce, and because of the changing values and motivations of this "new" work force, coming out ahead will involve much more than just salary and security.

2
The role of the employment function and the line departments

In discussing the separate roles of the employment function and the line departments of an organization in the employment process, it is fervently hoped that you are not simply looking for ways to justify the techniques and procedures you have been using; many of them are probably outdated, anyway. To fully understand the roles of the employment function and the line departments in the employment process, a clarification of the semantics should be helpful. Because of the simplicity of some organizations and the complexity of others, two basic terms will be used in the remainder of this book—employment function and line department. You can, at your discretion, relate the assigned tasks of your own organization to these terms. For instance, there may be a one-man personnel organization as opposed to one with a manager for each function (employment, wage and salary, benefits, etc.) in the personnel spectrum. In addition, there may be staff departments as well as line departments, depending on the size of the organization, but the use of one term should suffice here.

Employment is basically three processes: (1) *recruitment*—utilizing available sources to find candidates and developing an interest in that individual in your organization; (2) *selection*—through interviews, tests, reference checks, and medical exams, to arrive at the hire/not hire decision; (3) *placement*—the induction, introduction, and orientation of the employee, "which may be as critical as selection because it's often a question of measuring against the different requirements of several positions."[1]

---

[1]Milton M. Mandell, *The Selection Process*, New York: American Management Association, 1964, p. 11.

Because we are a highly technological society and oriented to mass-production techniques, the name of the employment game so often in the past has been "get me the bodies and we will get the job done." This is a rather narrow attitude in terms of the technological changes that are taking place, particularly in terms of the changing desires and attitudes of the work force. If the employment-function personnel allow such an attitude to persist, they are probably overly influenced by the line departments in doing their job and most likely are reacting to some unrealistic pressures. The answers and the most rational solutions will come about as both the employment function and the line department better understand their proper roles. What both have been doing is in all probability not enough to ensure the best in efficiency and economy. No one should ever accept the status-quo of any employment function, because like any other job, it can always be done better. Analyze and reflect on what is being done in terms of techniques and procedures. Develop measures and controls for the total process.

To really do a better job, the employment function will no longer be able to focus its efforts on a narrow area but will have to develop the skill to satisfy the continually changing demands of its organization and the even faster-changing goals and desires of the individual. Rather than reaction in the employment process, we need some common-sense thinking in filling jobs. Are there people inside the organization who could do the jobs in question with minimal orientation? If we go outside, where might we find the type of people we need? What are the comparative costs of the various sources that can be utilized? In other words, you need some realistic planning—manpower as well as recruitment planning—to be really efficient and economical.

2.1 MANPOWER PLANNING

So much confusion exists, even among manpower experts, as to the meaning and function of manpower planning. Some apply the global definition—forecasting needs, assessing current resources, planning and implementing recruitment efforts, selection and placement, training and development, compensating, and career planning. In short, they tend to view manpower planning as total *manpower resource management*. This definition is not necessarily incorrect or inappropriate. It is, however, confusing to those who view manpower planning as the basic ingredient of the employment function—specifically, determining future manpower needs and planning and carrying out programs to meet these needs. From the most practical standpoint, this latter definition provides a more meaningful framework upon which to make specific manpower staffing decisions.

The real difficulty in manpower planning is that so often management does not support it or does support it and the personnel function cannot come up with an acceptable plan. Too often, it becomes a multifaceted responsibility, with the controller and all functions in personnel involved. The most practical approach would be to have personnel coordinate the plans developed by line departments.

Before effective staffing action, whether involving increases to staff or reductions, can be taken, a decision must be made about future manpower needs. This decision can be made on the spur of the moment, based on hunch or inadequate information; or, it can be made thoughtfully, systematically, and based on adequate and relevant information. Formal manpower planning in this sense has as its chief purpose the *accurate and timely determination of the numbers and kinds of employees required to meet future business objectives.*

The "answer" to the manpower planning "exercise" may call for an increase to staff, or it may signal a reduction. Regardless of the result, the same basic dynamics are at work shaping future manpower needs. Two factors (and only two) generate needs for additional manpower—business expansion and attrition. Conversely, only one factor—retrenchment—causes reductions in manpower needs.

A careful analysis of the elements involved in the two factors—expansion and turnover—coupled with an accurate assessment of current manpower resources will provide the employment function with meaningful information about the extent and nature of the employment problem to be solved. The first critical question that must be answered for any given time frame is, "How many people with what skills will we need to run the business efficiently and successfully?" Reasonably accurate estimates based on objective historical criteria as well as judgments of future influences can be formulated by line managers working in conjunction with the employment function. Once future needs have been estimated, it is necessary to look at current resources to determine how many of the future needs are currently on hand. This assessment may get involved, but it should be a key part of the modern management-development process. Subtracted from current resources are anticipated losses of personnel. Attrition occurs as a result of: (1) resignations, (2) retirements, (3) terminations, (4) transfers, and (5) death. Historical trends and planned personnel actions will provide reasonably accurate projections of future attrition. The net balance—current resources less expected attrition—provides a picture of the resources expected to be on hand at any future point in time.

Future demand (FD, the numbers and kinds of people needed to meet business objectives) less current resources (CR)—adjusted for attrition—equals the *manpower gap* (MG), or FD – CR = MG.[2] Thus, MG, the manpower gap, defines the employment problem in any organization for a given time frame.

2.2 DEFINING THE JOB

The true creation of a job begins with the manpower forecast, which must be an integral part of an organization's general business planning. In order for the organization to achieve its goals and support its growth, each line manager should prepare long- and short-term objectives. If those objectives involve additional people, then manpower planning is initiated, and a job is created.

Working together, the line manager and the personnel function develop a position description which most accurately characterizes the function to be performed. The next step is for the personnel function to evaluate the position, then review the evaluation with the line manager, and gain approval from the compensation function and other appropriate parties.

While the position is being described and evaluated, the employment function consults with the line manager to develop meaningful man specifications, i.e., describing the potential candidate most likely to be selected and best able to succeed in the job to be filled. Such specifications as background, special skills, and personal characteristics should be listed. It is extremely valuable to divide these qualifications into two groups—those that are absolutely essential, and those that are desirable but not critical (see Chapter 8.2). Such man specifications should be detailed, should be agreed upon by all parties concerned with filling the job, and should be written down to serve as a sound guide for selection and placement. The personnel requisition form must require the approval of both the line manager and the personnel function before an individual

[2]From remarks by T.C. Mullins, Director of Personnel, Cheeseborough Pond Inc., at the Employment Management Association meeting, Boston, Mass., April 1971.

within the salary range established through job evaluation can be hired. When all necessary approvals have been secured, a copy of this form is forwarded to the employment function and constitutes authority to initiate recruiting activity.

The procedure is basically the same when hiring to fill an existing job. The personnel and employment functions, in conjunction with the line manager, review the existing position description and manpower specifications and update them if necessary. If there is a significant change in the duties, the personnel function will re-evaluate it and then follow the procedure employed when a new job is created.

2.3 RECRUITMENT PLAN

As is generally true with all planning, there seems to be confusion about recruitment planning. This can be a rather broad subject in its entirety, but hopefully the following definition will provide an overall perspective to what is a varied and difficult subject.

A recruitment plan must be established formally or informally to provide the parameters within which the recruitment phase of employment takes place. The recruitment plan should not be initiated unless there are unusual extenuating circumstances or until all possibilities of internal placement have been exhausted.

In its simplest form, a recruitment plan must take into account the following points:

1. The market place, i.e., the manpower concentrations with the requisite education, experience, and skills. Where are the markets containing people who could fill the open requisition? What kinds of organizations would have such people?
2. The primary sources, approaches, and media for reaching the selected segment of the population. What are the alternatives if the primary sources fail to produce in a specified period of time? How will channels of communication be maintained with these sources during the recruitment process?
3. The search itself, i.e., what degree of time and effort commitment has been obtained from the hiring manager? Who will participate in the employment process? What controls have been established to ensure that each participant in the process understands and carries out his role effectively?

The recruitment plan is thus a distillation of all the planning that went into the creation of the job and the translation of that job concept into action.

2.4 EQUAL OPPORTUNITY EMPLOYER

As has already been discussed, the passage of antidiscrimination legislation is probably the most significant thing that has ever happened in employment. This has brought a whole new perspective to the role of both the employment function and line department, because it is forcing abandonment of some of the historical employment generalities; women and minorities simply never applied for certain jobs because of what they knew were accepted hiring practices. Now, however, those practices have been challenged and are changing. But this type of change is not accomplished by simply having a key executive write letters to the staff about equal employment opportunity posture nor will it be accomplished by a slogan in employment ads, e.g., "We are an Equal Opportunity Employer." This, like any other employment problem will be solved only by a common understanding among those who have the responsibility.

2.5 EQUAL INTERNATIONAL OPPORTUNITY

While on the subject of equal employment opportunity, let's stretch the workaday definition to make a point about international employment. It would appear that some of the same basic EEO principles should apply here. There is a growing necessity for international organizations to make opportunities available to all of their employees, regardless of where they might be located—operating unit or country. There should be no discrimination on job openings, for example, by reserving them for nationals. Managers, regardless of where they are located, will more and more be expected to be knowledgeable and comfortable on the total scene. All of the old biases must be overcome if this is to happen.

To achieve equal international opportunity, a number of things must happen:

1. Top management will have to rid themselves of the doubts about nationals running part of "their" business.
2. Line managers will have to be more positive about having their good people transfer overseas *or* accepting a good transfer from overseas.

3. International experience will have to become a part of career planning. Top executives should have international experience.
4. There must be thorough planning and *real* jobs so that a transfer either way is a positive step.
5. A positive attitude about overseas assignments must be engendered to ensure that when "Fred" returns after three years in Europe, he is considered a better man for it.
6. People must be selected not for their passport, but for their skills.

2.6 CONTINUITY IS CRITICAL

All of the foregoing, then, tells us that there is a great deal more to the employment process than simply a determination of the presence or absence of a set of abilities to do a given job. Unfortunately, it is a reasonable assumption that practically any organization with enough time and money at its disposal can attract people. This is still too often the approach taken by many organizations with the misguided belief that the employment process can be turned on and off like a water tap if it is primed enough. The setting of employment goals and objectives and a concerted effort to provide continuity on the part of both the employment function and line department are two of the keys to success. To make that concerted effort an efficient and economic one also requires an in-depth understanding of the roles that both parties play in the total process.

Most of what is said in this chapter is common sense and fairly elementary, but like so much else in business, the basic principles are acknowledged in theory but too often neglected in practice. The remainder of this chapter, therefore, will not be a classical discussion of organization and manpower planning, because the diversity of companies in terms of their size, philosophy, geographic dispersion, and product lines would make it extremely difficult, if not impossible to provide the ultimate in functional organization charts and descriptions and planning advice. Suffice it to say that employment is the oldest part of the personnel spectrum and depending on the size of the organization, it may or may not be a separate entity. However, it would be safe to say that even in relatively small companies, it usually is a specialized activity. But whatever its size, the successful employment function does require logical thinking, planning, and the setting of objectives, as do all other functional areas of your business.

2.7 BASIC RESPONSIBILITIES

In defining the roles of the employment function and line departments, it will be necessary to establish some parameters. Depending on the size of the organization, the employment function may consist of a corporate staff employment department as well as plant or divisional employment departments, or it may be a function encompassed in the responsibilities of one personnel generalist. The responsibilities entailed in a specialized function such as employment can be spelled out in rather specific terms relative to the functional responsibilities for *both* a corporate staff as well as a plant, division, or one-man employment function. Basically, it is the responsibility of the employment function to administer and control the employment program. The line's role in the employment process is in many ways a more philosophical thing, but it also includes the all-important responsibility for making the hire/don't hire decision.

2.8 THE LINE HIRES

One of the most basic principles of employment (and a primary key to its success in any organization) is the understanding that the line manager does the hiring. It is his responsibility to make the final decision, utilizing all of the tools and inputs that the employment function puts at his disposal. Any organization that approaches this differently and allows employment, or for that matter any other people-related program, to be known as "Personnel's problem" is sure to guarantee failure of that program. No people program can be successful without the cooperation of all involved and a clear understanding of who is responsible for what. Personnel, and in this case the employment function, exists to provide guidance and assistance to the line department in the successful completion of their business objectives. Employment must be a major consideration of every manager because it will have great impact on his success in the final analysis. He must make the final hire decision, because the individual hired will be his responsibility and his alone, whether successful or not. When this principle is understood, the other pieces of the employment jigsaw will begin to fall into place.

2.9 LINE-MANAGER RESPONSIBILITY

Hopefully, we have now established that the line manager has the basic responsibility for the hiring decision within the framework of the policies, practices, and techniques established by the organization. The quality of these decisions will be a major factor in the success or failure of the organization. The employment function must bear in mind that the line manager has many other responsibilities in performing his primary function of running his operation, and therefore his time for participation may well be limited, for he has other personnel responsibilities as well. Therefore, it is up to the employment function to build a sound program that will assist him in meeting his responsibilities and still effectively fulfill his role in the employment process. The burden is on this function to establish rapport, to listen, and to communicate—which is really how proper understanding is achieved. (Proper understanding among the parties involved will prove a sound foundation on which to build a meaningful relationship.) Until you achieve the kind of relationship whereby the line manager expresses a positive attitude toward the employment function there probably will not be success. So, let's now explore the most critical things that the line department needs to do to assist in making employment a successful process:

1. They should continually attempt to improve the work environment:
   a) to reduce turnover and in turn replacement cost;
   b) to make the company a successful employer which hopefully in turn will make it a more successful recruiter.
2. They need to play an active role in the development, interpretation, and application of employment policy.
3. They need to understand that there is a significant cash flow through employment, and if for no other reason, employment decisions must get the same thorough thought that other business decisions get.
4. They need to stop thinking in terms of "job applicants" (the dictionary defines applicant as "one who applies; one who asks or requests") and to realize that more and more, the good people have to be sought out and are job *candidates* with all that implies. "Basic to the success of any employment program is a clear manifestation of

the company's interest in the candidate as an individual, and not simply as a cog in some great corporate mechanism."[3]

5. They need to take an active role in manpower planning, with particular emphasis on improving prediction of manpower needs and providing support for ongoing employment efforts.
6. They need to both eliminate the parochial view that exists in so many organizations concerning time and cost factors in getting the employment job done and understand that each job to be filled may require its own approach and technique.
7. They need to specifically identify:
   a) their manpower needs in terms of both *required* and *desirable* qualifications and understand that there is no such thing as "instant people";
   b) the parameters of their manpower needs over and above technical qualifications, e.g., time pressures, personal hangups, and salary conflicts. These things must be resolved before any recruiting action is initiated, if all that follows in the employment process is to be meaningful.
8. They need to be available to the employment function as necessary for interviewing as well as for providing information about the organization needed to sustain the whole employment process and the recruiting phase in particular.
9. They need to make sound and timely decisions, realizing that the good man is always in demand, and time is of the essence in attracting him.
10. Above all, they must understand that the selection process is not perfect, and it is seldom that the person hired matches completely the original specification.

These ten points may sound elementary, but as was stated previously, that may just be why employment is so often an inefficient and costly function—because the elementary things are not understood.

---

[3]D.Sweet, "Stretching the Employment Dollar," *Personnel Magazine*, November 1962, p. 1.

2.10 EMPLOYMENT-FUNCTION RESPONSIBILITIES

Now let's explore the specifics of what the employment function does to make the employment process successful and how it can ensure the development of the proper relationship with the line departments. As was stated in the introduction, employment is a full-fledged management function that affects all operations in an organization, and it can be fully effective only when close coordination with corporate plans and objectives is maintained. This must be accomplished in line with the policies and philosophy of the organization as well as with regard for its customers, its competitors, and suppliers, for any secret or proprietary information individuals from those organizations may possess, and in keeping with all applicable antidiscrimination legislation.

For employment to achieve its assigned role, we must first define the major tasks of an employment function and explore the problems of accomplishing them. These tasks, as delineated below, are in the context of a corporate employment function in an organization with decentralized operations, i.e., one which views employment as a decentralized process, as a "local" function. The only nonlocal, or centralized processes are college recruiting and executive-search activities. These exceptions are explained in detail in Chapters 4 and 6, respectively.

1. Provide day-to-day functional guidance to the divisions and plants of the organization on specific employment problems.
2. Assist in planning about manpower needs, budgetary requirements, and utilization of sources.
3. Train people in the methods and techniques of the employment process.
4. Direct policy development and interpretation as related to the total employment process.
5. Be responsible for university relations (including college recruiting as well as associated programs).
6. Direct equal employment opportunity programs, with emphasis on development and utilization of sources.
7. Be responsible for executive-search activities in terms of when, how, and who to use.

8. Assist in the development and utilization of the other employment sources, e.g., employment agencies, employee referral programs, advertising programs, etc.
9. Direct out-placement activities (see Chapter 10).
10. Provide the necessary economic and administrative controls to the total process.

2.11 LOCAL vs. CORPORATE RESPONSIBILITY

The primary difference in the tasks outlined above for the division or plant employment function as opposed to its corporate counterpart is best explained in terms of where the basic responsibility for making the day-to-day decisions rests. Logically, it rests with the division or plant employment function and is accomplished in concert with the appropriate line managers. It is really impracticable in this day and age to assume that even a big organization has a large corporate staff group capable of administering an employment program throughout the organization and able to solve effectively the multitude of problems that are every-day occurrences. That is the primary reason the author advocates "local" employment responsibility except for university relations and executive-search activities.

2.12 LONG-RANGE PROGRAM

The accomplishment of these tasks—whether corporate staff, division, or plant employment—efficiently and economically will be predicated on how the line manager views the function. A major obstacle here is that historically, the line has usually supported employment activity only to meet current needs rather than to develop longer-range programs needed to provide the efficient and economic continuity necessary to accomplish longer-range goals. Needless to say, the organization that continues to view employment as a "current" activity will suffer dramatically from manpower gaps in their not-too-distant future. Many companies learned a bitter lesson along these lines during the poor business years of the late 1960s and early 1970s, and it is an attitude that may haunt them again many times in the next several decades in terms of a shortage of back-up management talent. Although these comments may seem elementary, in reality, their logic is seldom appreciated.

2.13 ESTABLISH CONTROL

What are some of the practical things the employment function must do to solve some of the problems in dealing with the line and to provide proper controls?

1. Establish their role as the expert and get the line to delegate responsibility to them. As stated in section 2.9, the line manager's many other responsibilities necessarily limit his participation in the employment function. In essence, you say to him, "Mr. Line Manager, your time is too valuable for you to have to cope with all the necessary details of finding and selecting candidates. Your time is best spent on your primary responsibilities—running your operation—so let me assume the responsibility for serving up the one or two top candidates for your job opening. If I fail you, you have me fired. But, this is what I get paid to do, the same as you get paid to manage."

2. Involve the line with your sources. Don't feel that you have to hide the fact that you have outside organizations and people to help you do your job. You can bet that the average line department has also used consultants when they needed more expertise than was available in their operation. You may find that much definitive information will be exchanged when all three parties (employment, source, and the line) are involved that will be helpful to employment in terms of job specifics and general business information. (You really don't have all the answers, so don't try to continue to justify your techniques and procedures without change. You can always do the job better, and if you solicit ideas and listen, you will find that both sources and line departments will have some good ideas on getting the job done.)

3. Get to know your line manager. Know how many kids he has, what his golf score is, what his hang-ups and pet peeves are. Employment must be very personalized to be truly effective, and this aspect of it is no exception.

4. Don't compartmentalize your function so that you start saying no. You are a service function, so provide it. Carry any reasonable request by a line manager through to a conclusion satisfactory to him. If it involves something you can't handle, refer it to the appropriate person and follow him up. Don't say "that's not my area of responsibility." Remember, the farther up the line the manager is, the greater likelihood that he spends more time on people problems, and he may therefore lean harder on you for assistance and advice. That will be a real plus, because your help will get him totally attuned to being part of the employment team.
5. Adhere, within reason, to the old employment adage that a good employment man eats lunch *only* with candidates *or* line managers *or* sources and spends 50% of his time away from his desk. That means he is out developing relationships with the line managers and employment sources.

The employment function, then, has essentially two areas of responsibility in administering and controlling the program. One is the *doing* part of recruitment, selection, and placement. The second is *educating* the line to the economics and all the nuances of getting the job done. Even though employment decisions are joint ones, the ultimate go/no-go decision is the line manager's, but both parties must play specific roles. This assumes a relationship that necessitates the confidence and respect of the line. In short, *recruiting* is primarily an employment-function responsibility. The *selection* and *placement* processes are joint ones, and this is really where the definition of roles becomes so critical. At the risk of getting into Chapter 7, in which selection and placement are discussed more fully, it is appropriate to explain one critical point about the interview here. The interview comprises two assessments. One is the technical assessment about whether the candidate has the job abilities needed to perform the specific duties of the job, and this is basically the line's decision. The second is the environmental assessment, i.e., whether the candidate can function and grow in the organization as an individual, and this is basically an employment-function responsibility. There should always be flexibility in these assessments, however, and hopefully both parties can provide technical and environmental assessment inputs, but in the final analysis the "line hires" and must therefore be responsible for finalizing all of the inputs as the basis for the decision.

2.14 POLICIES AND PROCEDURES

To further ensure the greatest degree of efficiency and economy, there needs to be even more definition of the responsibilities and controls in the employment process. This is accomplished primarily by developing policies and procedures about the utilization of employment agencies and executive-search firms, relocation of new employees, and customer-competitor-supplier recruiting, etc. The basic philosophy of the organization and specific areas of responsibility should be spelled out to ensure that everyone involved in employment understands the "ground rules" and can thus provide meaningful direction to his phase of the employment effort. Let's bear in mind, though, that policies and procedures must be thought of as a *point of departure* in the decision-making process and *should never* be interpreted as the final say. Administer policies and procedures with the latitude and flexibility that each situation dictates.

Your company manpower policy will be spelled out in the employment policies and procedures that you implement, because they will really indicate the employment posture of your organization. Antidiscrimination legislation will of necessity play a major role in the development and implementation of these policies, and that will necessitate a regular review as new or revised legislation is implemented.

Definitions

The guiding philosophy in developing employment policy and procedures should be predicated on the organization's need for obtaining the skills and abilities of qualified people to specific jobs. The administration of your employment policies and procedures must be carried out with due regard for the ethical and moral considerations of doing business in our highly complex and mobile society.

What is policy? What is a procedure? Policy is set by top management and should meet certain criteria which will define its role in the overall philosophy of the organization. Thus, policy:

1. is an expression of belief or intent—the underlying principles governing what the organization does or hopes to do
2. should be stated in broad terms
3. must be long range
4. must be developed through active participation of top management

5. must have approval of the organization's highest authority
6. must be inviolate
7. must be stated in writing.[4]

Procedures, then, are really guides for achieving day-to-day objectives and must be developed at the operating level of an organization. Specifically, they tell the supervisors and managers that they "can or cannot do certain things." In a sense, they are a plan and a guide for getting the job done.

In reality, therefore, there are not many "policies" in any organization, but there may be innumerable "procedures." Whatever terminology is used, and for our purposes it will be "policies and procedures," they should be developed with the primary thought in mind that they will make decision-making simpler in the employment process and will also ease the approval process. If they do, they will make the employment function and the line work closely together. If they do not, efficiency and economy will suffer. Therefore, policies and procedures must be realistic, and their structure will be dictated to a great degree by the roles played in the employment process in a particular organization by the employment function and the line departments. Regardless of how they are structured, however, they must allow each party the flexibility needed to fulfill its role.

2.15 BASIC POLICIES AND PROCEDURES

Many organizations have policies and procedures that range from A to Z in the employment process. Realistically, we cannot cover every conceivable situation here. Therefore, we will focus on eight major areas of concern in the employment function in most organizations that require a statement of policy and procedures. These eight areas best reflect the roles of the parties involved in the employment process. These are:

1. overall employment policy
2. internal search
3. customer/competitor/supplier recruitment

[4]"Statement of Personnel Policy," *Studies in Personnel Policy #169*, New York: National Industrial Conference Board, pp. 5,6,7, and 8.

4. advertising
5. employment-agency utilization
6. executive-search firm utilization
7. equal employment opportunity
8. relocation of new employees.

Each of these will be discussed and presented in a format comprising a policy, responsibility, and procedure statement. Such sample statements encompassing the thinking of many organizations in these eight key areas will be more helpful than reprinting policy/procedure statements from specific organizations. Hopefully, these examples will provide a sound basis for you to develop or revise your own policies and procedures.

The Overall Employment Policy

This is the keystone for any employment function, inasmuch as it must set the ground rules for the organization. This in turn becomes the philosophy of the organization and will be a reflection of it in the industry, the community, and on the campus.

As this policy/procedure sets the stage for the others that follow, it would be well to explain the context in which it was developed. It was written for a fictitious organization, the XYZ Corporation. XYZ Corporation has a number of geographically dispersed operations, and it has employment functions at the local and corporate levels. Smaller organizations or nonindustrial organizations should be able to extract and adapt this information in order to develop or revise their existing policies.

EMPLOYMENT POLICY

Policy

The policy of the XYZ Corporation with respect to employment is to use every reasonable means available to select the best candidate for the position to be filled in order to achieve our objectives of profit and growth. It is corporate policy to fill position vacancies by promotion from within. When this is not possible, we will recruit externally. The employment procedures and practices shall be in compliance with all local, state, and federal laws. (There will be fair and equal employment opportunity for all, with no discrimination because of race, color, age, sex, creed, or national origin.) Recruiting activities will be conducted with due regard for our relationships with customers, competitors, suppliers, and other companies.

Responsibilities

1. Completion of Personnel Requisition Form #__________ is a joint responsibility of the Employment Function and the department with the vacancy. The Employment Function is responsible for obtaining the necessary approvals.
2. The selection of sources to be utilized will be the responsibility of the Employment Function. Line departments will communicate any source contact to the Employment Function to ensure maximum efficiency and economy in their use.
3. The Employment Function will be responsible for scheduling interviews with all candidates.
   a) All candidates should have a minimum of two interviews (one with Employment and one with the appropriate line department).
   b) Candidates for more senior positions will have enough interviews to ensure the best exposure for both them and the Corporation.
4. The Employment Function will be responsible for ensuring compliance with corporate policy on equal employment opportunity.
   a) Employment will inform all solicited sources of corporate EEO policy and of their expected compliance.
   b) Employment will communicate information about EEO laws, executive orders, etc., to all departments in the corporation.
5. References are the responsibility of the Employment Function and should usually be done by the person who conducted the interview.
   a) In certain instances the line-department interviewer should assist in checking references, particularly when an unusual or highly technical job is involved.
6. The Employment Function is responsible for coordinating the pre-employment physical examination with the medical department or with an outside physician.
   a) The medical department is responsible for interpreting results of the exam and notifying the Employment Function.
7. The Employment Function will be responsible for compiling and discussing all selection information with the hiring manager to arrive at the hire/not hire decision.
8. The Employment Function is responsible for extending offers of employment and for preparing the offer letter.
   a) All job offers will be approved by the appropriate line manager, with concurrence by the Employment Function. Disagreement on the dollar offer or other details will be resolved by the vice-president of personnel.
9. The Employment Function is responsible for organizing and coordinating the "formal" orientation program for new employees. The line department is respon-

sible for orienting the new employee to his specific responsibilities and to the departmental organization.

Procedures

1. The existence of a budgeted or replacement vacancy or a request for an addition to the head count in any department must be approved prior to initiating any recruitment activity. Personnel Requisition Form #________ specifies the necessary approvals.
2. The Employment Function must have the approved Personnel Requisition Form #________ to effectively recruit potential employees and ensure:
   a) compliance with the budget
   b) compliance with established salary ranges
   c) understanding of the requirements and responsibility of the position.
3. The Employment Function has full discretionary power to recruit (by best available means) and to recommend candidates for potential employment.
4. Initial interviews will be conducted by the Employment Function, with subsequent interviews (as necessary) conducted by the line departments.
5. All candidates will be required to complete and sign the Application for Employment Form #________.
6. All recruitment activities will be conducted in compliance with the corporation's policy of equal employment opportunity.
7. Reference checks will be conducted on all candidates of interest. This will be done to confirm interview results, as well as to elicit further information. Offers will not be extended until satisfactory information has been obtained. In unusual circumstances, offers may be extended contingent on satisfactory references.
   a) All reference activity will be conducted with due regard for the procedures required by the Fair Credit Reporting Act, Public Law 91-508.
8. All offers will be contingent on the candidate's passing a pre-employment physical examination successfully.
   a) Special tests or appropriate exams are recommended to potential employees over 40 years of age or to those assigned to duties involving an occupational health hazard.
   b) Potential employees not recommended for hire by the examining physician will not be extended offers. Exceptions to this must be approved by the vice-president of personnel.
9. The Employment Function and the hiring department will develop the offer, taking into consideration salary policy and the candidate's current salary, experience, potential, etc.

a) Offers should be extended verbally if possible and followed up by a letter specifying details. Salary will always be expressed in monthly terms.

10. Expenses involved in the employment process, with the exception of relocation expenses, will be charged to Employment Account #_______.

11. Each new employee will be required to attend an orientation program.

    a) The new employee will complete all required and necessary forms, e.g., W-2 form, group insurance, patent and inventions agreement, etc.

    b) This program is to acquaint the new employee with the Corporation and its policies.

Internal Search

Organizations, almost regardless of size, like to pride themselves on the fact that they promote from within. This presupposes a system of identifying individuals within the organizations—internal search. The essential ingredients of a policy/procedure statement for internal search should be to: provide maximum opportunity, improve morale, and reduce employee turnover. If internal search proves to be a successful program, it will also provide for real economies in overall employment costs.

A key factor in making internal search successful, and one that should be specifically defined in the policy/procedure statement is the determination of who in the organization is responsible for each of the various steps involved in effecting the employment process. There must also be flexibility in this policy/procedure that allows contact between managers throughout the organization in order for them to identify likely candidates. Above all, flexibility provides the means to overcome self-interest when one of "your own" is a candidate.

INTERNAL SEARCH

Policy

It is the policy of XYZ Corporation to fill open positions, wherever practical, through the transfer or promotion of qualified employees, in accordance with corporate policy on equal employment opportunity. The success of this policy requires that all employees known to possess the basic qualifications for the open position will be considered wherever they are located in the corporation. In this manner, all employees will be offered the maximum opportunity for growth and development; available manpower will be utilized to the fullest extent possible; the corporation will be protected from unnecessary loss of manpower from lack of opportunity; total costs of employment will be minimized; and employees will be provided with increased motivation. External recruiting will be initiated only after all qualified candidates within the corporation have been considered for all open positions, other than foreman or entry-level jobs filled by new graduates.

Responsibilities

The Corporate Management-Development Function is responsible for coordinating and administering the internal-search process as follows:

1. Reviewing personnel requisitions to determine the organization's potential to provide internal candidates
2. Establishing and communicating the basic parameters of the position to the appropriate parties
3. Obtaining the necessary clearances from the candidate's current department prior to informing the part of the organization with the open position
4. Maintaining up-to-date information on all employees through the Personnel Data Bank (PDB)
5. Preparing necessary records and reports relating to internal search.

The appropriate personnel manager is responsible for:

1. Preparing and getting required approvals, and forwarding the Personnel Requisition Form to the Corporate Management-Development Function
2. Contacting the appropriate people in other parts of the corporation to ensure that correct channels of communication are utilized (coordinating contact with candidates outside of the searching manager's immediate area of jurisdiction)
3. Taking appropriate referral action or closing out the candidacy of individuals after they have discussed their interest, or lack thereof, with their immediate supervisor
4. Ensuring that the manager with the open position has the opportunity to consider as wide a range of candidates as possible
5. Providing up-to-date information on all candidates considered to the Corporate Management-Development Function and the part(s) of the corporation supplying the candidate(s).

Procedures

1. Authorization for internal search will be receipt of the Personnel Requisition Form by the Corporate Management-Development Function.
2. The Corporate Management-Development Function will search the PDB for candidates meeting the basic criteria established.

3. Those candidates passing the initial screening will be identified to the Corporate Management-Development Function so that contact may be established to determine their interest.
4. All parties involved should try to ensure that no candidate is denied an opportunity to improve his job situation unless there are unusual extenuating circumstances.
5. There will be a two-week limitation for decisions after receipt of a candidate's information file.
6. If the candidate expresses genuine interest, arrangements for interviews are made through the appropriate personnel manager, with simultaneous notification to the Corporate Management-Development Function.
7. Costs incurred by the candidate in interviewing will be reimbursed by the part of the organization conducting the interviews.
8. The appropriate personnel manager will keep all interested parties informed about the progress of the candidate(s).
9. Offer/no offer decisions must be made one week after the final interview and will be communicated to candidates by the appropriate personnel manager.
10. The Corporate Management-Development Function should be apprised of any employee available for transfer (for any legitimate reason) so that they can attempt to locate a suitable position for him.

Recruitment from Customers, Competitors, and Suppliers

This is an extremely delicate and sensitive subject to most organizations. It is an activity that most organizations find themselves involved in at one time or another, but it is also one that is obviously given little external publicity. Most organizations, for obvious reasons, have become quite sensitive to the conduct of their employment activities in this area. Over and above the business relationships involved, recruiting becomes particularly critical when the individual possesses any proprietary or secret information.

The classic example of this is the "Space Suit" case involving the International Latex Corporation and an employee of B.F. Goodrich (*B.F. Goodrich* v. *Wohlgemuth,* Ohio Court of Appeals 1963). Wohlgemuth, a chemical engineer, worked for Goodrich as manager of the company's space suit engineering department. International Latex had a space suit contract from the government and offered him a job as a manager in the group handling the development work. He accepted the offer, but was told he could not perform the job at Latex without disclosing Goodrich secrets. He was warned that if he went to Latex, he would be sued by Goodrich. After hearings in several courts, Wohlgemuth was allowed to do space suit work for Latex. According to the legal opinion, "We have no doubt that Wohlgemuth had the right to take employment in a competitive business and to use the knowledge (other than trade secrets) and experience for the benefit of his new employer." Wohlgemuth assumed his new duties, but was under court order not to disclose any of Goodrich's space suit secrets. Although both parties accepted the decision, it did not solve the basic issue. The decision did, however, allow Wohlgemuth to improve his earnings and position on the premise that the space suit secrets were too complicated for Wohlgemuth to remember.

Most employees nowadays (particularly those in technical disciplines) are required by their employer to sign some form of patent and secrecy agreement stipulating, among other things, that if they leave his employ they will not "for a certain period of time become involved in activities of the same or related nature." Even without this type of document, however, there is a compelling moral obligation for both the organization and the individual to maintain confidentiality about secret or proprietary information. Of necessity, then, organizations need a policy/procedure statement on this subject, because a recruiting program of any magnitude will undoubtedly involve employees of a customer, competitor, or supplier. The main thrust of this particular policy/procedure statement is to provide a realistic and straightforward way to consider for employment employees of *any* organization without requiring the disclosure of any proprietary or secret information. Unfortunately, this aspect of employment is little publicized until an error in judgment is made, and then the lack of definition becomes apparent. Two good dissertations on this subject are *Engineers, the Law, and Trade Secrets* published by the National Society of Professional Engineers in 1966 and *Employee Patent and Secrecy Agreements*, published by the National Industrial Conference Board in 1965.

RECRUITMENT FROM CUSTOMERS/COMPETITORS/SUPPLIERS

Policy

XYZ Corporation will conduct all recruitment activities in a professional manner, with due regard for our relationships with our customers, competitors, and suppliers, as well as other companies, and we will not hire people for any proprietary or secret information they may possess. The corporation will, however, consider employees of any organization—within certain procedural guidelines.

Responsibilities

A basic judgment needs to be made about the value of pursuing a given candidate who has confidential or secret information of his present or former employers, i.e., can he be effectively employed without inevitably disclosing such information?

1. In the initial interview, the Employment Function must determine whether or not an employment contract or agreement exists.
2. The line department will be responsible for determining the specific nature of the work performed (without obtaining any secret or confidential information) and the feasibility of properly utilizing the candidate.
3. The Employment Function is responsible for obtaining clearance of candidates who have contract or agreement restrictions.
   a) Obtain a copy of agreement or contract with the candidate's present or past employers.
   b) Prepare a statement about the precise nature of his past work experience to identify areas in which confidential information has been obtained.
   c) Prepare a statement about the precise nature of work contemplated including proposed entry salary and how initial contact was made.
   d) Forward this information (a, b, c) for review by the corporate technical director or appropriate executive and determine any legal or corporate-wide business problem.
4. *No* offer of employment shall be extended until the necessary clearances have been obtained.
5. When an offer is to be made, the following paragraph *will* be included in the offer letter (retain a copy for the personnel file):

   "It is not the intention of XYZ Corporation to obtain from you any confidential knowledge or information obtained by you during the course of any of your prior employments. If you feel that any assignment which you may be given while in our employ requires the disclosure of such information, you should bring this to the attention of your immediate supervisor."
6. When an offer is made where clearance, as in item 3: a, b, c, and d is required, a copy of all pertinent information will be forwarded to the corporate employment function.
7. The corporate employment function will maintain and update a listing of important customers, competitors, and suppliers.

Procedures

1. The determination as to utilization of an individual without compromising any obligation of confidentiality he may have rests with the line department and ultimately with the corporate technical director or other appropriate executive.
2. Every technical or other candidate who may be in possession of confidential or proprietary information of his present or past employers, and who is offered employment at XYZ, will be informed verbally and via the offer letter of this policy.
3. All employment-contract restrictions that the candidate has with former employers must be cleared with the corporate employment function and legal department before an offer may be extended.
4. Employment advertisements should not be run in geographic areas where it is apparent that a customer, competitor, or supplier is the only source. Without prior approval from the corporate employment function, no one is authorized to recruit directly in any company.
5. We do *not* ask permission of *any* company to interview or hire personnel. Any individual may be considered who approaches XYZ directly, i.e., walk-in candidate, third-party referral, ad response.

Advertising

All of your policies and procedures must be specific in terms of people, regardless of their age, sex, race, color, religion, or national origin. Your advertising policy/procedure statement is no exception, and it must also comply specifically with section 704 of Title VII of the Civil Rights Act of 1964. This section, as quoted in Chapter 4.2, spells out the basic do's and don'ts of help-wanted advertising. The critical points that need to be considered in developing this statement are:

1. Definition of the goals and philosophy of your employment advertising program
2. The regulations imposed by Title VII of the Civil Rights Act of 1964 and any subsequent revisions or amendments
3. Control of the placement of advertising to avoid duplication of efforts
4. No obviously overt attempt to recruit employees from a competitor, customer or supplier
5. To identify the Employment Function as the liaison with the advertising agency.

EMPLOYMENT ADVERTISING

Policy

When appropriate, it is the policy of the XYZ Corporation to utilize advertising as a method of attracting qualified people for current or projected job openings. In its broadest context, this policy will comply with the Corporation's role as an equal opportunity employer.

Responsibilities

The responsibilities of the corporate employment function are to:

1. Establish and disseminate corporate employment advertising goals and philosophy
2. Review all employment advertising for overall impact on company image, public relations, audience appeal, etc.
3. Audit costs of employment advertising and review cost effectiveness and budget with the responsible individual in the operating unit's employment function
4. Meet periodically with operating-unit representatives and the advertising agency to plan strategy and campaigns
5. Serve as a collection point for feedback from management, operating-location employment functions, and the advertising agency about problems, criticism, and proposals concerning the employment advertising program.

The responsibilities of the operating-unit employment function are to:

1. Designate one person responsible for coordinating and placing all employment advertising. The person responsible:
   a) will ensure that the advertising agency is supplied with all the information it requires, i.e., job content, job environment, and general background information
   b) will ensure that the line department and the employment function are in agreement on necessary qualifications and job content
   c) will ensure enough lead time to develop advertising and provide a copy for review and change, if necessary
   d) will ensure that accurate records of response and associated statistics and costs of advertising are maintained.

Procedures

1. Corporate employment advertising goals and philosophy will be defined by the corporate employment function and communicated to our advertising agency and to the employment functions of the various operating locations (plants, labs).

2. Employment advertising will be considered as a source along with other external sources only after all internal search possibilities have been exhausted.
3. Employment advertising will be prepared and placed in accordance with the corporation's role as an equal opportunity employer and without regard for race, sex, age, color, creed, or national origin.

Employment-Agency Utilization

The economics of utilizing an employment agency requires a rather precise definition of the responsibilities of all involved. The major points of emphasis is this policy/procedure statement necessarily must be communication and contact responsibilities. To establish any kind of a meaningful relationship, both the agent and the organization must understand their "rights." A condensed version of this policy/procedure statement for use as a handout to the employment agency is outlined in Chapter 4. Because the policy/procedure statement is so self-explanatory, there is no reason for further detail here.

EMPLOYMENT-AGENCY UTILIZATION

Policy

It is the policy of XYZ Corporation to staff professional and managerial positions with present employees whenever possible. In situations where this is not possible, outside recruiting efforts may be initiated. A key source for professional and managerial employees is employment agencies, and to ensure their most efficient and economic utilization and compliance with our role as an equal opportunity employer, the following responsibilities and procedures have been developed.

Responsibilities

1. Because of travel schedules and other business demands, it may take us several weeks to determine a candidate's interest and to arrange for interviews. Therefore, it is our responsibility to keep the employment agency informed of the status of any candidate we may have interest in pursuing.
2. Since some agencies refer resumes on the same candidate to more than one operating unit, the operating unit contacting the agency or applicant first to express interest shall have preference on the referral. Any question that arises in following this procedure or any special coordination required should be referred to the corporate employment function.

3. Because of the high volume of resumes received from agencies, it is not practical to respond to them all. Agencies should be advised that we will contact them only about those applicants in whom we have interest. All other resumes will be discarded if they are not of interest.
4. It is the general rule that agencies work on the assumption that their referral is to the corporation rather than to a specific job.
   a) A time limitation on honoring referrals is necessary. Our policy will be to honor referrals 90 days from receipt. The initial referrer is due the fee despite any other agency referrals of the same applicant.
   b) Agencies should be informed that we do not have central control of applicant referrals. Referrals across organizational lines will carry the obligation of the initial recipient's agreement with the agency. This agreement must be indicated to the operating unit receiving the referral.
5. All agencies with whom we deal must be notified that we are an equal opportunity employer and expect to receive referrals on anyone, regardless of race, color, sex, religion, national origin, or age.
6. Employment agencies have the same obligations under law to refer people regardless of race, color, sex, religion, national origin, or age. Should it become apparent that they are not adhering to this, they must be discontinued as a source.

Procedures

1. Fees
   a) It is our policy to pay appropriate placement fees. These are paid as agreed after the individual has reported to work.
   b) All agencies from which we request and honor referrals shall provide a copy of their fee schedule prior to initiating any referrals. It is not practical to state fee guidelines corporate-wide because of the geographical and economic differences in operating-unit locations.
   c) Any special arrangements (retainers or special fee arrangements) that may have implications beyond the interested operating unit must be cleared with the corporate employment function.
2. Contracts
   a) All employment agency contacts must be made through the employment function responsible for filling the job opening.
   b) Contact with operating departments will be controlled through the local employment function. Approval must be obtained by the employment agency prior to initiating any direct contact with line departments.

c) The Employment Function must be notified of all referrals made directly to line departments. This will protect the employment agency by ensuring credit on fees should their candidate be employed.

3. Referrals/Identification/Obligation

   Because of the number of applicants that may be under consideration at a given time, particular attention must be paid to each individual to ensure that he is treated fairly and is properly advised of our interest. Each operating unit should spell out its policy about the identification of referrals and the period of obligation to each agency being utilized. The following basic guidelines will assist in determining this policy.

   a) Our obligation is to the employment agency that initiates the action which results in the individual being hired.

      1) We require that the employment agency forward a complete resume on all applicants recommended for consideration.

      2) All resumes referred must indicate contact information (applicant's name, address, and telephone number.)

      3) Telephone referrals should result in either a resume or an interview within 72 hours of the call (or an agreed upon time) in order to be honored over other referrals of the same candidate from other sources.

   b) Whenever feasible, prior to contacting the applicant, the referring employment agency will be made aware of the contact.

Executive-Search Firms

The major concern in developing a policy/procedure statement for this source should be to define guidelines about specific responsibilities for what is so often a misused and very misunderstood source and yet in terms of initial cost, one of the most expensive. Unfortunately, this is an area in which employment functions seem to have taken little initiative and as a result, this "level" of employment generally evolves from an arrangement between the line manager and the executive-search firm. The particular need for economy and efficiency in utilizing this employment source dictates a policy/procedure statement that makes particular reference to:

1. The level of the job or some other parameter, such as field of specialization, in order to have a determinant to provide guidance in the decision about whether to utilize this as a source. (In other words, these parameters must rule out the possibility of other sources being productive.)

2. The responsibility for the selection of a particular executive-search firm and the financial arrangements
3. The responsibility for the initial screening of candidates and the monitoring of the selection process.

EXECUTIVE-SEARCH FIRM UTILIZATION

Policy

It is the policy of XYZ Corporation to utilize the services of executive-search organizations when other manpower sources are not feasible; the salary of the job in question is in excess of $______ per year or pay grade ______ and above; or requires unusual, specialized skills. All search activities will be conducted with due regard for our policies and procedures toward customers, competitors, suppliers, and equal employment opportunity.

Responsibilities

1. The personnel manager of the operating unit will be responsible for initiating an internal search, as outlined in the internal-search policy, before any external search is begun.
2. The completion of Personnel Requisition Form # ______ and position description are the responsibility of the operating-unit employment function. Search activity will not be initiated until this has been completed and approved.
3. The corporate employment function has primary responsibility for conducting searches for all positions above level ______ and all Corporate management positions.
4. The operating-unit employment function is responsible for the conduct of searches for management positions at level ______ and below under the administrative guidance of the director of employment.
5. The operating-unit employment function will be responsible for reviewing candidates with the search firm and for scheduling interviews and maintaining an up-to-date "Candidate File." The scheduling of interviews with appropriate corporate functional heads and corporate officers will be made through the corporate employment function.
6. The corporate employment function will prepare monthly status reports on search activity. (The operating-unit employment function will be responsible for providing information on candidate activity and the status of those seen.)

Procedures

1. All contacts with executive-search firms will be made or coordinated through the corporate employment department.
2. The selection of an executive-search firm will be a joint decision of the director of employment and the operating-unit employment function. Search activity will not be initiated until both parties have approved a written proposal submitted by the search firm.
3. Bills for services from search firms will be sent directly to the operating-location employment function for payment, with a copy to the corporate director of employment for audit.
4. Exceptions to this policy will be cleared through the vice-president of personnel.

Equal Opportunity Employment

This is the most recent policy statement in most organizations and is possibly the most sensitive. It must set the ground rules and guidelines for minority/female employment in rather specific terms. It is also the policy that will require the most frequent review and revision because of the continuing development and revision of EEO legislation. Although a number of facets of this policy/procedure statement do not relate directly to the employment function, it has been included here because a major portion of its impact is on recruitment, selection, and placement.

EQUAL OPPORTUNITY EMPLOYMENT

Policy

It is the policy of the XYZ Corporation as prescribed by the president that all corporate departments and operating units of the corporation will recruit, hire, and promote for all job classifications without regard to race, creed, color, national origin, sex, or age, except where sex or age is a *bona fide* occupational qualification. It is also our policy that all decisions on employment and promotions will be based solely on an individual's qualifications as they relate to the valid requirements for the positions under consideration. This same policy applies to other personnel action, including compensation, benefits, transfers, lay-offs, recalls, terminations, company-sponsored training, tuition assistance, relocation assistance, and expense reimbursement. Company-sponsored events and social and recreational activities will be administered without regard to race, creed, color, national origin, sex, or age.

Responsibilities

The primary responsibility for implementing this policy is assigned to the director of equal-opportunity programs.

1. The director is responsible for ensuring compliance with federal, state, municipal, and company regulations governing employment practices such as: recruiting, selection, placement, training, and promotion. This responsibility will include the continuing development of policy, affirmative-action programs, and internal and external communication techniques. The director will be responsible for implementing an audit and reporting system in order to:
   a) measure effectiveness of operating-unit programs
   b) examine the need for remedial action
   c) evaluate the attainment of company goals and objectives
   d) keep top management informed of progress in equal opportunity programs
   e) keep line managers apprised of current developments in the field.
2. The director is also responsible for the implementation of programs of affirmative action and community relations by operating units.
3. Each operating unit will have a designated equal opportunity coordinator, and he will be responsible for assisting line management in that unit in matters of EEO compliance.
   a) The coordinator shall act as liaison with the corporate director of equal opportunity programs.
4. Responsibilities of the line manager include:
   a) assistance in the identification of problem areas and the establishment of objectives and goals for his operating unit
   b) active involvement in local minority organizations and community action groups
   c) periodic audit of hiring and promotion patterns to evaluate the achievement of goals and objectives
   d) regular discussions with supervisors and employees to ensure that company EEO policies are being followed
   e) review of the qualifications of all employees to ensure that minorities are given full recognition for transfer and promotion
   f) provision of career counseling for all employees
   g) formal business objectives shall include a requirement of EEO affirmative action
   h) the timely completion of all actions, programs, and reports required.

Procedures

1. This policy shall appear in the manual on corporate policy.
2. A statement of EEO policy shall be published by each operating unit.
3. Company news media, annual reports, company film, video tape presentations, etc., will include discussions of progress in areas of equal employment opportunity.
4. A statement of corporate EEO policy shall be posted on all operating-unit bulletin boards.
5. The various unions representing XYZ employees will be advised of the corporation's EEO commitment.
6. This policy shall be discussed in training programs for foremen, supervisors, and line managers.
7. A discussion of this policy will be included in the orientation of all newly hired personnel.
8. When employees are featured in company publications, both minority and nonminority employees will be included.
9. The director of equal opportunity programs will meet periodically with equal opportunity coordinators to assist in improving implementation of this policy.
10. Each operating unit will inform recruiting sources in writing of this policy, stipulating that the sources recruit and refer candidates without regard to race, creed, color, national origin, sex, or age. (See Chapter 8.1.)
11. Written notification of this policy will be sent to all subcontractors, vendors, and suppliers with whom the XYZ Corporation places orders valued at $10,000 or more per year, requesting certification as prescribed by the OFCC.
12. The operating units will incorporate an EEO clause in all purchase orders, contracts, leases, and other applicable documents.
13. All company recruiting literature, including display and classified advertising, will carry the footing "An Equal Opportunity Employer."
14. Employment functions will notify minority organizations, including but not limited to the Urban League, the NAACP, Concentrated Employment Programs, and the state employment services, of this policy.
15. Company advertising featuring employees will include minority and nonminority personnel.

Relocation of New Employees

This policy/procedure statement needs to be developed in detail inasmuch as it will be the control on the single most expensive item in the whole employment process. It will in all probability be less generous than your employee relocation amount, but in some instances it may require a more flexible interpretation. The primary purpose of this policy/procedure statement is to "ease the burden and not necessarily to cover every nickel of every expense." In addition, since this policy/procedure statement involves a number of other departments—traffic, insurance, and accounting—to a greater degree than do most other employment-related policy/procedure statements, the responsibilities of each must be detailed.

RELOCATION OF NEW EMPLOYEES

Policy

XYZ Corporation will pay to, or on behalf of, a newly hired employee reasonable relocation expenses incurred in moving himself, his family, and household goods to his new employment location. This policy will be administered by the appropriate personnel function.

Responsibilities

1. Personnel Function
   a) The appropriate personnel function is responsible for the administration and application of this policy.
   b) Exceptions to this policy must have the approval of the vice-president of personnel or his designee.
   c) Review, approve, and forward to the traffic department Request for Move of Household Form #________.
   d) Provide new employee with Expense Report Form #________. Review and approve for payment.
2. Traffic Department
   a) Prepare Moving Notice Form #________ when in receipt of Request for Move of Household Form #________.
   b) Distribute Moving Notice Form #________ to moving company, insurance department, new employee, and personnel function.

3. Insurance Department
   a) Arrange insurance coverage for movement and storage of household goods.
4. Controller's Department
   a) Determine withholding taxes required on expense reimbursements and notify new employee.
   b) Compute the percentage addition to regular reimbursement on taxable items and forward payment to new employee.

Procedures

Expenses covered are:

1. Travel
   a) Transportation for new employee from present location to new employment location
      1) Private auto—12¢ per mile based on most direct route
      2) Commercial transportation will be as dictated by hiring-unit practice
   b) One round trip, not to exceed four days, for spouse to visit new employment for purpose of house-hunting
   c) Transportation for new employee to return to former location to move family and household goods to new location
   d) Transportation of new employee and family to new employment location.
2. Living expenses (meals and lodging)
   a) For new employee while traveling to new employment location and for a period of up to two weeks unless permanent housing is occupied prior to that time
   b) For spouse during house-hunting trip
   c) For new employee and family while moving to new employment location
   d) For new employee and family for up to two weeks while awaiting availability of permanent housing at new location.
3. Moving household goods
   a) Costs of packing, transportation, storage, and unpacking within the following limits
      1) Up to 10,000 pounds of normal household and personal goods
      2) In transit, storage for a period not to exceed two months

b) The corporation will not be responsible for loss or damage to animals, currency, notes, securities, stamps, furs, jewels, watches, etc., and will not pay the cost of moving boats, trailers, frozen foods, or unusual items that require special handling or transport.

4. Federal income tax requirements

   a) Expenses paid to new employee with exception of items 2c and 3a are considered compensation income and as such are reportable on federal income tax return as "compensation for services." To assist the new employee in meeting this tax, X% will be added to the corporation's reimbursement on taxable items. This will be reimbursed as a separate payment to the employee at the end of the calendar year.

   b) The new employee is permitted to deduct expenses on his federal income tax return in the five categories specified by the law. These deductions will. within limits, be based on actual expenses incurred.

2.16 CONCLUSION

To achieve the level of understanding needed for the employment function and line departments to be really successful in fulfilling their roles is no mean task, and it will take all of your skill to make it work in the most meaningful manner. This will happen only when both parties understand the problems and misconceptions that each has fostered about the other over the years. So, the root of the problem is understanding, and hopefully this chapter has made its point if you now make a sincere effort to develop rapport, learn to listen, and communicate with one another.

3
Budget and cost

As we discussed in Chapter 2, practically any organization with enough time and money at its disposal can succeed in attracting people. It was also stated that this is unfortunate, because so little attention is paid to cash flow in employment in many organizations. Let's explore this lack of awareness. Employment *per se* is not a profit-and-loss function (P&L), but it impacts so dramatically on the effectiveness of the total organization that it has great bearing on the overall profit and loss.

Employment is often criticized for a lack of sensitivity to cost and controls, but many line managers are completely unaware of the costs of employment because they don't see them or make an effort to understand them. This could be a good argument for charging employment costs back to operating units if that practice weren't so difficult and expensive to administer. As an alternative to a direct charge, it is not unreasonable to notify the beneficiary of the services what costs were incurred on his behalf. This lack of awareness compounds the problem of cost by allowing employment to be done on a short-term, crisis, basis which in the long run has to be more costly. Continuity is the basic key to the economy of employment.

3.1 BASIC NEEDS

Because of the misunderstanding and lack of awareness, the basic needs of good cost control and budgeting in employment do not get enough attention, and this results in inefficiency and uneconomic practices. There are some "basic needs" that, if instituted, will help ensure better control and budgeting. These are:

1. *Need for planning*—manpower and recruitment plans
2. *Need for good relationships*—with line departments and employment sources
3. *Need for data*—timely accounting of historical data—records of who, what, when, where, and why.

To achieve full accord and understanding on those needs, there are some basic premises that the line manager and employment function must understand in their fullest context:

1. A "soft" labor market does not necessarily guarantee less expense in hiring.
2. The good man is always hard to find.
3. Generally, promoting internally and hiring at lower levels is more economical.
4. Unusual time pressures can affect employment costs dramatically; when done on crash basis, there is tendency to pay more for pre-selection help, e.g., an employment agency.
5. Try to avoid independent or individual programs such as letting the line departments go directly to sources.
6. Some aspects of employment costs should be centrally controlled.
7. Above all, the budgetary control should rest with the employment function, which in turn must delegate responsibility as required to ensure the flexibility to get the job done, e.g., allowing the local manager in large organizations to approve the field recruiter's expense accounts. Each of these points will be discussed in further detail in this chapter.

"The credibility of recruitment (employment) can be improved as the ability to describe current status and predict future operations improves."[1] The employment function must have data that can be utilized effectively to communicate with the line and ensure more realistic planning. There-

[1]Roger Hawk, *The Recruitment Function*, New York: American Management Association, 1969, p. 159.

fore, the discussion on budgets and costs will be divided into four sections: cost-per-hire, budget make-up, controls, and how to stretch the employment dollar.

3.2 COST-PER-HIRE

Cost-per-hire is one of the most controversial subjects related to the employment process, and in some organizations it would appear to be a more closely guarded secret than any proprietary product knowledge they possess. Even though most everyone involved in the process is cognizant of the great expense of achieving employment goals, it appears that few people want to really face the financial "facts of life." This unwillingness is a primary reason why there is so little agreement on what should be included in the data that comprise a cost-per-hire figure. A good approach to this subject is to standardize certain cost items that most logically comprise a cost-per-hire figure and to *stick with them* and build your controls around them. These items do not, in the author's opinion, have to include such intangible costs as interview time by the line department or costs incurred after placement (training costs). These costs may be measured in some other manner, if necessary, but they are generally extremely difficult to account for in this context of cost-per-hire. What we need to be concerned with here are the direct costs of *putting* the person on the payroll. We also have to take into account the fact that the employment function's costs may differ to a great degree as a result of such things as the scope of the particular hiring problem, geographic factors, the general image of the organization, and the product line. Accounting procedures, also, will vary from organization to organization, and that will affect the gathering and analysis of data. Therefore, you must determine what best suits your particular situation and set up your criteria accordingly.

In many organizations, cost-per-hire figures are high by design, because the organization is more concerned with selecting and retaining good people. In other words, a low cost-per-hire figure does not indicate success if there is high turnover.

Let's look at a standard set of items that can constitute cost-per-hire and provide a point of departure for setting up a system. Whether or not this includes all the items that any sample of employment managers would be unanimous about is in a way irrelevant, because this information is for your own use, guidance, and adaptation in your organization.

This set of items could, however, provide a basis for some standardization and hopefully some meaningful interchange among various organizations in different industries. This might eventually allow an organization to measure its employment function against some average figure for industry in general or within a specific industry. This approach does assume, however, that the employment function has been given the financial responsibility to get people on the payroll. The basic cost categories to be utilized in determining a cost-per-hire figure should be items which are easily identifiable and accountable in any organization. They can be slotted into two general categories—internal costs and external costs.

Internal Costs—expense of operating the employment function

a) salaries
b) benefits
c) overtime
d) travel expense
e) university relations
f) telephone and telegraph
g) publications
h) memberships
i) testing

External Costs

a) fees for employment agencies and executive search activities
b) advertising
c) travel expense for candidates
d) psychological assessments
e) relocation
f) brochures

How these specific items are set up in the budget will be elaborated on in the next section of this chapter. The primary point here is that each of these items is easily identifiable and should then be more controllable, even in a relatively unsophisticated organization. The total of these internal and external costs, when divided by the number of hires over a given period of time, gives you a cost-per-hire number which can then be the basis for "describing the current status of an employment program and for predicting future operations."

Let's emphasize that for this to be meaningful information for the future, *you must* determine what your internal and external items are to be and stick with them as your cost-per-hire criteria. Once you begin to deviate from the standard you lose all the value of having a "base figure," the figure which can be the basis for your future employment efforts. In essence, cost per hire probably has only one valid use—as a base figure for your own use and not as a figure to compare with some other organization to prove or disprove the success or failure of your employment function.

3.3 BUDGET MAKE-UP

Let's first accept the definition of a budget as an estimate of the amount of money that can and is to be spent for various purposes in a given time, i.e., a plan for spending. A good deal of the success in developing a budget and controlling it rests in the approach to budgeting in your organization. If you are in an organization that does not have a great deal of concern for controls, there will be less than a desirable amount of efficiency in the employment function. Budgets are not popular documents, because they are viewed as iron-clad controls. Realistically, however, a predictor of the future cannot be that iron clad. When a budget is submitted, the employment function should emphasize the factors that affect cost so that if circumstances change, the need for increases will be recognized more quickly. This frame of mind will help you achieve a better understanding and respect for your budget and its execution.

The following points should help provide some guidance for the employment function in achieving this frame of mind.

1. Run employment as a P&L center, that is, be a good "general manager."
2. *Know what things have the greatest impact* on your budget and develop controls.
3. Be flexible, because your manpower requirements change with the labor market.
4. *Know your basic cost structure*, e.g., employment agency fees, executive-search costs, man-day travel costs. This will help inestimably in ensuring the most effective utilization of your sources.

Without some historical data to work from, it is difficult to articulate the specifics of an employment budget. However, if you don't have it, there is a good deal of readily available information. For example, you will find it invaluable to keep records of all hires, with emphasis on their *source*. Source of hires will be a key factor in determining your "base figure," e.g., average fee paid to employment agencies, average cost per man day for campus recruitment. You should also keep track of the geography of your hires and the sex, race, and number of people interviewed for a particular job. All of these facts will help you to better determine the details of your budget. Knowing the average employment-agency fee paid and the number and level of hires over a given period of time in relation to other sources will allow you to calculate employment-agency expenditures for next year, based on proposed manpower needs.

Extremely critical to the development of an employment budget, and again it can't be emphasized enough, is the relationship established with the line departments. The magnitude of an employment budget is another reason why it is so important that they be involved. They must understand the dollars needed to do the job and the factors that affect the "doing." To influence the line with the importance of the budget, impress them with your skills as an "expense controller." Include in your monthly report comparisons of expenses incurred versus budget, reasons for variances, and particularly the results of any cost-cutting activity.

There are ten basic budget items (accounts) that if defined and recorded accurately should provide the data necessary for the all-so-critical "base figure." Within each of these ten accounts, it will probably be helpful to break out certain subaccounts. Your accounting system will have to be the determining factor in how finite your employment-cost records are, but if your accounting procedures cannot accommodate these suggested subaccounts, keep them yourself. Organize a simple set of books that can be maintained on a daily basis—it will prove to be more than worth the effort. It will provide an accurate day-by-day accounting of all your expenditures. This really is a plus, because an accounting department usually provides only a monthly summation of expenditures. So any specifics you may need during the month are at best estimates. The employment function should be half-way home toward thinking like a profit-center manager if it keeps these records. The employment function will know its costs on a timely basis and will be in a much better position to control them.

Let's review the ten basic accounts and subaccounts that are suggested to provide your cost-per-hire statistics. These should be easily adaptable to most employment functions, large or small.

1. *Salary and Overtime Pay.* The normal rate of pay for all people in the employment function will include proposed increases during the budget year.

2. *Taxes and Benefits.* A percentage of salary and overtime is established by your accounting department and includes such items as workmen's compensation, group insurance, and FICA.
3. *Travel.* It will be helpful if this includes two subaccounts: one for *employment-function personnel* (expenditures for transportation, lodging and meals, tips, meals and entertainment for others, e.g., other employees, source people, candidates); and another subaccount for *candidates'* expenditures for transportation, lodging and meals, and tips.
4. *Advertising.* This category will be more meaningful if also broken into two subaccounts: *campus advertising*—all the advertising that is related to your university-relations program (Chapter 6); and advertising directed to the *"experienced"* job market.
5. *Professional Services.* This account consists of costs incurred for the payment of employment-agency fees, retainers, or "seed" money; for any psychological services, e.g., assessments and testing; and costs of printing recruiting brochures, pamphlets.
6. *Executive Search.* This was purposely omitted from the account above because of the flexible nature of this activity. This is an extremely difficult part of any employment plan. Set this account up as a "contingency account," with X dollars budgeted on the basis of executive manpower turnover during the past two or three years.
7. *Relocation.* There should be two subaccounts: one for *employment-function personnel* relocation costs, and one for *new-hire* costs. As is the case in many organizations, the new-hire cost may be charged to the hiring department. If so, arrange with your accounting department to provide you with these data. It is very critical in establishing the "base figure," and in most cases this will be the single largest cost for an individual hire.
8. *Campus-Relations Aid.* This account should be structured to cover a miscellany of subaccounts, e.g., aid to education (grants and other monetary gifts to universities and colleges) and cost of satellite programs (equipment donations, materials, and speakers' bureaus).
9. *Telephone and Telegraph.* This account is self-explanatory.
10. *Miscellaneous Services.* This can include expenditures for such things as memberships in professional organizations, cost of publications,

books, and registration fees for professional meetings. This also can include those "other" expenditures that don't fit elsewhere.

In summary, then, it certainly will make the whole system a lot easier if your accounting department is structured to accommodate some or all of the suggested subaccounts. In many organizations, this probably is not practical; therefore, do not hesitate to set up your own books so that you know the daily status of your budget. As the employment budget is prepared, remember that it is particularly difficult to foresee every conceivable situation that might arise. The best you can do is to use good judgment in making your predictions; no one can predict the future that accurately.

The employment function's relationship with the line should pay off here in getting general inputs about the business, e.g., the pending acquisition that may affect the manpower plan and thus employment activity. Remember the peculiarities of the labor market under different circumstances. Remember that each job may require a different approach and that what was successful last time may not work now. Go and talk with the controller or accounting manager and get his advice and counsel about the best approach for structuring the budget. These people may also be able to provide assistance on the subaccounts, and in all probability they will have some helpful planning guides. Also, this kind of contact will help establish even more, your credibility as a P&L-oriented manager.

3.4 CONTROLS

The controls that employment is able to institute will generally be only as good as the internal relationships that have been established. If the employment function has achieved a level of professional credibility in the eyes of the line, then in all probability, authority for getting the job done will be theirs. If not, the line will assume responsibility for determining how, for what, and by whom the money budgeted will be spent. There must always be a willingness, however, to delegate authority as the situation dictates. This will be particularly critical in larger organizations where the accounting system is usually more cumbersome and time-consuming.

Many of the controls needed to make employment as economical and efficient as possible will be spelled out in your employment policies and will emanate from one basic statement in a majority of organizations—

"It is our policy to fill available positions, wherever practical, through the transfer or promotion of qualified employees." The importance of this statement is that once it has been determined that there are no transferable or promotable employees, the "meter starts running." Decisions need to be made. What are the specifics of the types of people we need? What sources(s) should we use (advertisements, employment agencies, executive search)? What time pressures are there? (The less the pressure, the more economical the sources utilized.)

As was indicated in Chapter 2, the primary responsibility for directing employment activity and utilizing various sources should rest with the employment function, which logically gives approval for expenditures and thus is accountable for adhering to the approved budget.

Approval control for all budget accounts makes the employment function's task easier, particularly in dealing with any sources that charge for their services. With controls, the employment function can insist on adherence to its *modus-operandi,* because it will be responsible for paying the bills. For example, the employment function can ensure that no one deals directly with the line departments, employment agencies and executive-search firms in particular, thereby avoiding the inefficient and uneconomic use of management's time and energy.

By keeping its own set of books, the employment function will be able to identify at any point in time the exact status of a specific account. Also, on a calendarized basis it will help in spotting potential overruns, thus allowing adjustments to be made. These records can be utilized for a quarterly analysis of progress of the program to date, which will be particularly critical in communicating with the line.

Similarly, it is important that your own chain of command be kept informed. This type of communication accomplishes several things. *First*, it helps to prove that the employment function is cost-conscious, alert to, and on top of its budgetary situation. *Second*, it will make a request for additional funds, if needed, less traumatic and will help prepare management for a possible overrun at the end of the year. An employment function organized with these types of controls will be alert to any warning signs as the year progresses. Necessary adjustments can then be made with a lot less anguish and will be more palatable to management.

To reiterate, the most important aspect of budget control is to have the initial decision-making responsibility vested in the employment function. This provides the leverage to make things happen in an orderly way, with particular reference to utilization of sources. The level of expenditure approval will vary from organization to organization. However, authorization to utilize a particular source within the framework or the overall budget should belong to the employment function, as should control of those sources and the responsibility for results.

Controls on sources have to be predicated on the cost of those sources, and this should always be well understood before any action is initiated. For example, the employment agency should provide a schedule of fees; the advertising agency, a breakdown of all costs in preparing and inserting an ad; the executive-search firm should spell out the cost structure, including expenses, in writing for *each* search.

Travel and entertainment expenses involving other persons in the organization (e.g., campus recruiters and job candidates) should be spelled out. What class of air travel? What expense items require receipts? Are other employees allowable as entertainment/meal expenses? Approval of these expenses should be delegated in larger or more decentralized operations because of the time element involved in accounting procedures. Ultimate approval, however, must rest with the employment function. Obviously, this assumes initial approval, because there will be other levels of approval in most organizations based on the amount of the expenditure. Don't hesitate to get some idea of how effective your controls are by comparing some specifics (such as travel expenses) with other companies or with other functions in your organization.

Without controls there will be no real accounting, and without that there will be chaos in employment. Therefore, control on key budget items is essential to a well-run employment function, but it also must be understood that "you get what you pay for" and "you have to spend money to make money."

3.5 STRETCHING YOUR EMPLOYMENT DOLLAR

Like all other expenditures in business today, the employment dollar is under continual scrutiny. However, like costs in any other part of the organization, those of running an employment function continue to increase. As discussed in Chapter 1, there are new factors influencing the labor market which tend to intensify the cost problem. For example, just try to estimate the cost of restructuring the various jobs in your organization and its implications with reference to employment. Things are changing so rapidly on the manpower scene that they are not noticeable until they have occurred, and it is only then that we realize the true cost impact. Inefficiencies that are costly today could be disastrous in terms of dollar expenditures in the future.

If this is true, what are some of the things that can be done to make your employment dollar go farther? Other chapters have or will elaborate on a number of points that will help you stretch your employment dollar, but at the risk of repetition, let's take each of the ten basic employment-budget accounts and determine how best to get the maximum out of each dollar in them.

1. *Salary and Overtime.* This account will be stable in that to accomplish the job, you will need a certain number of people; to do the job more economically, you will want to have the most competent people; and in all probability, to get them you will need to pay good salaries. So, there just aren't many ways to cut corners without at the same time decreasing quality. The clerical staff, however, may lend itself to some dollar-stretching, particularly if you have a good feel for the pattern of activity, e.g., campus recruiting, which tends to slow down in June, July, and August, may not require a full-time staff year round. Using part-time students in your clerical jobs, for example, may be another answer.

   Are there typing pools in the organization? Off-peak times in other departments? If you have large volume of correspondence, check and find out if it might not be handled more economically by an outside service; this will be particularly valuable if there are known peaks and valleys in the activity.

2. *Travel.* There is a great deal of potential for stretching the employment dollar here. The most significant may be to schedule travel on a geographic basis. Organize the campus recruiting schedule according to the location of schools, and consolidate the use of recruiter(s). (Using different recruiter(s) at geographically compatible schools is one of the biggest wastes in a campus-recruiting budget. See Chapter 6.10.) When recruiting experienced workers, take advantage of the geography of a given problem. With a job to fill in New York City and four or five candidates in and around Chicago and Detroit, go there for interviews rather than have each candidate make a trip to New York. You can sometimes negotiate candidates' travel costs, particularly lodging costs if you are in an area where there is competition among the hotels and motels. A caution here; to avoid any future ill

feelings, be sure to standardize the class of travel and level of accommodations used by both candidates and your employees. It is only logical that the candidate should know what the rules about travel are. This is the time for him to find out that you fly tourist class or pay 10¢ a mile for automobile mileage, or limit meal expenses to a certain amount.

3. *Advertising.* Know your media and take advantage of newspaper advertising contracts; you can ride on the coat-tails of other advertising your organization does, because it all counts toward total lineage. Don't feel that the size of the ad is necessarily a criterion for the number or quality of responses. If you use an agency, be sure that it has a thorough understanding of your organization and the structure of the jobs so that any ad the agency prepares is meaningful and not a lot of words about a lot of mundane things. The ad agency will know the best time and media needed in any geographic area to reach your intended audience. The agency can also keep you up to date about new publications and trends in the labor market. (See Chapter 4 for further ideas on maximizing the advertising-dollar investment.) A good ad agency will work hard to maximize your dollar expenditures, but you should also get it involved so that it knows the environment and the problems of your organization. Then and only then can the agency develop ads that will reach the potential employee and help stretch your employment dollar.
4. *Professional Services.* Nowhere else will "you get what you pay for" be truer in the employment process than here. As was mentioned on p. 62, be sure to know what the costs are for these essential outside services, and don't hesitate to use them. But be sure you are using the agency to the maximum extent possible. For example, the employment agency should be providing a *complete* service in terms of getting people on the payroll—not just referring resumes. It should be involved as an objective sounding board for the candidates; it should be involved in reference checks. (Other points on full utilization of this source are given in Chapter 4.) Don't hesitate to use a little "seed money," i.e., with a particularly capable employment agency, a few dollars now and then for an advertisement or miscellaneous expense can put you on top of the referral list for the best candidates from the agency.

In developing your recruiting literature, slant it toward jobs and job content and the overall philosophy of your organization rather than merely its immediate needs. Your objective should be to ensure the longest life to the literature and to take advantage of volume costs by purchasing several years' supply at one time.

5. *Executive Search.* It is difficult to stretch your dollars here, because it is a source that should be utilized only when the use of other sources has been ruled out for whatever reason. If we use the pure definition of "search" (seeking the individual who is not looking), it becomes obvious that it really will not make much sense to use this source for jobs under $30,000 a year or so unless there are some highly unusual characteristics in the job, e.g., a very narrow technical specialty that is in great demand.

   Once it has been decided to go this route, be sure that the ground rules are spelled out about all the financial aspects of each particular search. Costs may vary considerably from search to search. Ask some questions. How is adjustment to be made between retainers paid and the final, total placement cost? Is it base salary or base salary plus bonus (total package)? What are rules about expenses and when will you require approval—$200 a month, $300 a month?

   Some problems may arise in using this source to stretch the employment dollar. But by spelling out the details and having regular communication and good rapport with the firm doing the work and the line manager involved, you will be able to realize some economies.

6. *Relocation.* This should be well detailed in your policy statements for both employees and new hires (see Chapter 2.15). On the average, the major cost of employment is relocation of new employees; therefore, this account should lend itself to some dollar-stretching. The major objective is to make the move simple and expeditious for the new employee and not necessarily to cover every dime of expense. Even though flexibility in interpreting your relocation policy is important, you still must make sure that the applicable restrictions and limitations are spelled out. Discuss all the pertinent implications of the policy with the new or potential employee so that there will be less probability of misunderstanding when the final bill is submitted. Your biggest opportunity for stretching the dollar with this account can be achieved with a few minutes of specific conversation to ensure complete understanding of "the rules." If you have a potential new

hire who for whatever reason requires some bending of the rules, handle this in person (see Chapter 9.1 for an elaboration of this point).

7. *University Relations.* Because of the complexity of this type of program in a large organization, the key to maximizing the employment dollar is central control. Campus recruiters should be selected assigned, and evaluated from a central point. Referrals of recommended candidates should be controlled from a central point to ensure maximum exposure to the organization. The aid-to-education program, which is a substantial sum of money in most larger organizations, needs "someone in charge" to ensure maximum publicity value for the *whole* organization rather than have it reflect purely local interests.

   Central control seems to be the name of the dollar-stretching game in this account in order to avoid duplication of efforts, eliminate local interests, and ensure the involvement of the best people—regardless of function or discipline.

These are the primary areas in which the employment dollar can be stretched. This does not mean, of course, that there are not many other situations in any organization that don't hold the potential for economies. If the employment function is really doing its job, it will continually be seeking ways to stretch the dollar and will never be satisfied with the status-quo.

In summary, then, the employment function needs to establish a businesslike credibility; it must have approval authority and in turn must delegate responsibility for control; it must budget within the budget; and it must audit each month. If it adheres to these responsibilities, it will be able to measure the effectiveness of the employment program, which in turn will help immeasurably in keeping costs in line and avoiding budget overruns.

4
Employment sources

Once you have determined that you have specific manpower requirements and have completed the specifications for the job, you are ready to seek job candidates. To do this intelligently, you need to understand the various manpower sources and their advantages and disadvantages. The key to the success or failure of any employment function will be predicated on how well it develops and utilizes all of the available technical/professional manpower sources. To seek a potential employee efficiently and economically, it is imperative to know when and how each source should be utilized. Everyone involved in the employment process must forget the generalizations and prejudices that they may have developed over the years about various sources. Even though each source may be more productive under certain circumstances, there will be occasions when you may need to tap all of them and make your own determination about which are the most efficient and productive. At times, for example, it will be cheaper to pay an employment-agency fee or the cost of retaining an executive-search firm than it will be to advertise.

A very important point in selecting the source to be utilized on a specific recruiting problem is *lead time*. What are the pressures to get the job filled? Is it a situation for which all the stops need to be pulled? Your own experience with your own organization, of course, will be a major factor. Your geographic location, your product line, your salary structure, your reputation, the general economy—all will affect what sources you use and how you use them. But, a major factor in how you use or misuse your sources may well be the degree to which you have "educated" your organization to the importance of the employment function in relation to the total business. The burden is on the employment function to know the sources and the associated costs and to build the confidence of management so that the job can be done effectively and economically.

4.1 INTERNATIONAL SOURCES

It would be remiss not to mention the international aspects of this subject in terms of the modern employment function. It is safe to assume that in discussing employment sources in organizations with an international orientation, the basic philosophy of utilization is not too different. There are differences in technique in certain countries due to accepted historical practices or laws. But as the world grows smaller and we move into the era of a world-wide manpower market, procedures and techniques will tend to become standardized.

At this time there is a great deal of dependence, maybe too much, on internal sources for staffing international jobs. Nationalism is still a big factor and prevents, to a degree, the development of the true international manager.

All of the symptoms and patterns that we have in the United States labor market appear to be developing in international employment—job hopping, underemployment, a middle-management shortage—and these are compounded by a general lack of sophistication in the international-employment process, which has generally been neglected over the years and becomes important now because of these problems.

On the plus side, the procedures and techniques of entry-level recruiting are improving. Search firms (both American and foreign) are proliferating and are developing more flexible attitudes about national boundaries. Although this may be truer in Europe than in other parts of the world at this time, there appears to be a greater sophistication in general.

4.2 MAJOR SOURCES

Let's take each of the major sources that are available to any organization and discuss each one in terms of what it can contribute and how best to utilize it.[1] These sources are not necessarily discussed in any order of

[1] *The Recruiter's Encyclopedia*, a looseleaf service of Recruiting Trends, 20 N. Wacker Drive, Chicago, Illinois, discusses a number of off-beat sources that relate to specific industries.

priority or level of productivity. However, there will be more emphasis on the three most expensive, and possibly the most misunderstood and misused—advertising, employment agencies, and executive-search firms. It is important to always think of and utilize all the sources that any organization may have as an "extension" of the employment function and to understand *that* relationship well enough so that you get your money's worth out of each source.

Advertising

Unless you have specific experience to go on, it will be hard for you to spell out specific advantages and disadvantages of this source to your organization. Since it is impossible to talk about every organization's specific employment advertising problems, we will have to generalize.

Most organizations that have any sizeable volume of manpower requirements utilize the services of an advertising agency. There are many reasons for this, but the primary one is that you need to handle advertising for what it is—a business problem—so get a "pro" to do it. Select your agency on much the same basis as you do your other sources (see the next section). However, once you have selected and have begun to use an agency, don't try to second-guess them; they are the experts and have the staff, the contacts, and the "know how" necessary to get the job done. The agency's primary role is to look at your problem, develop a program that best meets your needs, create and place ads, and pay the bills. Remember, employment advertising is a difficult communication problem, and most organizations will probably need all the assistance they can get to make this the productive source it can be.

The effectiveness of advertising is influenced considerably by the type of job, the level of the job, and by its placement, i.e., the media used and the content of the ad itself. In a technically short labor market, technical or industry magazines or journals appear to be the best media because they are seen by active as well as potential candidates over a longer period of time; also, because of their tenure, they tend to do a better job of image-building for an organization. You should not necessarily expect a large initial response from this media, nor is it feasible in many cases to trace hires directly to these media because of their longer life. For example, an ad in the February issue of *Chemical and Engineering News* may be seen by a potential candidate in May or July in a technical library, and only then may the organization receive a direct inquiry. Because of the long-range value of industry journals, general job specifications can be listed and special problem areas can be concentrated on better, because you are reaching a more specific audience. Newspaper ads, on the other hand, lend themselves better to two situations and are logically targeted to the "active" market:

1. Recruiting in a particular geographic area. (In doing city recruiting, newspaper ads should run prior to and concurrently with the recruiting effort.)
2. "One-shot" ads for specific jobs.

Regardless of the market, the number of ads run should be carefully considered. No matter how good they are, ads run too frequently can easily suggest that the organization has a high turnover rate, is poorly organized, and may not be the best place to work. Ads should never be run (and/or rerun) merely to pacify an impatient line manager. Radio and television have been used to some extent as a media over the years but have not proved particularly successful except for nonexempt jobs. It appears that the best media still are newspapers, consumer magazines, business magazines, professional journals, and industry publications.

Once it has been determined which media to use, the next problem is whether to run an "open" ad with corporate identification or a "blind" ad with no identification. Blind ads generally do not draw as well as "identified" ads for several reasons. First, the anonymity of a blind ad often negates its drawing power and will, in all probability, preclude response from many well-qualified people. Second, the candidate may be reluctant to respond to what he fears might be his own organization. You can probably figure that a third to a half of the potential respondees won't answer a blind ad. Although you have no obligation to answer blind-ad respondents if you have no interest, this should never be a determining factor in selecting this source. There are other, more productive methods of recruiting for openings sensitive enough not to be broadcast generally under your organization's name.[2]

[2]Postal Regulation 261.23H prohibits concealing identity of a firm or employment agency in blind ads with only a P.O. Box # given. The interested party may inquire at the post office and pay an inquiry fee to receive the identification of the advertiser. This ruling does not apply, however, if a newspaper box number is given in the ad.

There are six basic criteria that determine what constitutes a good employment ad. They should provide some realistic guidelines, but also remember that no one type of ad appeals to every discipline or to every individual.

1. Select the right paper or magazine and the right section of that paper or magazine. As mentioned earlier, technical or industry magazines are probably the best for technical disciplines. Sunday editions of newspapers are recommended because the person actively looking will usually take time to read them more thoroughly. In most cases it is best to use the section devoted to employment advertising, although this may not necessarily be the "Help Wanted" section, e.g., the Sunday *New York Times* "Financial Section." The paper does not have to be the "best" paper or have the largest circulation in a given area, but it should be the one that is generally known to carry the largest number of employment ads.
2. The dignity of the ad is important. Cuteness is deadly when dealing with what to the interested reader is a very serious subject. The ad should project the best possible image of the organization. Visual aspects are important, but irrelevant illustrations should be avoided.
3. If there are a number of openings at different levels in a specific functional area, an ad emphasizing the work and responsibilities of the whole function may bring a larger volume of response. Care should be taken, however, to avoid "a large number of" approach, which tends to be impersonal. On the other hand, the details of a specific job opening should be spelled out. Verbiage about such things as benefits and living area should be minimized; rather, emphasis should be placed on "selling the job." The ultimate key to advertising for a specific position is detailed job information. Ads generally tend to exaggerate the qualities necessary for *getting* the job, so don't do it; you want respondents who have the qualities for *doing* the job.
4. Salary information should not, in most cases, be included in an ad. If it is, it may well eliminate some good potential candidates before the organization has an opportunity to sell the job. It may also cause some negative reactions among current employees. A well-written ad will, in all probability, reflect the level of the position without limiting the response.

5. How often should ads be run? The best rule of thumb is to set a criterion which can be measured, i.e., how many responses of interest are being received? Longer range, how many invitations to interviews are ads producing? What is the cost per interview and hire as compared to other source costs? It is reasonable to assume that a continuing program in technical and industrial magazines will prove more fruitful than a volume of newspaper ads, particularly for professional/technical needs. Newspaper ads tend to be more productive on a one-shot, short-term basis. This does not necessarily hold true for ads run for a company by a "third party," but the logic involved in that instance is different.
6. Ads should provide for ease of reply. It should be as easy as possible for the first contact to be made. Time is always critical in the employment process, so cut it down whenever you can. If feasible, a telephone contact is best; otherwise, a simple request for a postcard or a business card with a brief description of background (degree, job title, present employer) provides enough information to enable the employment function to follow up. (It is better to telephone to see what mutual interests exist before you spend time and money having a candidate complete an application form and processing the paperwork.) If the candidate is interested, you can request a resume. To follow up any response with a standard letter requesting completion of an application form usually wastes time. If an application is essential, a resume need not be requested.

In terms of cost, advertising is a rather broad and complex area, but there are a number of publications available that will answer most questions that might arise.[3] (If you use an advertising agency, it can provide this information.)

Advertising, like all sources, has been affected by antidiscrimination legislation. The primary ruling affecting advertising is Section 704 (b) of Title VII of the Civil Rights Act of 1964.

[3]Standard Rate and Data Service books; rate cards available from all media; Nationwide Advertising Service publishes a *Classified Ad Guide* covering all U.S. papers (free—write to them at 465 Investment Bldg., Cleveland, Ohio 44114); *The Directory of the College Student Press in America*, Oxbridge Publishing Co., Inc., 150 E. 52nd St., N.Y., N.Y. 10022.

> It shall be unlawful employment practice for an employer, labor organization, or employment agency to print or publish or cause to be printed or published any notice or advertisement relating to employment by such an employer or membership in or any classification or referral for employment by such a labor organization, or relating to any classification or referral for employment by such an employment agency, indicating any preference, limitation, specification, or discrimination, based on race, color, religion, sex or national origin, except that such a notice or advertisement may indicate a preference, limitation, specification, or discrimination based on religion, sex, or national origin when religion, sex or national origin is a bona fide occupational qualification for employment.

There are other implications of antidiscrimination relating to the placement of ads, e.g., use of "Male" or "Female" columns in newspapers, but this is primarily the media's problem and, again, the type of problem your agency can handle.

Organizations would be well advised to consider utilizing ethnic publications for their minority recruiting efforts. Believability is so critical with this audience that your ad in the *Wall Street Journal* with "Equal Opportunity Employer" on it just may not come across. The best approach when placing an ad in ethnic media is to be direct and straightforward about the requirements for doing the job. Don't try to explain all the things your company says its doing about equal employment; it won't have any more impact than an illustration showing only black employees, for example. Minority groups are extremely perceptive and sensitive to employment practices, so don't try to appear to be other than what you are. *A Guide to Black Media*, a publication prepared by Deutsch, Shea, and Evans, Inc., is an example of an excellent aid in recruiting black employees.[4]

Third Parties (Employment Agencies and Executive-Search Firms)

These two sources are perhaps the most misunderstood of all of the sources of professional/technical personnel and this results primarily from a lack of communication. Before discussing these sources in more detail, let us first define the basic differences between them. An employment

[4]Deutsch, Shea, and Evans, Inc., 49 E. 53rd St., N.Y., N.Y. 10022.

agency, which receives payment for its services only when it has placed a candidate, cannot afford to provide in-depth service to a company on specific individual jobs, but it can provide broad coverage for a number of needs with some immediacy and/or commonality. Executive-search firms, on the other hand, are "consultants" and are paid for their *time*, whether or not they place a particular candidate. Therefore, they can provide in-depth service on a specific job because they are not attuned to nor interested in handling volume.

Employment Agencies

Employment agencies date back to the Roman Empire, but nowhere have they developed as fast or become such a factor in business as in the United States. Today, there are approximately 10,000 employment agencies in the United States.[5] Most states require agencies to be licensed and have laws governing their operation and the fees that they can charge.[6]

Employment-agency mechanics are relatively simple. Through advertising and word of mouth, they develop candidates and refer their credentials to client companies. Should the candidate be hired, the agency collects from him a specified percent of his starting salary, although the general practice is for the hiring company to pay the fee for professional/technical people.[7]

The primary problem most organizations have in utilizing this source is selecting the one(s) that can be most productive. There are three basic criteria that should help an organization determine the right agency to use. Bear in mind that *you* should make this decision after weighing all the facts, because the success an associate or another organization may have had will not automatically ensure success for your organization.

1. What is the agency's *reputation* in particular functional areas, disciplines, or industries? Some agencies, of course, specialize in functional areas, and all of them usually are better in some area(s) than others.

---

[5]The National Employment Association (NEA) reports that the "average" agency placed 379 people during 1970.

[6]The United States Department of Labor Bulletin 201, "State Laws regulating Private Employment Agencies," can be obtained from the National Employment Association in Washington, D.C. It answers specific questions pertaining to the operations and charges of employment agencies.

[7]According to NEA, 54% of "*all*" placement fees in 1970 were paid by employers.

2. How *professional* is the agency? Does it really make an effort to get the "right" man? How much of an effort does it make to get to know your organization? Is it willing to invest the time to build a relationship? Does the agency have an interest in your problems over and above its fee?
3. How is the *personal chemistry* between you and the agency? Do you have confidence and trust in each other *or* can it be developed? Most organizations find it difficult to work effectively with an unlimited number of agencies, so this personal aspect becomes critical.

Once your organization decides to use a particular agency, you must determine how to use the agency most effectively. To a degree this will be predicated on the relationship you have already established. There are five basic things you can expect the employment agency to do:

1. Interview or *at least* screen potential candidates. Hopefully, the relationship will become good enough so that the agency's evaluation means an automatic referral and interview by your organization.
2. Make appointments for interviews and get feedback from the candidate after his interview with you.
3. Provide accurate inputs about compensation and be instrumental in the negotiations between the candidate and your organization.
4. Check references, as requested. The agency will be able, at times, to check people that you might not.
5. Serve as an objective third party in interesting and selling the candidate if he's right for the job. An agency doing its job can be the candidate's "sounding board," i.e., he might ask questions he wouldn't ask you.

Those things take time, and of course this is the key to client-agency relationships. How much time is the agency willing to invest in working with a client? That is always the option the agency has and will be based to a great degree on how well they know you, your organization, the problems you have, and the type of talent you require. On the other hand, you also have an option; if the agencies don't adhere to your standards or have a fee structure that you feel is reasonable, then you don't have to do business with them. There are 9999 more to work with.

To ensure the greatest mutual success, there are specific procedural matters that should be spelled out so that both parties understand each other. The agencies have their contract and/or fee schedule, and you should have some guidelines. A detailed policy that is generally applicable and adaptable to most any size organization is shown in Chapter 2.15.

A summary of that policy for use as a handout to your employment agencies follows. All organizations that utilize agencies should consider a similar handout to avoid confusion and misunderstanding.

EMPLOYMENT-AGENCY GUIDELINES

It is the policy of XYZ Corporation to staff professional and managerial positions with present employees whenever possible. In situations for which this is not possible, outside recruiting efforts may be initiated. One key source for professional and managerial employees is employment agencies. To ensure their most efficient utilization, and in accordance with our role as an equal opportunity employer, we have developed the following procedures:

I. Fees

1. It is our policy to pay appropriate placement fees. These are paid as agreed after the individual has reported to work.
2. All agencies from whom we request and honor referrals shall provide a copy of their fee schedule prior to initiating any referrals. It is not practical to state corporate-wide fee guidelines for XYZ Corporation because of geographic and economic differences.

II. Contacts

1. All employment-agency contacts must be made through the employment function responsible for communicating the job opening.
2. Contact with line departments will be controlled through the employment function. Approval must be obtained from the employment function prior to initiating any direct contact.
3. If you make any referrals to line departments you must copy the employment function to insure credit on fees if candidate is hired.

III. Referrals/Identification/Obligation

Each operating unit will spell out its policy about the identification of referrals and period of obligation to each agency being utilized. The following points will provide basic guidelines for determining this policy.

1. Our obligation is to the agency that initiates the action that motivates the process, which results in the individual's being hired.
   a) We require that you forward a complete resume on all applicants recommended for consideration.
   b) All resumes referred must indicate the applicant's name, address, and telephone number. Agencies with coding systems are so advised.
   c) Telephone referrals should result in either a resume or an interview within 72 hours of the call (or an agreed-upon time) in order to be honored over other referrals of the same candidate from other sources.
2. Whenever feasible, we will notify you before we contact the applicant.
3. You are advised that we will contact you about only those applicants in whom we have interest. All other resumes will be discarded.
   a) Our policy will be to honor referrals 90 days from receipt. The initial referrer is due the fee, regardless of any other agency referrals of the same applicant.
   b) XYZ Corporation does not have central control of applicant referrals.

IV. Equal Employment Opportunity

1. By this statement you are notified that we are an equal opportunity employer and that we expect to receive referrals on anyone, regardless of race, color, sex, religion, national origin, or age.
2. Employment agencies have the same obligations under law to refer people, regardless of race, color, sex, religion, national origin, or age. Should it become apparent that you are not adhering to this policy, you will be discontinued as a source.

In addition to reaching an appropriate understanding with the employment agency, there are things that any organization will need to do on a continuing basis to ensure maximum success in utilizing their agencies.

1. Maintain employment statistics by source and indicate total referrals, interviews, offers, and acceptances. These statistics determine productivity. The gross statistic of number of hires is not the sole measure of effectiveness; the best measure is the ratio of candidates interviewed to offers made. If this ratio is small, then the agency is probably a good one, that is, their referrals generally result in offers.
2. Visit agencies on a regular basis in order to know the staff and its *modus-operandi.*

3. Invite agency representatives to visit your operating units and meet your key managers. Agencies which have this exposure will be able to both make more intelligent referrals and recommend the organization as a "good place to work."
4. Provide up-to-date, realistic information on openings, and notify the agency as soon as possible when a particular job has been filled.
5. Provide the agency with any background information about your organization such as annual reports, news releases and reprints.

Many employment agencies have branched out into "semi-search" operations. Their methods of scouting potential candidates are, however, generally more limited than those of executive-search firms, since their primary business is based on contingency, and they can ill afford to spend a lot of time on a particular job without an imminent payoff.

One effective way to utilize an agency is to advertise under its name, thus using the agency as the response point. This cooperative advertising generally yields much greater results per dollar than does advertising under your organization's name, because it offers the job-hunter a chance to investigate the opportunity in some confidence without incurring any obligations.

Another effective way to utilize this source is to use retainers. If you have a particularly knotty problem in terms of numbers of jobs, special skills, time pressure, or if you have on-going needs in a particular discipline or function and you need a reliable captive source, "X dollars" a month can buy a lot of attention from your good agency sources. Negotiate whatever amount seems reasonable for the specifics of your problem and try to arrange to have the retainer deductible from placement fees. The idea behind this arrangement is to insure priority and/or first referral from your key source(s).

In terms of costs (fees), the charges in most states are regulated by the competition. Service charges may vary from agency to agency, depending on their overhead and the calibre of service they render, but their fee is either set forth or can be calculated from a schedule in their contract. In general, the placement fee ranges from 7% to 20% of the new hire's starting annual salary.

One final critical point about agencies is how to measure their effectiveness as a source. The only really fair criterion is "how many people did they refer to you who received offers?" If your offers are rejected, that's your problem. But if the referrals aren't good enough to get offers, you are using the wrong agencies.[8]

Executive-Search Firms

The continuing shortage of good executives and the intricacies of the executive job market have made this source increasingly valuable for many organizations. Unfortunately, as with the employment agency, there is a great deal of misunderstanding about what has become an international business of some magnitude. The total annual expenditure in the United States for executive-search services in 1971 was estimated at more than 75 million dollars.[9] In comparison to the others, these firms are a relatively new source, having entered the employment picture in a significant way only since World War II, with a majority of them having opened their doors in the past 15 years.

The key to this source is the word "search," which in this context means to find and introduce the individual who isn't actively looking for a job. This is a source that with few exceptions should be used only at the more senior levels. Indeed, many search firms will not accept assignments below certain minimum salary levels, because the market is too big and their techniques are not economical or particularly applicable to those conditions. Exceptions to this however, are jobs in a highly specialized functional area. This source is particularly valuable when an organization cannot compromise itself in an industry in which many customer relationships exist or when there is a need to maintain confidentiality. Last, but not least, executive-search firms can minimize the costly burden of finding, screening, evaluating, and negotiating with a large number of candidates with the subsequent involvement of top management's time.

The mechanics, although more sophisticated than those of the employment agency, are basically knowing people (as candidates and as candidate sources) and having a broad, albeit general, knowledge of industry and government. After developing the specific parameters of a job, they research companies in related industries and compile dossiers on the appropriate management people. After reviewing their files, they may in

[8]Questions about employment agencies—practices, problems, etc.—may be directed to the National Employment Association. 2000 K St., N.W., Washington, D.C. 20006.
[9]From information compiled by the Association of Executive Recruiting Consultants, Inc.

some instances resort to advertising. They also use a "come-on letter," which is sent out to any number of executives in the field of interest being searched. Typically, this letter follows the format of "as a leader in industry you may know of someone qualified to serve our client company as VP of Manufacturing. . ." Two results are sought: the recipient will either repond with personal interest or suggest someone else. The approach is fairly impersonal and perhaps loses some of its effectiveness for that reason.

Once candidates have been identified, the direct contact, typically a telephone call at home, starts the actual selection process. Interested or not, the recipient of the call is usually flattered. Such a call adds a personal touch to the initial contact and can be used to excite the individual about the job and the organization.

Search firms must be used selectively, since there are varying degrees of competence among and within firms. You must take a balanced approach to search: search assignments should not go out if you are able to fill the position internally; indiscriminate use of search firms may cause the marketplace to become wary of your organization; continual evaluation should be made of performance against time and costs; and acceptability of the "searcher" in both the organization and the marketplace must be ascertained. In the final analysis, the results achieved against time and cost factors should determine the selection and use of search firms.

To ensure optimum effectiveness when using an executive-search firm, the following guidelines should prove helpful.

1. Once your decision to make an external search has been made, the search firm should be involved immediately. Finding good candidates takes time. Searches are 85% successful if given enough time—generally from 90 to 120 days. If a search firm is called in after some real crisis has developed, and the need has been broadcast throughout the marketplace, candidates may be more reluctant to express interest.
2. Detailed and accurate information must be given to the firm about the position; don't assume that *you* know everything the firm needs to know. The firm's access to the organization and its executives is vital.
3. All the persons involved must have a clear concept of the position to be filled and the type of individual needed to fill it.

4. If the specifications change, tell the firm immediately.
5. The salary established must be at an equitable, attractive, and competitive level.
6. The search firm should assign one man as liaison with the company and the appropriate executives.
7. Provide the firm with immediate and thorough feedback on interviews.

Inasmuch as the use of this source involves an immediate expenditure of money, it is critical that progress be audited continually. If no worthwhile candidates are identified within approximately 30 days or if the search firm loses its objectivity/productivity because of its long-term contact with the industry or the specific problem, a decision to terminate their contract may be in order. The termination of the services of a firm is sensitive. The decision to terminate should be explained in a direct manner, and services rendered to that point in time are paid for.

Selecting an executive-search firm should involve some research on your part inasmuch as the time and money you will invest necessitate the right selection decision. The best approach is similar to that outlined in the section on advertising, with the addition of several other checkpoints. What is the background and experience of the various staff members of the search firm? Who are some of their clients? What is their *modus-operandi* (including charges)? Also, you might contact the Association of Executive Recruiting Consultants (AERC) for general information about specifics on costs and method of operation.[10] In addition, there are a number of published lists and directories that are quite comprehensive in their coverage of executive-search firms.[11] Don't overlook the checking of their references; talk with some of their clients.

Cost, of course, is critical when using this source. It is the *single* most expensive *direct* cost item in your budget. That, however, should never preclude the use of this when necessary; that's when it may be the cheapest. Executive-search firms are not included under state licensing laws, so they use a variety of methods for charging for services performed.

---

[10]Association of Executive Recruiting Consultants, Inc., 347 Madison Avenue, New York, New York 10017.

[11]For example, the *Directory of Consultant Members*, published by the American Management Association, 135 W. 59th St., New York, New York 10020.

The best explanation about "fees" is given in the AERC booklet *What Every Executive Should Know about Executive Recruiting* as follows:

> Executive recruiting consultants use different ways to calculate the professional fees paid for their services by clients. The most commonly used methods are these:
>
> - A percentage fee, usually equal to 25 to 30 per cent of the first year's agreed-upon compensation of the executive recruited.
> - A flat fee, fixed in advance on the basis of estimated time and difficulty of the search.
> - A retainer fee for professional services over a stated period.
> - A straight time formula, based on actual time spent on the search, but sometimes governed by an agreed-to maximum.
> - A per diem fee for any candidate appraised and recommended by the consultant and hired by the client.
>
> In addition to the fee, there are also expenses. These are mainly for travel and communications, and they will vary, depending on the complexity of the search and the distances between client, consultant, and candidates. It is customary for clients to pay for candidates' travel expenses to interviews. It is also customary for clients to pay additional fees, if they hire more than one of the candidates recommended by a consultant.
>
> Invoicing also varies from firm to firm. However, most favor monthly billings for professional services and expenses during the search, and a final payment of the balance due after the candidate has accepted.[12]

Since this is a substantial investment, it certainly behooves any organization that utilizes it to institute some procedural controls. It makes sense to assign the responsibility for executive search to the employment function rather than to have it in the executive suite, which can waste a great deal of expensive executive time. The employment function must first prove, however, that it can assume the responsibility for this activity, since most search firms generally try to deal directly with the hiring executive. Seldom does the executive have the time to

---

[12]Reprinted by permission from *What Every Executive Should Know about Executive Recruiting*, New York: Association of Executive Recruiting Consultants, 1971, p. 11-12.

devote to ensuring that the consultant develops the on-going, in-depth relationship needed to gain a real understanding of the organization.

In summary, the primary advantage of using an executive-search firm is the complete anonymity it offers both the organization and the candidate. It allows an organization to reach the well-situated executive who is not looking and is happy where he is and therefore has no motivation to make a change. It allows the screening of a score of candidates without jeopardizing either party. It brings an objective view of candidates to the line manager with a key position to fill. Search firms provide candidates with a "middleman." Last, but not least, the source is used to attract the executive who is not out of work and applying for a job, and that takes specialized knowledge and techniques.

4.3 OTHER SOURCES

Computer Systems

This is the newest of the sources and has evolved with the growth of computers. There is still some debate about its overall usefulness, and most people would agree that although it is far from perfect, it does appear to hold great promise. There are a number of computerized job-bank systems in existence which provide data and information ranging from computerized prescreening systems for college students so that company and student may check each other out confidentially, to on-line systems which provide data on experienced professional/technical people.

The utilization of this source probably makes more sense for the larger organization with numbers of requirements and a capability to screen large numbers of potential candidates. The costs of using this source will vary from a small monthly retainer plus to so much per referral to a regular placement fee. The Grad II system, run by the College Placement Council to provide employers with a preselection of seniors and graduate students, is a good example. The Council charges a basic annual fee of $100 to list four job categories, e.g., accounting and mechanical engineering. For each additional job category, there is an additional charge of $25.00. To those charges is added a "point charge" to placement offices, which differs depending on the number of students in their pool. A variation of this job-matching service is that provided by National Personnel Associates (NPA), which has instituted a computerized retrieval system which encompasses 150 employment agencies in 100 cities across the

United States to provide the widest possible search capabilities for employers and job seekers.[13]

The computer is also a necessary tool if an organization hopes to have an effective in-house manpower inventory and internal search effort. The real value of computers is based on the premise that they are timely and accurate banks of information.

To sum up computer sources, it appears that they are far from accepted and really have not been developed to their fullest potential. With the proper understanding and support, however, the almost unbelievable capabilities of existing or proposed computer-based systems could begin to become a reality.

For more information on the various computer sources available now, contact *Recruiter's Encyclopedia,* 20 North Wacker Drive, Chicago, Illinois 60606, and the National Industrial Conference Board—Conference Board Library, 845 Third Avenue, New York, New York 10022.

Position-Wanted Ads

These advertisements run by individuals advertising their availability can be an extremely economic source. The Sunday *New York Times*, the *Wall Street Journal*, many of the professional-society journals, and various industry publications carry such ads on a regular basis. This source merely requires that you write to a box number in order to receive the individual's resume. This source is particularly valuable in a soft labor market (see Chapter 10).

Unsolicited Inquiries

Unsolicited inquiries may come to your organization as a result of your product ads, by word-of-mouth, from people who have seen your product ads or have heard friends or others talk of the company, or possibly just a completely random contact. In general, the "walk-ins" or direct "write-ins" are less important as a source of good people in a tight labor market, but proper attention must be given to this source because over a period of time, many capable people may use a direct approach (see Chapter 10.8). Whether or not you have immediate employment needs, you should still be concerned about the public-relations aspect of unsolicited inquiries. If not potential employees, people who apply for jobs are nonetheless poten-

[13]National Personnel Associates, 100 Fifth Ave., Pittsburgh, Penna. 15222.

tial customers, stockholders, or suppliers. Also, proper attention to these inquiries will help build your files with candidates for future openings.

To ensure proper and consistent handling of these inquiries, the employment function should arrange to receive all inquiries to the organization for review and reply. It is very important that those involved in handling these inquiries be aware of all the openings throughout the organization. If there is more than one location involved, compilation and distribution of job openings should be a regular procedure so that the best possible results from this source can be obtained.

Unsolicited inquiries tend to fall into two broad categories—the fairly senior management-level individual who is now, or shortly will be, out of work and the younger man making his initial change. Regardless of the level of the individuals, unsolicited inquiries should never be given cursory attention; they should receive the same courtesies given to inquiries from any other source—promptness of reply and straight facts about the job situation in your organization.

These same basic principles should apply to walk-in candidates, with the added caution that your receptionist, guards, or anyone who has initial contact understand the organization's policies and procedures, particularly EEO rules and regulations.

City Recruiting

This can be a highly productive source if properly planned and organized. If not, it can result in a tremendous waste of time and money. The primary advantage of city recruiting is that a minimum investment of time and money can lead to face-to-face discussions with a number of candidates, and a basic "employability decision" can be made prior to investing in a "plant visit."

In planning city-recruiting trips, take the time to analyze the town or general area in terms of overall condition of the labor market; the location of organizations in your business or related lines; which of your customers are there (be sure to brief the on-site recruiters about the sensitivities of this); the most appropriate media for your ads (think in terms of the whole-area, local papers, ethnic papers, nearby papers); any "third parties" that might be helpful; review your files for people in the particular area; present employees from there who might be able to recommend candidates. You could go on and on, but this will give you some ideas.

There are several other thoughts that may be helpful in maximizing the potential of this source. Develop some prescreening techniques (specific questions about the product, process, or manufacturing techniques) to use in phone-screening, particularly if you are involved with technical jobs. Such questions will help screen out people who do not have the specific skills you seek without your having to schedule an interview in your hotel. Use these trips, also, to cultivate your third parties in the area and to develop a better analysis of the overall market and other organizations in the area. This will prove to be of real value in setting up records that will provide helpful answers when the next trip is planned.

Combine all of your resources—your employment agencies, advertising, and "people known" from your files. Give enough advance notice to your third parties so they can arrange interviews. Have your advertisements run prior to (preferably the Sunday before) and during the period of the visit, and make phone calls to "people known" so that you can explore their interest and schedule interviews. If feasible, establish some type of phone coverage prior to your arrival that will provide you with at least basic information about each individual who responds. Adequate interviewing facilities are mandatory, since a candidate's first impression of your organization will be made at this time.(As a matter of fact, the facilities should probably be better.) Interviewing schedules should be arranged with the convenience of the candidate in mind; generally, weekends and evenings are best. In interviews, use a team approach, i.e., have a representative from both the employment function and the hiring function available to interview candidates in some depth. Be prepared to invite good candidates on the spot for further interviews.

Another advantage of city recruiting is to take advantage of layoffs in other organizations when it is known that a number of qualified people will be available in a given geographic area. More and more, personnel departments of organizations undergoing cut-backs or reorganization are willing to cooperate with recruiters from other organizations in placing the people affected.

Banks, Consulting Firms, and Public-Accounting Firms

In discussing these as potential sources, the consulting firms referred to are the general, management-consulting firms such as McKinsey and Company or Arthur D. Little—*not* the executive-search firms.

Both banks and consultants can be very productive sources (particularly if your organization is doing business with them), yet they are frequently overlooked. They have several things in common that can be extremely advantageous to you in identifying candidates. First, they are very responsive to a client/customer *or* potential client/customer. Second, they have widespread personal contacts among all types of businesses and disciplines. Banks are generally very alert to proposed growth and expansion of businesses, for obvious reasons. The consulting firms, of course, are attuned to technology, new products, and new markets. They also have good pipelines into industry and government.

Public-accounting firms are also a good source, particularly for financial candidates. Again, they are particularly responsive to client needs. As a matter of fact, a number of these firms have entered the recruiting business—not unlike the "third parties."

Establish the kind of rapport with the principals of each of these sources that will allow you to go to them for help on a periodic basis with specialized needs. But even if your organization does not have contacts with these potential sources, you should be able to establish them through friends or associates on some mutually beneficial basis.

Colleges and Universities

Chapter 6 discusses the total concept of university relations in some detail, so only a few key observations will be made here. Suffice to say that this is one of the key sources for any organization, and in some it is the primary building-block for professional technical manpower.

The key points in the maximum utilization of this source relate to continuity of the program and good administrative control. There must be continuity because it takes time to develop meaningful relationships on campuses, and it is extremely difficult to be successful if there is a continual shrinking and expanding of the program. Control, preferably central control in large organizations, becomes necessary for economy and efficiency's sake when dealing with a number of geographically dispersed parts of your organization and campuses. The logistics alone necessitate one person's being responsible, much as the campus has its placement officer. The College Placement Council, a nonprofit organization representing the mutual interests of some 1200 colleges and universities and 2200 employers, is an invaluable source of information on all aspects of college-trained manpower.[14]

Alumni-Placement Services

A number of colleges and universities run a placement service for their alumni. These services are usually an adjunct of the Placement Office.

[14]The College Placement Council, Bethlehem, Penna. 18001.

Unfortunately, many of these services operate on a fairly limited budget and as an additional responsibility of an already busy placement department. However, more and more schools are making serious efforts to upgrade this service.

This source generally services the more recent graduate (the man dissatisfied with his first job) who has not had sufficient exposure to, nor experience in, the job market to know best how to "market" himself. To cultivate this source, use your campus visits to update your needs and strengthen the relationship with the school. Remember, this is not an employment agency; rather, you are being provided with a free service, so be very specific about your needs and be sure and follow through on referrals. The burdens of communication and initiative are on you once an individual has been identified. Examples of better alumni placement services are those at Cornell and MIT.

State Employment Service

Under the auspices of the United States Employment Service, the state employment services have branches in all large cities and representatives in many smaller communities and are a significant source of manpower, but they do require careful cultivation. Continuing efforts to improve this service both technically and financially have helped dispel some of the generalizations that many organizations have had about it, e.g., that the generally poor competence of the counselors makes this a poor source for the "good" professional.

This source has usually proved to be most productive for nonexempt candidates. However, Executive Order 11598—Hiring of Vietnam-Era Veterans, which requires that you list all your job vacancies with your state employment service, is a more tangible reason to attempt to cultivate this source. If you make a sincere effort at establishing a relationship, it may prove useful in a number of ways, over and above the fact that it should result in more selective referrals. It can also be a source of information for such things as manpower surveys and interpretation of legislation affecting manpower and employment.

All organizations must occasionally use every manpower source available. Even though there is still much to be done by state employment services to increase the public's confidence and patronage, it cannot be overlooked as a potential source. Bear in mind that all persons who file for unemployment benefits must report to their local state employment office.

Former Employees

This can be a very good, direct source of candidates or of leads to candidates. Its value is directly related to the organization's relationship with the employee when he left. Only if he left in a positive frame of mind will he be approachable as a source for new employees. If your exit interviews or "outplacement" efforts (see Chapter 10) were positive, you shouldn't hesitate to tap the former employee. To fully utilize this as a productive source, stay in touch with all of your good people after they leave. A simple technique is to correspond when you have an appropriate reason to do so—when the annual report comes out or when significant press releases are issued. Don't overlook stopping by to see them in your travels. Some organizations go to great lengths to keep track of their former employees for purposes of rehire (that, of course, depends on the organization's policy), but "sourcing" former employees generally poses no policy problems.

Professional Societies

This can be a particularly economical source, but it does require a fair amount of effort. Most professional societies now have procedures for acting as intermediaries between job hunters and employers. The effectiveness may vary, but nonetheless it is a source that should be utilized.

Conventions and meetings of professional societies provide a logical approach to searching for potential candidates. But when considering investing your time and money to "source" one of these sessions, you must understand that most attendees are there to participate in the planned activities. The basic city-recruiting techniques apply here for planning and organizing your efforts, but bear in mind that a number of associations have now either banned or instituted strict controls on any overt employment activities at their meetings. Exceptions to this are societies like the American Chemical Society, which actively provides assistance to job seekers at its meetings. Be sure and check with societies' secretariats to determine their procedures; your approach will have to be predicated on their regulations.

In addition to holding meetings and conventions, a number of professional societies publish a listing of members and/or jobs available. The American Institute of Chemical Engineers (AICHE), for example, provides a free listing in their *Openings for Chemical Engineers Bulletin* for any advertiser in the magazine *Chemical Engineering Progress* (CEP). They also mail to employers of chemical engineers their *Available Chemical Engi-*

neers Bulletin, which lists people available to industry and academia. This is a good source, because there is no initial cost other than an ad in CEP magazine, and this will more than pay for itself when this source begins to yield results. This is a good source in a technically-oriented soft market, and as long as it's free or can be utilized at a minimal cost, you can't afford not to use it.

Employee Referrals

This is a productive and relatively inexpensive source, and it has a distinct advantage in that the people referred by your employees will tend to be above average. Your employees can provide a realistic picture of your organization, and because they will feel some responsibility for his performance should he be hired, it's doubtful that they will refer a person who isn't capable.

Many employees enjoy being involved in the staffing process. However, the burden is on the organization to provide direct communications about manpower needs and programs. Use all of the available internal communications to tell your story: company paper, bulletin boards, management meetings. This type of employee involvement can also be a significant morale factor by involving them in the long-range future of the organization.

As with any source there are disadvantages to relying on employee referrals. Management problems may be caused by "friends" forming cliques. In the extreme, hiring large numbers of employee referrals may result in inbreeding, i.e., same schools, same experience, same age.

This source may be better suited to the smaller organization because of its easier internal communication about needs and programs. This source is not necessarily adaptable to all types of jobs, nor will it necessarily produce the right man at the right time. However, if properly administered, it can be a good source of manpower.

Over the years, various incentives, such as cash bonuses or gifts, have been offered to stimulate referrals. That may pose problems in terms of the number and the quality of the referrals. It would appear that the best incentive is still the loyalty and interest employees have in the organization, which results from good relations between management and employees. In utilizing this source, be sure your employees are alert to customer-competitor sensitivities.

The key to the productivity of this source will be greatly influenced by how easy a "system" you have to follow up on it. If you have communicated needs and programs, the "referral" can be as simple as the business card of the individual with his *home* phone jotted down. If he does not have a business card, you can ask him to put his name, address, phone number, and title or function on a three-by-five-inch index card. This gives you the basic information you need to make an initial phone screening.

The primary rule in effectively utilizing this source is to always respond quickly, and be sure to express the organization's gratitude for the referral.

Internal Search

There are three basic methods an organization can use for internal searches, and each has its advantages. The *first* method is as simple as holding regularly scheduled conversations with various segments of your organization about manpower needs and determining who might be upgraded or transferred. A *second* approach is to post a list of job openings which essentially puts the responsibility on the employee to make himself a candidate. The *third* method, and the one getting the most attention today (in the age of the computer), is to develop a computerized personnel data system.

A major factor in determination to use any of these methods is the size and location of the organization and a thorough analysis of why you need the capability to look inside, over and above the fact that "everyone has a system, because it's a fad." There can be a multitude of reasons for developing this capability ranging from: "We have an opening, who is the best man in the organization to do the job?" to "Are we overlooking any new areas of business for which we have the skills in-house?" However, regardless of the need for any system to work, top and middle management must understand, accept, and play their roles in the development of the system and its operation.

The *first* method, "word of mouth," can be quite effective in a smaller organization where there is a good deal of personal contact and exposure among the total staff. Advocates of the second method, job-posting, say that job mobility and improved morale are benefits to employer and employee. Each person can make his desires known without being penalized for "passing up" an opportunity. The third, the computer-based method, presents the strongest arguments, particularly in larger organizations which can develop a sophisticated skills inventory (a list of skills, areas of knowledge, and special abilities possessed by a company's employees) and has the equipment to store and retrieve the data. This data system really becomes an "electronic resume" and provides a systematic and thorough means of finding people who fulfill certain requirements. It does *not* however, select individuals to fill jobs.

All of these methods produce varying degrees of information that should facilitate consideration of employees for positions available anywhere in the organization. As a source, internal search does several important things and depending on the method used and management's commitment, it can be one of your most economical. Specifically, internal search:

1. Provides employees with opportunites for growth
2. Utilizes available manpower resources to the fullest
3. "Protects" the organization's manpower from unnecessary loss
4. Reduces employment costs.

It has become standard policy (see Chapter 2.15) in many companies to consider qualified employees for promotion or transfer before hiring outside; therefore, internal search should be developed to its finest degree of effectiveness.

In summary, all of the sources and methods that have been discussed have merit, although some, obviously, have been overrated, whereas others have been underrated. The superiority of any one approach, however, depends both on your individual situation and your evaluation of which ones produce the most satisfactory employees for you in the most efficient and economical manner. If an employment function is really doing its job, it will appraise each source and each technique in those terms.

5
Equal opportunity employment

INTRODUCTION

It is apparent that the passage of various antidiscrimination laws is perhaps one of the most significant things that has happened to any employment function during this past decade. This legislation will probably hasten the day when there will no longer be "male" or "female" professions and when individuals will get jobs based on their skills and advance according to ability rather than according to their sex, color, or age. A lot of things must happen though, before those things become reality. And that is what this chapter is all about—how to solve, or at least begin to solve, the minority and female-employment problems that most organizations face.

The significance of this subject is obvious, and the fact that special legislation was required for most organizations to become equal opportunity employers is indicative of the magnitude of the problem. It is doubtful that even the cost of discrimination, i.e., the waste of this reservoir of manpower, would have opened doors in many organizations had not the government intervened. As is true of so many social and community problems today, economic necessity is the only factor that prompts organizations to take action—in this instance, the fear of losing business. If an organization is a government contractor, it "must" adhere to certain employment rules and regulations. The impact of this is obvious when you realize there are approximately 250,000 firms in the United States today with government contracts. In the same vein, no organization is doing the job for its stockholders simply by earning as large a profit as possible this year, unless it is also helping shape an environment in which it can continue to earn a profit five or ten years from now.

5.1 EQUAL EMPLOYMENT OPPORTUNITY LEGISLATION

The increasing complexity of the employment function's responsibility is brought into focus once we begin to understand the whys and wherefores of the federal regulations that pertain to industrial employment. To simplify the discussion, these regulations have been grouped according to the appropriate regulating agency.

First, there are the laws, regulations, and guidelines administered by the *Equal Employment Opportunity Commission (EEOC)*, which was established by the Civil Rights Act of 1964 and became effective on July 1, 1965. Title VII, the key part of this legislation pertaining to industrial employment, established the EEOC as an independent agency reporting to the President and gave it the right to investigate complaints from any individual based on discrimination in employment by reason of race, color, creed, sex, or national origin.

As originally enacted by Congress, the Civil Rights Act of 1964 empowered the EEOC to investigate complaints, subpoena records, and make every effort to conciliate the differences between the employer and the charging party. However, if conciliation failed, the only further recourse available to the EEOC was to advise the charging party that he had a right to sue the employer in federal district court. The Civil Rights Act of 1964 was amended by Public Law 92-261, effective March 24, 1972, which granted the EEOC the additional power of going directly to the federal district court and sueing an employer in behalf of a charging party. Although the EEOC has exercised this power only a few times since March 1972, it is now enlarging its staff, and it is anticipated that there will be a dramatic increase in the number of cases that will be filed for litigation in the courts.

The EEOC has issued regulations governing procedures to be followed in investigation and appearances before the Commission and in formulating records and reports that will be required. The EEOC has also issued guidelines concerning discrimination on the basis of sex, religion, and national origin, employment testing, disclosure of records, and pre-employment stature inquiries.

On September 24, 1965, Executive Order 11246 was issued, which banned discrimination in federal employment, on all federal contracts exceeding $10,000, and on federally assisted construction contracts. *The secretary of labor* was assigned the responsibility for administrating Parts 2 and 3 of the Order dealing with nondiscrimination by government contractors and subcontractors. The responsibility for administrating Part 1 dealing with nondiscrimination in government employment was assigned to the *Civil Service Commission*.

As originally issued, Executive Order 11246 did not cover sex discrimination. Part 2 was amended on October 13, 1968 to add sex as a prohibited basis of discrimination. Under the general guidance of the *Office of Federal Contract Compliance (OFCC)*, advisors to the Department of Labor, the various federal contracting agencies, were assigned to review the performance of their own contractors to ensure compliance with the executive order. Subsequently, the regulations were amended to assign companies to various government agencies according to their industry classification. Therefore, it is conceivable that if your organization is involved in different industries, you may have a number of different government agencies conducting compliance reviews. The OFCC gains its power from its right to reject and/or cancel federal contracts if it believes that a contractor is willfully violating the letter or spirit of Executive Order 11246.

Revised Executive Order 4 was issued December 4, 1971 to furnish guidelines to federal contractors. Affirmative action, as required by Executive Order 4 and Revised Order 4, indicates how it should be accomplished. This order is the basis on which the periodic compliance reviews by the various agencies are made. In essence, it requires a contractor (an organization with a contract for $50,000 or more and 50 or more employees) to analyze his own performance in providing equal employment opportunity, pinpoint his weaknesses, and spell out his plans for improvement, including the setting of goals and timetables for such improvements. In employment it essentially concerns what you have done, are doing, should do, and how it will be accomplished.

It should be pointed out that the agency does not set the goals or timetables; rather, it approves or disapproves those set by the contractor himself. Executive Order 14 was issued by the OFCC in March of 1972 to provide a standardized compliance procedure for all of the agencies, and an implementation memorandum for Order 14 was issued on June 29, 1972. The question of how arduous it will be for contractors to comply with the requirements of Order 14 will depend on the way in which the agencies interpret the requirements of the order. The OFCC will in all probability be reasonable in this regard, but the order as written does permit the issuance of "show cause" notices, with very little regard for the contractor's problems in effecting his affirmative-action program. It is too early to say what the effect of Order 14 will be, but it will obviously create more paper work for organizations.

Particularly critical to the issue of sex discrimination, as has been pointed out, are Title VII of the Civil Rights Act of 1964 and Executive Order 11246. Possibly equally important is the Equal Pay Act of 1963, an amendment to the Fair Labor Standards Act—Wage and Hour Law. The Equal Pay Act calls for equal pay for equal work. These three laws, when fully effective, will ensure a "unisex" employment process; the only criterion will be the individual's ability to perform the job.

On February 12, 1965, Executive Order 11141 made it illegal for federal contractors to permit discrimination because of age. The question of age discrimination was not really solved by this order, however, and on June 12, 1968, Public Law 90-202 (Age Discrimination in Employment Act of 1967) was enacted. This law prohibits discrimination against people between the ages of 40 and 65, thus putting them in a protected class. *The Secretary of Labor* was assigned responsibility for implementing the law, and the Wage and Hour Division of the Department of Labor is charged with investigating compliance with this law. Enforcement can be provided through the courts in the same manner as cases are now processed under the Fair Labor Standards Act. It should be kept in mind that discrimination can occur in favor of a 50-year-old person over a 60-year-old person, as well as between a member of the protected class (40-65) and a 30-year-old.

5.2 UNLAWFUL EMPLOYMENT PRACTICES

Rather than attempt to outline the detail of all the legislation applicable to equal opportunity employment, let's just highlight the basics of unlawful employment practices. Copies of the various laws, regulations, and guidelines may be obtained from the appropriate governmental agency.

Under existing legislation, it is an unlawful employment practice to:

1. Refuse to consider for employment, or otherwise discriminate against, any individual because of his race, color, religion, sex, national origin, or age
2. Classify any individual for employment on the basis of race, color, religion, sex, national origin, or age
3. Indicate in job advertisements a preference for or against individuals based on race, color, religion, sex, national origin, or age, *except*

when a bona-fide occupational qualification (BFOQ) exists, e.g., in the extreme, a wet nurse or sperm-bank donor)

4. Make pre-employment inquires about sex, religion, or national origin if the inquiry expresses, directly or indirectly a limitation, specification, or discrimination based on those three points. This is not applicable when a BFOQ exists.

Age

It is against the law to refuse employment or otherwise discriminate against any person because of age or to cateogrize any person for employment based on age. This includes advertisements as well as any printed or published notices. It is permissible, however, to ask a person his age when, for example, there is a statement on an application form to the effect that "Federal law prohibits discrimination in employment based on age," and his age is not used directly or indirectly for an illegal purpose.

Sex

You cannot refuse to hire a woman because of her sex or based on the generalizations of employment characteristics or abilities of women. Examples of such generalizations are: women are too emotional, women are absent more, and women are not aggressive. Another example is the refusal to hire women because separate facilities would have to be provided. Unless you can prove that the expense of providing such facilities is unreasonable, you have no argument.

On the other side of the coin, traditionally women's jobs cannot be denied to men unless there is a BFOQ. In essence, BFOQ's must be given the strictest interpretation, and organizations will have to stop thinking in terms of jobs for any "grouping"—be it sex, age, or national origin. However, your application form and your interviewers may ask for a designation of male, female, Mr., Mrs., or Miss as long as the request is in good faith for a nondiscriminatory purpose.

Religion

An organization must "make reasonable accommodations to the religious needs of employees and prospective employees" when this can be done without imposing an undue hardship on the employer's ability to conduct his business. An undue hardship might exist when an employee's work cannot be performed by another qualified employee during the period of absence for religious reasons.

Quotas

The "law," contrary to popular belief, does not require any organization to have a quota of a certain category of employee. However, if an organization has an obvious imbalance in its work force as compared to its labor area, a quota may have to be set. Thus, the real burden for avoiding a "quota" rests with the employment function, since in judging compliance, the government generally looks first at the employment process and attendant procedures.

5.3 COMMITMENT TO EOE

The only real key to an organization's achieving success as an equal opportunity employer rests at the highest levels. The chairman, president, or chief executive officer must assume the responsibility for formulating a policy of equal employment opportunity. The policy must state unequivocally the organization's commitment, its present equal opportunity situation, and its future potential.

How a policy is received and implemented in any organization will be directly related to the effectiveness of communication channels. The critical point in disseminating a policy (or for that matter, any new plans in this subject area) is to ensure that top management's approval comes through strong and clear. The equal employment opportunity policy must be communicated to all employees, to all job candidates, and to all employment sources, as well as to the community. A primary mistake that so many organizations make is to *overpublicize* their efforts outside; external publicity on this subject should be fairly low key unless there has been an unusually significant accomplishment.

Communicating this policy requires the involvement of all executive, managerial, and supervisory personnel in the organization. To repeat, however, this process will work only when the top executive lets his commitment be known and reiterates it on a regular basis. This can best be done *internally* by:

1. Including a statement in the organization's policy manual (see Chapter 2.15)
2. Publicizing the policy regularly in all of the organization's publications, e.g., newspaper, magazine, and annual report
3. Having the top executive conduct special meetings to reinforce his commitment to key managers with instructions for them to do the same

4. Making it a regular subject of discussion in staff meetings, departmental meetings, orientation sessions, and training programs throughout the organization
5. Posting policy on bulletin boards.

This commitment and policy can best be disseminated *externally* by:

1. Informing all employment sources verbally and in writing of the policy and what is expected of them
2. Notifying minority and womens' organizations, community leaders, etc., in writing
3. Communicating overall EEO philosophy to candidates.

As a general rule, don't count on managers and supervisors to follow through unless top management gets the message across on a continuing basis. Because the line managers have the hiring responsibility, they must be educated to all the nuances of minority and female employment. These aspects should be a primary educational responsibility of the employment function.

Even with a well-thought-out policy statement and an excellent communications program, an EEO program should not depart too dramatically from established administrative procedures, thus avoiding the risk of causing reverse discrimination or a backlash from other employees. To maintain proper control of the program, the smart organization will utilize existing procedures, record-keeping, and functional assignments within the employment process, but will not hesitate to update them as necessary to meet the letter of the law. However this is accomplished, the organization must also establish the need for the "extra effort."

5.4 THE EXTRA EFFORT

An extra effort is usually required in any organization, about any subject, when people don't, or don't want to, understand something well enough to do it successfully. For an employment process to be successful in relation to minorities and females, it is imperative that the employment function and line managers make an "extra effort." Line managers do the hiring, and their example, particularly, will set the tone for success or failure of the program.

To really make the "extra effort" work, an organization must ask some questions about its employment process:

1. Who is really held responsible for success? For failure?
2. What do our minority and female employees think of the employment process and the organization?
3. Who screens the interviewers? Are they sensitive to what is going on?

In other words, ask the same sorts of questions about this as you would about any other phase of your operations that aren't performing up to standard or meeting their objectives.

This extra effort has to include accountability for the objectives of the EEO policy and the affirmative-action plan. There must be the same intent as with other business objectives, and when there is nonperformance, the results will be the same as on other objectives. The extra effort, in essence, is best exemplified by an affirmative-action program that *exceeds* the parameters of Revised Order #4.

Affirmative Action

As defined by the OFCC, affirmative action means applying management techniques and controls over personnel actions that are normally applied to any other program that the business wants to succeed. It means analyzing the methods, procedures, and results of personnel actions to determine whether they have resulted in the exclusion of qualified or trainable workers because of race, sex, color, national origin, or religion.

Revised Order 4 requires the development of affirmative-action plans by all organizations which are affected by Executive Order 11246. To quote from Revised Order 4, an affirmative-action program

> is a set of specific and result-oriented procedures to which a contractor commits himself to apply every good faith effort. The objective of those procedures plus such efforts is equal employment opportunity. Procedures without effort to make them work are meaningless; and effort, undirected by specific and meaningful procedures, is inadequate. An acceptable affirmative action program must include an analysis of areas within which the contractor is deficient in the utilization of minority groups and women, and further, goals and timetables to which the contractor's good faith efforts must be

directed, to correct the deficiencies and, thus to increase materially the utilization of minorities and women, at all levels and in all segments of his work force where deficiencies exist.

The truly committed organization will not be satisfied with merely attempting to meet those goals. In other words, affirmative action is not just employing someone who is qualified to perform a job for you, because you would do that anyway. For instance, with a continuing shortage of chemical engineers, any organization with an opening would hire a black or female chemical engineer. Affirmative action must be creative and aggressive efforts to hire people you would not "normally" hire.

Affirmative action is not fully achieved until some "average minority and female candidates" are hired, as is true with some of your white male candidates. Ability to do the job is the criterion for upward movement. The problem is in no way solved if the best qualified candidates are hired and there is no room to move.

The *Federal Register* published on December 4, 1971 contains the complete text of Revised Order 4. Copies may be obtained from the Department of Labor, Office of Federal Contract Compliance, Washington, D.C. 20210.

In summary, then, the federal rules and guidelines are spelled out, and we can assume that enforcement will become more and more stringent. Organizations can be consistent with their responsibility to the "bottom line," stockholders, and the community by making equal employment opportunity a business objective and holding people accountable for the results.

The remainder of this chapter will explore the details of "getting the job done."

5.5 MAKING IT ALL WORK

Making a total EEO program work is difficult, to say the least, for there are so many road blocks that need to be removed, and the most difficult are the social and psychological ones. Organizations must have the motivation and knowledge to change. In the final analysis, this will really require a change in attitude–going from apathy to affirmative action, which in itself requires more than merely meeting quotas.

A watchdog committee can be the guiding force in making it all work in any organization. This group should be responsible for the overall direction of EEO programs on a corporate-wide basis and should comprise a representative group of key management people. The guiding philosophy for this committee should be "what doesn't get followed up doesn't get done." It should be the committee's responsibility to ensure that there is proper planning, the setting of realistic objectives, and the availability of real jobs. This can be accomplished by instituting control through regularly scheduled meetings and progress reports from all parts of the organization. For example, every hire should be reported in enough detail to allow a determination of the total effort required in a particular operating unit (see Chapter 8.1).

5.6 MINORITIES AND FEMALES

When we speak of minorities, we are usually referring to the Negro, Oriental, American Indian, and Spanish-surnamed American. Although these are the standard government classifications, we will expand this definition to encompass two other groups who, because of all of the generalizations about them, have been victim to almost the same degree of discrimination—women and older (age 40-65) workers.

Women are not a minority in terms of numbers, but in terms of opportunity. Women, as a matter of fact, are a majority in numbers, but a true "minority" in employment. They are seldom paid on an equal basis for equal work; they seldom have the opportunity for jobs other than the traditional ones—teacher, sales clerk, secretary. In some respects the employment of female professional/technical workers poses a much more difficult problem than does the hiring of any male minority. Richard Clarke, President of Richard Clarke Associates, a minority-group recruiting firm, states this problem quite succinctly.

> The problem will be even more difficult for companies to come to grips with, because women have, by and large, been nonpersons in American industry. Blacks' pigmentation has at least been a visible irritant to the corporate "go slower"; women are just beginning to challenge the male sanctuary of the executive suite. Those in management positions have reported hearing discussions among male managers that are painfully reminiscent of those held 10 years ago about Blacks.[1]

[1]Reprinted by permission from "Publisher's Statement," *Contact*, July 1972, p. 5.

Realistically, it must be understood that change is quite difficult, because both sides (the organization and the candidate) must change their frame of mind. The primary burden must necessarily fall on the organization, because it must fill the jobs. The organization will change only when it faces up to its biases and sincerely tries to develop an insight into the problem. In some organizations, it isn't even bias, it's just lack of concern, which is almost as bad. In order to develop that insight, the organization will need to provide both *real* jobs rather than special jobs and the same degree of personal-development assistance to all employees.

The real problem is that in a sense, the white male candidate is "innocent until proved guilty," i.e., it is assumed that he can do the job until it is proved that he cannot. On the other hand, the minority or female candidate is "guilty until proved innocent," i.e., such candidates get an opportunity only after proving they can do the job.

Minorities

Although most discussions about minorities focus on the black worker, the overall context of the employment problem relates to all minorities. The primary problem of minority employment is the tendency to hire into classical (traditional) jobs without any, or very little, regard for the facts or logic and to be unduly influenced by three basic factors:

1. The differences in the educational system and training opportunities, i.e., most minority-group members receive an inferior education, which in turn compounds the problem of entry into training programs. Until equal education is a reality for all, none of the problems discussed in this chapter will be solved.
2. The so-called language and social/cultural barriers which are a great cop-out for tests, although governmental guidelines have or will eliminate that in the near future. This particular point is a big factor in the "credentials" game—credentials for getting the job which may have no effect on the candidate's ability to do the job.
3. Outright discrimination, or more and more today, a more subtle discrimination whereby a "token" minority-group member is hired. Or, in another form, an organization may publicize its intent and activity without holding anyone really responsible for results.

The historical generalizations (generally all negative) about black people or other minorities must be dispelled. Instead, an attempt must be made to understand the "cause and effect" of the problem; otherwise, there can be little hope for success in the employment process. People *must* be judged primarily on their ability to *do* the job.

Over and above the historical generalizations about minorities that have been talked to death and written about *ad-infinitum*, there are many facts and practicalities about minority employment that must be understood by everyone who is party to the employment process in an organization. First, it is a fact that more and more minority-group members are entering college. As pointed out in Chapter 1.4, the increase in black enrollments is 20+% as compared to 5.7% for whites during the last several years. In 1972, 50,000 of the 900,000 college graduates who received bachelor's degrees were black. However, there is still a dearth of minority technical graduates. In 1971, there were 43,000 engineering graduates in the United States and only 407 were from minority groups.

Accreditation of the predominantly black schools continues to be a problem and will continue to result in the matriculation of many of the better students (particularly technical) to white campuses. This in turn will place more and more of a hardship on the already financially pressed minority campuses. There are some bright signs in all of this, however. Howard University is starting a Chemical Engineering Department, which at this point is one of a kind. Its importance is highlighted by the fact that only 20 minority chemical engineers were graduated in the United States in 1972; yet it continues to be the technical discipline most in demand.

To compound the problem, more and more organizations are using the black campus as a source. In fact, while the number of campus visits has been going down on most campuses, they are up at the minority campuses. This, of course, is consistent with the continued efforts by many organizations to increase numbers, but it also causes monumental problems associated with supply and demand.

Second, it is estimated that less than 3% of the line managers and officers in American industry are blacks. In a sense, this figure really capsulizes the whole problem of minority employment and causes endless discussion and debate about supply and demand, cause and effect, etc. But there are some realistic facts that should be considered by any organization that is sincerely trying to meet its EEO commitment, because most organizations are ill-prepared for hiring minorities. Without some prior planning, these organizations will continue to "react," and usually not very logically, to whatever pressures are brought to bear, i.e.,"The government told us we have to hire some minorities, so get out and get some." Such an ill-conceived approach has several unfortunate results:

1. When the minority employee is hired, he will continue to be thought of as a "minority employee" and not as an "employee."
2. Other employees will attempt to give special treatment to the minority group member without understanding that what the new minority employee really wants is equality of opportunity.
3. Training and management-development programs will be a little more inaccessible to the minority employee. When he realizes (and it won't take long) that there is little opportunity to develop his skills in order to compete with peers, he will leave. This will be another mark against the organization's reputation as an employer, and you can rest assured that the word gets around fast in the minority community.
4. The minority employee has to be performing at the next higher level before he gets moved to it. There will be less willingness to "give him the chance to show what he can do." In all probability, he will have to show more skill and ability in doing the job than his peers.
5. There will be no "audit function" to determine what is really being accomplished across the board in minority employment.

Third, to counter some of the impact of those "reacting" problems, the forward-thinking organization that wants to be successful will:

1. Understand that all the legislation in the world can do only so much. There must also be a program of "education" for, and a real effort by, all employees in an organization if there is to be any success. Many *organizations put more time and effort into their United Fund drive*, for example.
2. Provide support to the employment function by ensuring that realistic standards are established for jobs and credentials for doing the job become the dominant selection factor. Jobs must be real jobs and and not just "urban affairs and special markets" positions. As a matter of fact, a minority employee may be not better than anyone else in a "special job." They may in a sense pose a real credibility problem. What really counts here is the commitment of the organiza-

tion to make ability to do a job the primary criterion and to ignore all the peripheral generalizations, i.e., put the best person in the job!

3. Upgrade the placement phase of employment to ensure that any new employee is not overplaced or underplaced which in most situations just leads to rapid turnover.
4. Instill more determination in the selection process by being as willing to take a chance here, on measurable potential as they might be with an existing employee's measurable potential for a promotion.

The Older Worker

The older worker is victim of many of the same generalities that are applied to other minorities, and in a sense this is a real enigma. Medicine and technology continue to provide ways to make people live longer, but organizations are always thinking of ways to get the older employees out of organizations by lowering the retirement age. The arguments for this are all too familiar to the other minorities; generalizations categorize an entire segment of the work force. In this instance, the primary arguments are that the older worker is less able to learn new things, has less energy to work long hours and travel, has a greater impact on benefit costs, etc.

The real facts to be considered are that some people are "old" at 42, whereas others are still "young" at 60. Therefore, the real criterion should be professional competence and physical health. United States Government studies consistently show that a worker's peak earning period in industry is his early to mid- 50s. The bulk of the knowledge and know-how in most organizations is vested in the 40-65-year-olds. Also, a majority of the key management people in most larger organizations fall in that age range.

Organizations that are concerned about their future manpower needs will do well to hire and promote on the basis of skills and motivation and not on the basis of chronological age. To do otherwise is the same type of short-sighted thinking that precludes hiring a well-qualified person because of his color or sex.

Females

As suggested earlier, "women have been *non persona*" in the business world. So much of this problem continues to be perpetuated by generalizations, e.g., "Women are the weaker sex," "Woman's place is in the home," "Women don't want business careers," "Women get pregnant,"

"Women are too emotional," an aggressive woman manager is "overbearing," whereas her male counterpart is "efficient and tough minded."

Women today have greater freedom than they ever had before, e.g., birth-control devices and liberal abortion laws. The array of convenience food and household items and appliances available make housekeeping a lot less demanding than it was even a decade ago. The key here is that this new freedom has given women a much longer potential work life. In addition, according to the Women's Bureau of the United States Department of Labor:

- 50% of all women between 18 and 64 work
- Approximately two out of five workers are women
- One out of three women are still employed in clerical jobs
- Approximately 43% of the 1972 college graduates were women
- In 1970 women earned 64% of what men earned ($5323 as compared with $8966).

These facts should provide some food for thought for any organization with manpower needs. Also, according to Department of Labor statistics, women, on the average, have about the same turnover and absenteeism rate as men. Women change jobs for the same reasons as men, the primary one being boredom. The motivations, attitudes, and values of women toward a job are really not much different from those of anyone else.

However, changes in thinking about women in any job other than "women's jobs" will certainly be more difficult, because the problem is more inbred. Even those organizations that have done a reasonable job of minority employment haven't even scratched the surface in female employment. Revised Order 4 is beginning and will continue to have a real effect, but both women and organizations must also provide some initiative in this. One of the most critical needs is for realistic counseling in our schools about nonstereotyped opportunities for women. (Organizations can be instrumental here by directing more of their university-relations efforts to predominately female campuses.)

In college, women have tended to major in the low-demand, over-supplied fields such as education, social sciences, home economics, much as the minorities have done, because they led to the "safe" professions. That merely compounds the problem. This may be one of the primary reasons that women, on the average, have been less able to take advantage of scholarships and aid-to-education funds. Women haven't been taken seriously as a factor in the professional/technical labor market. "Four years of college to learn to be a housewife; she should have learned to type in high school"; how many times have you used or heard those expressions? In the technical disciplines, for example, women account for only 10% of the nation's 350,000 scientists, according to the National Academy of Sciences. Here, too, women have tended to gravitate to the oversupplied technical disciplines—chemistry and biology, not engineering.

Organizations will have to stop thinking in terms of "women's" jobs and "men's" jobs (Title VII has spoken to that with reference to employment advertising). There will, however, have to be a more concerted effort in all media to show women in other than the secretary or sales-clerk image. The United States Navy took a big step in 1972 when it opened up shipboard billets to women; for decades women have worked aboard ships in many foreign countries. Mobility of women in organizations is almost always limited; it is assumed that when "she" is hired, she will stay only until she gets pregnant, finds a husband, or makes enough money to take a trip. That would be funny if it weren't such a widespread belief.

5.7 SOURCES

It is a fact that in judging compliance, the government will almost always first review employment practices and procedures. A primary problem many organizations have in this respect is their reliance on "walk-ins" and "word of mouth" referrals. That will generally be viewed as a positive sign of discrimination. Organizations must take the initiative to identify and cultivate additional sources and ensure that hiring standards are directly related to job performance.

There are a miscellany of sources available for developing minority and female candidates. They run the gamut from standard sources (Chapter 4) to the American Association of University Women, the League of the United Latin American Citizens (LULAC), and the Urban League. There are literally scores of local and national organizations that can prove helpful.[2] Don't overlook individuals who may be helpful in your

[2]Several references that may prove helpful are the *Directory of National Urban Affairs, Organizations and Urban Oriented Publications*, published by the Public Affairs Council, 1601 18th St., N.W., Washington, D.C.; Chapter XII in *Equal Employment Opportunity for Minority Group College Graduates—Locating, Recruiting, Employing* by Robert Calvert, Jr., Garrett Park, Md.: Garrett Park Press, 1972.

organization's "local community." The principal of any predominantly one-race school, the head of the YMCA, ministers, and any well-regarded businessmen or women may also prove helpful.

The "extra effort" is particularly critical here, with emphasis on the quantity and quality of personal contacts. More effort has to be made to prove the average organization's sincerity and thus its credibility to whatever group is being tapped—black, Spanish-surnamed American, or female. This sourcing requires real affirmative action. An organization must do more than what is normal for achieving employment goals and must prove its willingness to hire people based on skills and abilities to prove that sincerity and establish the credibility.

To gain the most from any minority source, you will need detailed and thorough communications. You may want to put more emphasis on plant tours. Utilize (on a volunteer basis) your existing minority and female employees as spokesman and recruiters, e.g., key-man concept. Publicize in the community, using college brochures, annual reports, and news releases. Explain at every opportunity your job structure and the selection process Above all, let people see for themselves. No organization can really tell its equal opportunity story and make it sound credible; the proof is in the practice. Make someone responsible for coordinating local contacts. Let that person become Mr. XYZ Corporation to the various sources and individuals.

Advertising

Advertising programs should meet all the criteria outlined in Chapter 4.2. Advertisements to reach the minority community, in particular, must be in media directed specifically at an ethnic group. Nothing should be overlooked—newspapers, magazines, radio, and TV. The Deutsch and Shea *Guide to Black Media*, for example, will prove most helpful here.[3] Be sure and emphasize some media directed primarily at women.

These ads must clearly reflect the organization's attitude toward equal employment opportunity. It is not just a question of *saying* you are (everyone does), but rather *showing* that you are. Show a mix of employees

---

[3]In addition, the *Directory of Newspapers, Magazines, and Trade Periodicals*, published by N.W. Ayer & Sons. Other good examples are such periodicals as *Black Enterprise*, Earl G. Graves Publishing Co., 295 Madison Ave., N.Y. 10017 and *Contact Magazine*, Richard Clarke Associates, 1270 Ave. of Americas, N.Y. 10020.

in any illustrations used. Feature employees who have "made it"; this is the best way to get the point across that there is opportunity. It isn't enough just to prove you hire—can people progress based on ability? Don't show minority or female employees in only such traditional jobs as sales clerk or secretary.

State Employment Service

Traditionally, this has not been a particularly lucrative source for professional/technical candidates, because most organizations have such a variety of other sources available to them. It should be given some degree of attention and effort in this context, however, because no stone can be left unturned when demand so outstrips supply. However, because it is part of the "establishment," it generally has a poor reputation in the minority community.

Employee Referrals

Organizations with good orientation programs and credibility in their EEO efforts will find this an excellent source. No one source can communicate your image into the community or segment of the work force better than a satisfied employee. If they understand the organization and its goals and their roles, they will want to refer good people. But, you must also be sensitive to the fact that this can also be a negative source, as was discussed earlier.

Minority Community and Business Leaders

Identifying and establishing rapport with these individuals should prove to be of real value, not only in terms of potential candidates, but also in communicating the organization's sincerity to the community. This will have real impact on your credibility as a real equal opportunity employer. These people can also be extremely valuable in assisting in the development and implementation of various aspects of your affirmative-action plan. They will have particular knowledge about the composition of the local labor force, the skills available, where the organization's assistance and support will do the most good, etc. In communicating with this source, be specific and realistic about jobs and requirements. Emphasize the developmental and training aspects. In other words, prove that there are *real* opportunities based on the need for *skills* to do the job and *ability* to perform.

Third Parties—Employment Agencies and Executive-Search Firms

As would be expected, there has been a proliferation of employment agencies in the past few years that handle minority or female candidates exclusively. A good deal of their success is based on the usual reluctance of the minority and female job seeker to utilize the old-line firms. This is a historical problem; when organizations had no pressure or real incentive to find minority or female candidates, employment agencies and executive-search firms did not bother, in fact, discouraged them as potential candidates. As a result, the average employment agency or search firm still has little credibility. The Civil Rights Act of 1964, however, confronted them with the same obligations for nondiscriminatory practices as it did other organizations. This obviously has had some effect in improving their credibility, but it will take time and in the interim, this new breed of third parties is a valuable key to this segment of the labor market. (All of this is compounded by the fact that few organizations have enough believability to attract the candidates they need from their usual sources. In addition, the shortage of experienced technical/professional minority and female candidates really makes for a competitive seller's market.)

The identification of these firms is not too difficult, because they are relatively few in number and are usually well publicized by word of mouth. It may be difficult, however, to cultivate and develop a meaningful relationship, because you will need to put forth an extra effort in terms of both time and money. A majority of these firms have as many or more clients as they can reasonably handle. They will react the most positively to those organizations that prove to be the easiest to work with, i.e., organizations that provide rapid and thorough follow-through on a given candidate and that have realistic job requirements and credibility in terms of minorities and females who have "made it"; in short, organizations that deserve to be known as equal opportunity employers. Don't overlook the fact that your organization will lose all of its credibility if you attempt to merely "use" these sources to show the government where you have listed your jobs.

The two most important things that an organization should do to develop rapport and credibility are:

1. Make regular visits to the offices of the firms to update them on your current needs, activities, and problems. Invite them to visit your organization, at which time you need to involve the line departments and provide tours of your facilities and community. Let them see what

you are. None of these things can be a one-shot deal; they must be scheduled on a regular basis.

2. "Seed money" can be extremely valuable with this source. Support advertising programs and provide support to their general recruiting effort, e.g., expenses to go see potential candidates or to bring them to a central point. All of this should be done with first-refusal privileges, of course.

Executive search, in its pure definition, is obviously limited by the dearth of minority and female "executives" (generally thought of as earning $25,000 and above). The techniques, however, are being utilized by a number of firms to seek out individuals with particular skills and also to overcome the historical reluctance of minorities and females to respond to the usual sources utilized by many organizations when they have job openings.

In a sense, then, the techniques are similar to those recommended in the sections on employment agencies and executive-search firms in Chapter 4. It really comes down to a question of spending more time in developing a relationship. The initiative must be taken by the organization, however, because there is so much competition for a few people.

Interviewing

Interviewing is an imperfect art for a variety of reasons, which are discussed in Chapter 7. In principle, interviewing minority or female candidates is no different from any other type of interviewing; yet it must be tempered with a great deal of sensitivity and understanding. Chapter 7 also emphasizes the fact that a good interviewer faces up to his biases. We must also, of course, recognize that the interviewee has biases, and these must be recognized if you hope to achieve any real degree of success. Those biases generally center on the following:

1. Minority and female candidates will probably expect unfair treatment because of their past experiences and belief that the organization's efforts are the result of government pressure rather than sincerity.
2. Minority and female candidates will generally be more perceptive than other candidates and know that they do what "we" want or run the risk of getting left out.
3. They will feel that they have to be better prepared than other candidates for interviews, e.g., know what's available and what their rights are.

4. They will feel that credentials to get the job are more critical than their ability to do the job. They may also feel that requirements are not based on those for similar jobs, but rather on what the interviewer feels they should be for someone like them.
5. They will blame the interviewer for rejection rather than their lack of qualifications; they will feel that the white interviewer probably won't play it straight. In fact, the minority candidate will most likely be mistrustful about white interviewers, period.

With those points as examples, it begins to become quite clear that the interviewer needs to have a great deal of empathy and understanding. To help develop that empathy and understanding, let's review some facts:

1. It is safe to assume that a large percentage of the minority candidates with a college degree got through school because they wanted to and not because it was pre-ordained or expected of them.
2. Since past performance is a critical predictor of the future, interviewers must gain a real understanding of the circumstances and environment in which the average minority candidate has lived; it is quite foreign to the average white, and it will be difficult at times, therefore, to understand the attitudes of minority candidates.
3. The female candidate has to overcome not only the housewife/mother syndrome that she has been taught all her life, but also she has to cope with an interviewer who in all probability thinks the same way. The black female candidate, of course, has a doubly difficult role; she is both female and black.
4. Women are generally as well educated as men. In 1970, 50.5% of the high school graduates were women, and 43% of the bachelors degrees and 40% of the master's degrees were awarded to women. The school dropout rate for women is about half that for men.
5. Women make substantially less than a male with comparable education ($3 to each $5 paid the male). They realize that the average organization will try to pay less, assuming that women don't need to make as much money, but they also realize that you don't pay people for the number of dependents they claim on their income tax. You cannot expect a woman (or any other employee) to have much enthusiasm or job satisfaction if she *knows* she is underpaid.

6. Minority and female candidates, like recent graduates, may not have has much work history for an interviewer to relate to. There may be more gaps or possibly more unrelated work experience than with other candidates.
7. Chronoligical age does not necessarily preclude ability to learn, energy, or ambition. Experience is the best teacher.

In initial contact with these candidates, recognize reservations they may have based on bad experiences. Bear in mind that they may have had less exposure to the interview process; therefore, you may want to explain in more detail the whys and wherefores of job structure, the appraisal system, and career pathing. If you don't, the candidate may assume that you don't have a real interest. In addition, these candidates will in all probability have had less experience in evaluating opportunities and may therefore require more information on points "we" might take for granted, e.g., relocation process, travel.

Interviewers

Anyone involved in the interviewing chain must be attuned to the differences and sensitivities of minority and female candidates. Don't be fooled into thinking that a black or female interviewer is any panacea for success. Interviewers must be highly objective and secure in their jobs to be really effective. Black or female interviewers, while probably more perceptive, may set tougher selection standards than their white counterparts. Therefore, it is entirely possible that they may end up being more "biased" in a sense.

Whoever the interviewers are, they must have an understanding of the organization's philosophy and commitment, as well as a real understanding of the motivations and attitudes of this part of the labor force. They should also have an in-depth knowledge of the organization and a sincere interest in helping solve this "problem." They must also understand that real determination is needed in selection and placement to overcome all the generalities and misconceptions that exist.

Interviewers must learn to adapt themselves to interviewing minority and female candidates. To do that with any reasonable degree of success will require that they have a thorough understanding of their function so that they can objectively evaluate people with different beliefs, motivations, and attitudes.

Interview Guidelines

In orienting and training your interviewers to the sensitivities and nuances of minority and female interviews, concentrate on the following items. These are by no means all of the things that must be considered, but they should provide a solid point of departure.

1. Set stage for interview(s) by explaining in some detail the procedure, the roles of each person, the purpose, etc.
2. Do not try to explain the organization's EEO posture; it just won't sell to these interviewees. Don't rattle off the names of the black or female employees unless you can do the same for any group–Irish, German, etc.
3. In the initial interview, concentrate on job and job experience and try to avoid the personal aspects of the candidate's background. Particularly with female candidates, stay away from the domestic and personal aspects.
4. Don't be ingratiating or try to BS; it will only come across negatively. These candidates have been "put down" too many times for this.
5. Make your questions meaningful, objective, and job-related. *Don't* ask "Do you take the pill?" "Are you serious about a career?" "Do you belong to any militant organizations?" In other words, don't ask questions you wouldn't ask of other candidates. You cannot request information of female candidates that you don't request from men, e.g., marital status, contraception practices, unwed parenthood. Indeed, you may want to consider revising your application form to include "Ms."
6. Avoid making or implying stereotyped comments. Let's face it, most organizations employ divorced men who have responsibility for children, and there are unstable and emotional white male employees. You must be very aware of the socially prejudiced context of the job, e.g., "Will she fit in?"
7. Assume that a majority of women will have had less interview exposure and possibly will be more guarded in their responses.
8. Don't assume that women can't accept jobs involving travel and relocation. Explain the requirements of the job, then let her decide.

9. In the same vein, don't assume that the minority candidate won't relocate to the South because of the "housing situation; that is his option. Explain the job requirements and location openly and honestly.
10. Do not be swayed by appearance; you probably weren't hired because you had "good legs" or had "nice" features. If you don't make hiring decisions and placement on ability, it will smack of special treatment and will surely irritate employees.
11. Be sure that the existing job structure does not favor men over women. If the organization has commitment, you should be hiring for the candidate's ability to do the job.

The application for employment form becomes very critical in the selection process of minorities and females because there are so many factors that might be considered a violation of the law. The Employment Management Association has compiled a listing of questions which might violate Title VII of the Civil Rights Act of 1964 or other laws.[4] These questions are not unlawful in themselves, but the use of the information gathered may be, dependent on its purpose. There are different considerations, however, when gathering information for an affirmative-action program. The general areas of concern are:

1. Age? Date of birth?
2. Arrests? Convictions for other than traffic violations?
3. Availability for Saturday and Sunday work?
4. Children under 18? Number? What arrangements will you make for their care?
5. Citizen of what country?
6. Credit record?
7. Color of eyes? Hair?
8. Fidelity bond ever refused?
9. Friends or relatives working for us?
10. Garnishment record?
11. Height? Weight?
12. Lowest salary will accept?
13. Maiden name?
14. Marital status?
15. Mr., Miss, Mrs.?
16. Prior married name?
17. Sex?
18. Spouse's name?
19. Spouse's work?
20. Widowed, divorced, separated?

[4]Detailed listing available from the Employment Management Association, P.O. Box 385, Weston, Mass. 02193 (Technical Advisory Program, August 14, 1972).

Obviously, each of these points may pose particular problems, and it would be difficult to list all the details here. Suffice it to say that this is another indication of the necessity for understanding and sensitivity by all those connected with the employment process.

In controlling the interview process, particular attention must be paid to a number of things:

1. Be sure that all people who will have contact with minority and female candidates (gate guards, receptionists, secretaries) are aware of the sensitivities involved. Every candidate should be treated like a guest.
2. Make all interviewers write their comments. Make them explain turndowns and structure their comments to job-related items.
3. Have a well-planned interview schedule, and pay particular attention to any delays or gaps that may occur. Don't leave the candidate to his own devices.
4. Give your sources honest reasons for your rejection of their referrals. They can be most instrumental in providing you with insights and guidance to assure better results in the future.

5.8 REMEDIES

We have talked about the problems of equal employment opportunity for minorities and females. There is no simple answer or formula, and the problems will certainly not be solved by government regulations alone. The problems will be solved only when organizations realize that discrimination is too costly. Discrimination costs money (taxes) but more importantly, it excludes or makes it difficult for people to enter or perform in the work force at a level commensurate with their skills.

Realizing that a problem of this magnitude will not be solved overnight, what are some of the things that can be done to help expedite solutions? Most organizations can immediately improve their minority and female employment process and retention rate by giving serious thought to the following:

1. What really is the philosophy of the organization and its beliefs about the employment process as related to minorities and females?
   a) Are policies written and administered to encompass the total labor market?

b) Are responsible managers held accountable for their record in hiring and promoting?

c) Is the selection phase really geared to identifying credentials to do the job?

d) Is the subject of minority/female employment a regular agenda item at various management and staff meetings like other "personnel" subjects?

2. The whole "people system" at times encourages discrimination and will continue to do so unless the organization begins to:

   a) Review any testing procedures being utilized. Other than skills tests (e.g., typing), all such procedures are required by law to be validated.

   b) Review job specifications regularly. Otherwise, the odds are pretty good that they are outdated and reflect a structure that precludes most otherwise qualified minorities and females. Are the required qualifications realistic?

   c) Review its development, stewardship (or whatever other title is used) program to ensure that upward mobility is a reality for any qualified employee. (This may be the most crucial factor for minorities and females. Most organizations, once they have a commitment, can hire, but can they retain workers?)

   d) Review turnover statistics realistically. Don't compare female v. male, or black v. white, or mail boys v. engineers and use these figures as justification for not hiring. Rather, review nonexempt and exempt personnel separately or one discipline against any other discipline, e.g., engineers v. chemists.

3. Organizations must make that most difficult of decisions—that commitment to this subject is not an "on-again off-again" thing. Commitment cannot be tied to quarterly profits. Decisions on this cannot be postponed. Employee and community relations are very critical to most organizations, and the new generation of bright, young graduates—white and black—will be turned off by organizations that play games with their EEO responsibilities.

4. Social responsibility doesn't end with paying taxes. There are innumerable programs that most any organization can support that will have a highly visible and credible payoff for a minimal investment.

a) Tutoring programs—providing volunteer instructors to inner-city schools or predominantly minority campuses.

b) Career-guidance assistance at both the secondary and university levels.

c) Plant tours and summer jobs.

d) Aid-to-education (see Chapter 6.9).

5. Expend your dollars and effort in planning and implementing positive programs rather than in trying to determine "what do we have to do to stay out of trouble." It is as foolish for an organization to compromise its employment criteria and process as it is to ignore what must be done to attract more female and minority candidates.

   a) Make certain that *all* employees and sources understand the seriousness of this effort, and remind them often of your commitment.

   b) Involve the minority and female "community" to be sure they understand the organization, its needs, and its criteria.

   c) Offer salaries that reflect the requirements of the job rather than the candidate's current earnings. You don't get a 100% effort out of anyone who is not rewarded equitably.

   d) Identify those parts of the organization in which employment efforts to recruit minorities and women have not succeeded. Ensure that any new or existing openings get only minority or female referral—no options.

   e) Be willing to hire a good candidate regardless of head-count, which should be a year-end figure, anyway.

6. Be sincere and direct in the whole employment process by understanding that minorities and females understand us a lot better than "we" understand them. They have been in a position for a long, long time of doing it the way "we" wanted or being left out.

5.9 SUMMARY

The problem of equal opportunity employment is really more a question of unwillingness and apathy in most organizations. It is a program that requires an extra effort to be successful—an extra effort by everyone in an organization and particularly top management. The employment function must ensure that the employment process is up to date in all respects of understanding the practicalities of getting the job done. It must also ensure that in the final analysis, people get hired for their ability to do the job. With the proper understanding, the hiring of minorities and females will become an accepted fact of life.

6
University relations

6.1 INTRODUCTION

A few short years ago, a book on the subject of employment would in all probability have entitled this chapter "College Recruiting." But like all other aspects of business and almost regardless of the type of organization, things are changing, and campus-industry relationships are no exception. These changes have been brought about by necessity and have been *aided* by the economic downturn of the early 1970s, *not caused* by the downturn. These changes would have occurred anyway, but they were expedited by a slow economy. Forward-thinking organizations were either already adjusting to or planning changes in their campus approach. The problems in the economy merely highlighted these necessary changes.

The downturn of the early 1970s did not change the fact that the "good man" was hard to find; to the contrary, competition for the "good man" became even stronger. Organizations had to change their business philosophy because of rising labor costs, foreign competition, and job openings. In many instances, therefore, they were willing to interview more candidates in order to find the "right" one. Fortunately, at the same time the emphasis began to shift from credentials to *get* the job to credentials to *do* the job. The college graduate with military experience became a most sought-after commodity. Experience is becoming a prime criterion, even overcoming, in many cases, the advanced-degree syndrome that has been prevalent in so many organizations.

Realistically, a lot of this changed or changing thinking has in all likelihood been brought about by the rather dramatic *decrease* in the "bodies game" of the 1950s and 1960s that was perpetuated in many respects by the government's tremendous budgets for electronics and aerospace and its rather loose approach to contract awards and administration. Also, the general affluence of society since World War II has increased the numbers of young people on campus; 50% of our high school graduates now go on to college.

While the costs of education have increased, the overall quality has decreased. There are too many young people on campus without the basic skills or motivation; they are there because it "is expected" of them. The quality of education has not really improved over the past several decades, but college attendance in our society is much like having two cars or two TV's. All of this has had rather dramatic impact on our campuses. First, when demand for college educated people was so high in the 1960s, there was generally little effort made to provide worthwhile counseling or placement assistance; it just wasn't needed during those hectic days. Organizations recruiting on campus were really scrambling and scratching to get their quota. Quality was not as important as numbers and degree level.

Now, the picture is changing dramatically. For example, the military is going to become an all-volunteer force, which will take some edge off of the student's desire to be in college in order to avoid the draft; some of the traditionally "high-demand disciplines" have lost their glamour; but maybe the most important point is that organizations are becoming more realistic. They can no longer afford to have a surplus of people or to retain marginal people (see Chapter 10) *or* to overhire. The latter point may be a key to the future. How many professional jobs are there in your organization that *absolutely require* a four-year college degree or an advanced degree? Two-year colleges, junior colleges, and community college will become an increasingly important factor, as will re-evaluation of job requirements to realistically reflect the level of education needed.

6.2 DEFINITION OF UNIVERSITY RELATIONS

The changing direction and emphasis of campus-industry relationships make it almost mandatory that a different approach to this source be developed. In its broadest definition, this approach should encompass all of those activities necessary to ensure that the right candidates are provided to the organization as potential employees. The basic employment philosophy of any organization is reflected in its employment policies and procedures. As a general rule, most organizations attempt to fill openings by promotion from within, and when that is not feasible they recruit externally. If an organization is concerned about its future manpower potential, one of its prime external sources should be the campus.

Competition will increase as the years go by, and the organization that hopes to be successful will have to use all the tools available to it. The goals must be to acquire the caliber of people necessary for the future of the organization; to continually seek better ways to achieve that goal; and to assist in improving the total education process through more industry-campus contact and support. University relations, then, must be all-encompassing, running the gamut from aid to education to summer employment, with recruiting being one aspect of the total process.

To summarize, we can assume that a university-relations program exists to facilitate the yearly acquisition of a sufficient number of new graduates to assist the organization in meeting its business goals and objectives. This should be accomplished within the established economic framework and with due regard for relationships with the faculty, staff, and student body of the colleges and universities of interest.

The approach as spelled out in the remainder of this chapter will emphasize that organizations will no longer be able to only *show up* on campus once or twice a year *nor* will the campus be able to function as if its domain is strictly a seller's market. There will have to be more equality in the relationship with neither party "demanding" more than it is willing to give.

6.3 ORGANIZATION

The structure of an organization's university-relations function is predicated on a number of things, including business volume, geography, total employment, philosophy, type of product or service, and so on. There are some basic principles involved, however, and it is hoped that they will be applicable and of assistance to any organization that utilizes or plans to utilize the campus as a source of manpower.

As part of the *people function*, the area of university relations is part of the personnel spectrum. In all probability, who it reports to within that context will depend on the size of the organization. In a large organization, it logically is the responsibility of the individual in charge of the employment function; in any organization, however, it should be part of the employment function. For university relations to have maximum success, there must be a strong functional relationship within the organization with the appropriate top management people—technical director, marketing director, manufacturing director. These people need to be apprised of and made party to all the significant problems, undertakings, and accomplishments of the program. The positive aspect of this is having them "on the team," which will be a particularly significant factor in the continuity of the program. It should also simplify the problems of justifying your existence in slow business years and educating the rest of the organization to the whys and wherefores of an ongoing university-relations program.

Hopefully, by now the point has been made that university relations connotes more than just campus recruiting, which no longer is the only answer to the problem of getting the right people for your organization from the campus. Competition and the generally more selective attitude and approach of more and more organizations have broadened the scope. More and more, activities directed at the campus become a two-way street, with a truly mutual cooperation necessary to solve all the problems involved in such a rapidly changing environment. Organizations can now be more demanding of the campus *if* they are organized in such a manner as to provide the assistance, support, and communication necessary to make this a mutually advantageous relationship.

Centralize or Decentralize

This is a classic problem of organizations, and in this context one that is not necessarily dictated by the basic philosophy of the organization's structure. In other words, regardless of the parent's structure and dependent primarily on the geographic spread of the organization, university relations can be centralized or decentralized. Generally speaking, though, it is advantageous to maintain at least a degree of central control over the administrative aspects of university relations. There is no room for a duplication of efforts or for confusion in a program of this importance in your organization or on the campus. Centralization will help minimize the parochial view and self-interest that are often generated when each operating unit runs its own campus program. Central control provides continuity and, if organized and administered properly, will be instrumental in instilling the concept of the "Corporate Recruiter," i.e., all recruiters *represent the corporation* and by so doing, self-interest is limited to finding the best candidates, regardless of where in the organization they may finally be employed. Students become confused and at times frustrated when an organization competes with itself by allowing individual operating units to do their own recruiting. An organization's image will be only as good as the worst unit's methods. Also, the campuses have their own problems in getting the job done and will respond best to the organizations that provide the easiest channels of communication.

Ideally, placement directors would like to have one individual in a given organization as a contact point, and they generally prefer that all divisions or operating units be represented on one "corporate date." Competition within an organization is inefficient for both the organization and the candidates, who get confused about the organization. Placement under such conditions is not as effective, because you need more systems and paper work to ensure maximum exposure of a given candidate; there is a greater risk of a mistake and the ultimate loss of the candidate to the competition. Remember, your handling of a candidate through the employment process can be a major factor in his decision about you; it will indicate to him what kind of an organization you really are.

Centralization then, appears to be the answer to university relations for any multilocation organization because of its efficiency and economy. Centralization will help avoid duplication, and duplication means duplicate costs, less mileage out of an individual candidate, poor communication, less management support and involvement, with a resultant loss of the competitive edge to the other organizations. Forward-looking organizations that follow this centralized approach will find that they can do more with less. In other words, by penetrating fewer campuses in more depth and by developing closer campus ties through more significant supplemental programs that meet campus interests, organizations can achieve better results at less cost.

Coordination is the Byword

In the context that it is used in this chapter, centralization refers to the coordination of a number of supplemental programs that in actuality are directed toward one major goal—to identify and, hopefully, to employ the best people for your jobs from a given campus. In accomplishing that objective, though, there are other advantages. For example, an aid-to-education program is a primary way for any organization to support education as a basic building block of our whole economy; a speaker's bureau should really exist to impart practical, expert knowledge into a given discipline rather than to be a platform to sell good old XYZ Corporation. By coordinating all efforts of this type, the organization's image will necessarily be improved, which in turn has a positive effect on its reputation as a good employer.

6.4 RESPONSIBILITIES

The definition of responsibilities in a university-relations program is important because of the large number of people and schools that may be involved, the highly competitive nature of the campus, the numbers of candidates, and the relatively short period of time available to complete the employment process. Overriding all the various responsibilities in a university-relations program is the necessity to build a long-range program; a meaningful relationship with a college or university is a long-term one, not something that can be turned on and off.

Difficult Role of the Recruiter

Traditionally, most organizations' recruiters have attempted to function in a dual role—as interviewers and as liaison with a particular school that they visited once a year. It is difficult for interviewers to evaluate an unscreened group of candidates on the basis of a 20- or 30-minute conversation. Yet the individual recruiter is also expected to provide liaison with the faculty to gather and develop the information necessary to help build a really meaningful mutual relationship between his organization and the campus.

Unfortunately, that has not worked well for many organizations. Recruiters who are trying to identify, locate, and interview the better students all on the same day seldom have sufficient time to see faculty members or placement-office personnel. This problem is also compounded in most organizations by recruiter turnover, which results in a new face showing up on campus each year, with a subsequent loss of continuity. As a consequence, establishing the "right" relationships has not been accomplished very effectively, and overall results on campus have generally been poor.

6.5 KEY-MAN CONCEPT

To solve some of those problems, programs directed at the campus must be reoriented. This can be accomplished by instituting the *key-man concept*. A "key man" is one of your professional employees who has an existing or potential relationship at a specific school. This individual will establish himself as "Mr. XYZ Corporation" at that school—in a sense he becomes all things to all people, providing the necessary communication with the faculty and pre-identification and access to the better students. The key man will also be responsible for assisting in the establishment of liaison between the school and XYZ's staff and for coordinating all supplemental programs directed at that campus.

For this concept to be established and developed into a viable program, an organization will have to make the best people available, and this can be done only if management provides a long-term commitment to support university relations, including continuity of the individuals in the program, regardless of their level and responsibility.

Because the key man assumes extra responsibility, there must be a method of recognizing this contribution. There must be some incentive for the individual and some method of making this "important." It must be part of his career development plans, or it won't be successful. It must be sold to management as such, and appropriate recognition must be communicated to the individual's supervisor and his personnel record. The key man, at a minimum, should function as follows for maximum results:

1. He should visit the school at any time he feels it is appropriate to develop and maintain the right level of rapport. He *must* visit the school prior to regularly scheduled recruiting date(s) to discuss specific job needs and seek faculty recommendations for interviews and to contact recommended candidates and arrange interviews for the upcoming campus visit.
2. He should be the primary funnel for the allocation of *all* university-relations resources (supplemental programs, Chapter 6.9, e.g., speakers bureau, materials, aid to education).
3. He must coordinate the actual campus visit, assisting the recruiters in orienting to that campus.

6.6 EMPLOYMENT-FUNCTION RESPONSIBILITIES

Under the centralized principle of organization and with a key-man program, the employment function should assume responsibility for these activities:

1. Organize a program that will maintain a capability to provide "x" number of people per year to satisfy the organization's manpower requirements, in line with degree level and discipline requirements. (This program should be *geared* to provide the number required in a "maximum" year.)

2. Develop and maintain contact with campuses by coordinating key-man activities.
3. Identify candidates for the organization's job openings.
4. Coordinate logistics of campus visits.
5. Promote liaison between the campus and staff of the organization.
6. Administer the supplemental programs.
7. Cultivate the organization's image in the academic community.
8. Select, assign, and evaluate campus recruiters and key men.

This centralized concept requires a team approach to the actual campus recruiting. Teams should consist of operating-unit personnel with the appropriate academic discipline and level relative to the potential candidates on a specific campus, plus an employment-function representative. Thus, for example, a team recruiting accountants would require an accountant and an employment-function representative; a team recruiting engineers would require an engineer, and so on. These operating-unit people *should not*, however, be members of a full-time centralized staff, as is the case in some organizations.

The key to success on campus is continuity. This approach allows much more flexibility than having a large central staff, and in addition facilitates efficient and economical utilization of manpower.

On-Campus Responsibilities

One member of the campus team should be assigned as visit coordinator. His specific responsibilities include:

1. Previsit
   a) Contacting, well in advance of the scheduled visit, the other team member(s) to coordinate plans (each member should handle his own travel and motel arrangements) and to arrange an appropriate meeting place.
   b) Checking the "central office" on the day prior to the visit to determine the size and composition of the student sign-up. The coordinator should relay this information to the team member(s) and also reconfirm all arrangements.

2. During the visit
   a) Interview students and prepare comments on the interview report form (see Chapter 8.2).
   b) Review departmental and placement-office files and discard outdated literature and organization fact sheets.
   c) Discuss with placement-office staff those topics about which information is sought on the campus report form (see Chapter 8.2).
   d) Indicate, on the campus-report form, *suggestions* for visit dates for the following year. Specific dates will be determined by the team's geographic swings.
   e) Order transcripts of those students being referred and request that they be forwarded with a bill to the central office.
3. Postvisit
   a) At the end of each interviewing day, the coordinator collects all student resumes and interview-report forms and forwards them to the central office.
   b) After the visit, the coordinator makes sure that the team members call or write those contacts who helped during the visit to express the organization's appreciation.

The team members' responsibilities should include:

1. Previsit
   a) Contacting appropriate faculty contacts (usually dictated by discipline of team members) as listed on the campus-report form, well in advance of the scheduled visit to make luncheon or dinner arrangements in order to gain their assistance in stimulating student interest.
2. During the visit
   a) Interviewing students and preparing comments on the interview report.
   b) Discussing recruiting effectiveness with faculty members to determine what steps might be taken to improve access to the better students and to gather information for the campus report. Update and supplement the information on this report for use in subsequent visits.

c) Renewing existing faculty relationships and/or establishing new ones so that the university faculty who are in a position to influence the student attitudes understand the opportunities that exist in the organization.

d) Meet with faculty to obtain their evaluation and recommendations about students who have been interviewed.

e) After the campus visit, call or write those contacts who helped during the visit to express the organization's appreciation.

All of the people who represent your organization on campus must be concerned about the total program on a long-range basis and not just "today." They should be very aware that they are:

1. Recruiting for the entire organization and must be as objective as they can be in determining the most suitable referral point for each candidate
2. Responsible for seeking out any top students who did not sign up to see your organization, even though the schedule at a given school may be full
3. Making referrals only as indicated by the entry-level manpower requirements unless there is an unusual situation or the candidate has unique qualifications
4. Responsible for indicating the speculative nature of the referral if a recommended candidate is marginal or possesses a background not generally sought.

To ensure that the best possible "total recruiter" represents your organization on a given campus, include a summary sheet of the past history of relationships with the particular campus, the number of graduates hired and their progress, and an aid-to-education record. This summary might also briefly explain the organization's philosophy about its social responsibility and corporate-citizenship objectives, both of which are subjects of increasing scrutiny and complexity.

6.7 OPERATING-UNIT RESPONSIBILITIES

In many respects, the success of the university-relations program will be only as good as the operating units make it. They must realize that they are the ultimate key to success, and without their complete cooperation, all of the organization's university-relations activities will be for naught. The operating units should be primarily responsible for:

1. Planning the entry-level manpower requirements and communicating details to the university-relations function.
2. Assisting in identifying and evaluating campus recruiters and key men and ensuring continuity to their efforts.
3. Assisting in administering the supplemental programs by providing equipment, materials, and logistical and manpower support.
4. Coordinating "*local* campus recruitment" efforts so as to avoid conflict with the central program. (There may be circumstances that will dictate the use of local schools as a recruiting source, and this should be encouraged *if* it is truly productive. "Local schools," however, should *never* be schools that are on the central schedule, and they should not "interfere" with accomplishing the primary objectives of the overall university-relations program.)
5. Coordinating all referral activity, i.e., arranging interview trips, handling the plant interview schedule and followup, communicating with the central office on the status of referrals and all details attendant to an individual candidate considered at that location.

6.8 TRAINING AND ORIENTATION

The centralized, team approach to the campus is not without drawbacks, and a major one is that you have to ensure, as best you can, that your man on campus is the "compleat man." This really means that no organization can afford to have recruiters who don't know the organization in depth. If they are to truly represent the organization, they must be knowledgeable about more than their own work environment. If the days of "Let Charlie take that campus trip because he isn't busy or competent" are gone, then so, too, should the day of the "location recruiter." Recruiters today must be "organization recruiters" representing the total operations and not just their own operating units and attendant self-interests.

Orientation

To effectively prepare recruiters to play a total role on campus, they must have an opportunity to be exposed to each operation in the organization, or at a minimum, a representative sampling of the operations, i.e., at least one plant in each separate product area. A simple, practical way to accomplish this is to arrange a round-robin visit to the appropriate operating units for all campus recruiters. This should be completed before any campus visits are made. The scheduling should provide for the least disruption of the recruiters' and operating units' schedules. The visits should include: a "plant tour" with a good, *practical* indoctrination into all the operations and problems, meetings with appropriate department heads for discussions about their particular needs, problems, and future goals and objectives; and a community tour, which should include a representative sample of the whole area—housing, churches, shopping facilities, transportation, and general cost of living (taxes, food, housing). Once continuity is developed in the program, then the problem is simplified inasmuch as only new or replacement recruiters will need this exposure.

Training

Training for *everyone* involved in the university-relations program, and particularly the campus team, is a must and should be an annual activity. The campus scene changes as rapidly as do the desires and motivations of students, and organizations must stay in tune or run the risk of losing their competitive edge.

As a prelude to the training for the new campus year, it would be well to critique the past year's activity and results. This can be arranged any time after the last campus dates have been concluded. If possible, the critiques should involve *all* of the key men and members of the campus teams. The critique itself should be an open discussion session, with particular emphasis on how to improve the overall university-relations program.

The training program should include a thorough review of the previous year's program, including results, problems, and inputs from the critiques. There should be a thorough discussion of the upcoming program, with emphasis on the overall philosophy of university relations and particular reference to continuity, economy, and efficiency. Interview training should be an integral part of the program (interview techniques can always be updated and improved), and all recruiters should be exposed to "campus interviews" via role-playing. The emphasis on interview training must be on the difficulty of gathering sufficient data in the allotted time to make that critical decision which, when positive, will result in a further investment of time and money in a "plant visit."

A Handbook

It will pay real dividends to prepare some type of a campus recruiters' handbook as a supplement to any orientation and training program. Your campus recruiters can utilize this valuable tool as their guide to the total program. It should be a "working book," with brief, practical information on all aspects of the system and the program. A suggested table of contents would include the following items:

1. *Introduction*—a brief history of the program and the philosophy behind it
2. *Campus Procedures*—the responsibilities of key men and the recruiting team in:
   - a) general responsibilities on campus
   - b) conducting interviews
   - c) faculty contacts
   - d) completion of paperwork
3. *Schedules*—this year's schedule for date(s) at each campus, recruiter(s) assigned, and disciplines sought
4. *General Information*—to provide information on:
   - a) supplemental programs
   - b) recruitment of foreign students and visa requirements
   - c) military obligations
   - d) salary policy
   - e) benefits information
   - f) development and training programs
   - g) statement on equal employment opportunity
   - h) information on corporate involvement, e.g., community and public-service programs
   - i) statistics on results at scheduled schools in previous years
5. *Placement Office*—listing of key people on the placement staff
6. *Operating-Unit Information*—brief description of each major operating unit, including:
   - a) general background of the facility, including numbers of employees and significant achievements

b) product information, including the process or method of producing

c) community information: size, cultural and educational aspects, housing, leisure-time activities

7. *Sample forms*—all paper work necessary to the program, showing type of information required on each.

For economy and efficiency, this type of handbook is best prepared in a loose-leaf format so that revisions and up-dating can be made easily.

6.9 SUPPLEMENTAL PROGRAMS

Basic to the success of a university relations program is an in-depth knowledge of the campuses of interest. This, of necessity, must go beyond merely identifying the best students. Success on campus depends on how much you know about the total environment. What department could use an unrestricted financial grant? Where are the critical centers of influence—placement office or department heads? What is the general attitude toward your organization? Do departments need speakers, materials, equipment? There are others, and the list might get quite lengthy; however, these examples indicate that it is crucial to penetrate the campus in depth and to know at all times what the pulse is. To repeat, the long-range goal is to establish a rapport with the school and faculty that will assure your organization of a high priority in everyone's mind in terms of the good students, both those ready to graduate, as well as those coming along in the pipeline.

The professor who talks about what a great organization you are; the set of textbooks that you donated to the new library; the speaker from your treasurer's department who talks to the class on finance—that's the kind of influence you want. But *none* of those things can be accomplished in the traditional manner. So a major part of the non-traditional approach must be to develop and utilize supplemental programs. There probably can be innumerable supplemental programs, depending on the individual organization's approach. However, there are five basic ones that most organizations should be able to provide and support to some degree, and all of them will pay dividends in building and furthering campus relationships:

1. aid to education
2. speakers bureau

3. materials bureau
4. equipment bureau
5. facility tours/faculty employment.

Aid to Education (ATE)

Aid to education has been a major factor in the continuation of higher education in this country, and the magnitude of this program required formation of a formal advisory council, the Council on Financial Aid to Education (CFAE).[1] This council was formed by a group of industrialists who believed that if there was a return in giving to colleges and universities, organizations would be more likely to give. Over the years, based on experience with a broad cross-section of organizations and schools, the CFAE has developed some basic guidelines that should assist any organization in setting the parameters and administering an ATE program for maximum results.

1. Corporate support to ATE is not philanthropic in nature, but is a business investment with anticipated returns.
2. The size of the gift is not as important as is continuity in giving.
3. Direct departmental grants are more effective than are university grants.
4. Gifts should receive adequate publicity.
5. Scholarships provide only transient rewards.
6. Customer-related donations apart from aid programs should be used.

Speakers Bureau

What better way to get your organization in front of students of interest to you than having one of your employee "experts" talk with them. It is an excellent opportunity not only to get to the students, but also to bring a broader or more practical point of view to the specific discipline. A financial analyst can certainly open up some new areas to an accounting class; an R&D chemist may bring a new practicality to some lab routines.

This type of program will also assist in developing a more realistic liaison between the faculty and your organization's staff. Depending on

[1]Further information may be obtained from the Council on Financial Aid to Education, 6 E. 45th St., New York, New York 10017.

your budget, speakers may be furnished as part-time lecturers or even as lecturers "in residence" for a year. However you accomplish it, it will pay real dividends for a minimal investment of time and money.

Materials Bureau

If your organization has a product line that either ties in to the curriculum or complements the expertise of a particular campus, a materials bureau can be a real plus. For a chemical company to be able to put a hundred-gallon barrel of acetic acid (with your logo on it) in the campus lab has to be an asset. How else can you get the organization's name in front of a captive audience every day? If it also helps save a few dollars in the departmental budget, the department head and instructors will in all probability be boosters of "good old XYZ."

Equipment Donation

How much obsolete equipment, books, tools, or equipment has your organization thrown away over the years? Aside from the good will that donating this to a campus will provide, there is also a tax benefit in many instances. Don't assume that just because your organization can't utilize a particular piece of equipment any longer, it's worthless; it might have several more years of practical, worthwhile service left. On the other hand this program has no room for broken or inoperable equipment, which may cost more to fix than would be worthwhile.

Facility Tours/Faculty Employment

These two things are unique in creating a favorable image in the minds of both students and faculty. Facility (plant and lab tours) tours provide a very practical insight into your organization—physical set-up, working environment, exposure to staff, all of which allows the individuals to better relate to what kind of an organization you are and the requirements you have. Faculty Employment has the very obvious advantage of direct mutual personal contact with the organization and its problems, accomplishments, and needs under very practical circumstances. A caution however, neither of these programs should be attempted without very thoughtful planning and with specific objectives in mind to be achieved. A poorly organized tour or a meaningless job for a faculty member may cause irreparable damage to the organization's image as a potential employer.

However these supplemental programs are utilized, always ensure the maximum in publicity on the campus to continually promote your organizations image as one that shows real concern for industry-campus cooperation.

6.10 BUDGET AND PLANNING

If your organization, as so many others do, operates on calendar-year budget and planning cycle, this phase of university relations is difficult. The timing of university-relations activities is confusing in the average organization's scheme of doing business because of the June-to-June aspect. Unless this is recognized and understood by everyone involved—employment function, line management, the controller—the effectiveness of the program may suffer markedly. To avoid as much misunderstanding as possible, the following points should be understood by everyone:

1. A recruitment season encompasses two budget years, and any increase or decrease in spending levels will be reflected in the actual expenses for two years.
2. The time lag between the initiation of a given year's program and the resulting hires can be 16 months or longer.
3. A majority of the preplanning and commitment of resources takes place prior to the time that operating units initially indicate their manpower requirements.
4. If the operating units change their requirements, there is little flexibility to make a corresponding change in the level of recruitment activities for that current season.
5. August is about the earliest that campus recruiters can be informed of firm trip assignments for the coming season, so they must make their plans and set their objectives accordingly.

In a sense, then, the year is a June-to-June cycle, with major expenditures occurring in late fall and early spring, when a majority of actual campus activity takes place. The months of April through August, although not months of major expenditure, are the time for planning, scheduling, training, orienting, and developing the program mechanics—scheduling recruiters, revising or developing literature, advertising programs, developing requirements, and on and on.

A very real fallacy about college programs that hurts their effectiveness and economy to a great degree is the mistaken belief that a college program is dormant during the summer. This point must be made very clear: *the real heart of the program is the summer*. This is when it all gets put together and will determine the success or failure of your campus-recruiting program.

Budget

Chapter 3, "Budget and Cost," covered budget makeup in some detail. There are, however, specific monetary items that are peculiar to university relations, and those particular items need some elaboration to further clarify the concept of the program.

First, travel expenses, which were originally categorized according to expenses for employment-function personnel and employment candidates, can be broken down further, into three subaccounts. One such subaccount is for the *campus recruiter's travel* expenses. Under the principles espoused in this approach to the campus, the central employment function says, in effect, to the campus recruiter, "While you are on campus working for me, I will pay your way." This subaccount includes *all* costs associated with getting the individual from his work site to the campus and back, and does *not* include his salary. The objective here is to make it more palatable for the operation in which the recruiter works to give complete support to the program—by paying the freight. A second, centrally charged subcategory should be for *orientation and training travel expenses*. The third subcategory should be your *key man travel* expenses. This breakdown will give you some fairly definitive facts on costs, as well as the control necessary to help achieve continuity.

Second, advertising expenses should be divided into *campus advertising and experienced advertising*. You may be able to improve your total effort with this source by establishing subcategories—*campus magazines, campus newspapers*, and *campus-oriented publications*. The real value of defining these expenditures will depend on your efforts to track responses to each of these categories. This task is always difficult, but an accurate analysis will help you determine where best to spend your "source dollars."

Third, expenses for campus-relations aid should be structured into at least six subaccounts: *aid to education, equipment donations, materials bureau, speakers bureau, scholarships* (if applicable), and *plant visitations*. You should discuss this account with the controller and your tax department to be sure that the right information is recorded and maintained. The employment functions must serve as the control point for these programs, particularly in larger organizations where "local-interest" requests and pressures for these types of help are magnified because of the number of operating units.

Fourth, there are expenses for *professional services*, primarily campus-oriented recruiting brochures and other literature. In larger organizations, this constitutes a substantial sum of money and should really be a separate subaccount—*campus literature.*

Because the university-relations budget will in all probability involve large sums of money, much detail, and many subclassifications, the employment function should pay particular attention to the four points discussed in Chapter 3.3 about the *right frame of mind* toward budgeting.

Planning

The planning of a university-relations program is intimately tied to the organization's attitude toward entry-level recruiting and its necessity in terms of the organization's future goals and objectives. This planning process should be similar to that for formal manpower planning (Chapter 2.1). Thus, university-relations planning should be an "accurate and timely determination of the numbers and kinds of activities required to provide the entry-level candidates necessary to meet future business objectives."

The chronology of a campus season points up the variety of problems in the overall planning process that must be understood in order to minimize misunderstanding and confusion.

1. *February*—contact schools to be visited the following fall and spring to establish recruiting dates. Coordinate those dates into meaningful geographic swings.
2. *April and May*—complete the school information sheets from placement offices, specifying by degree and discipline the general types of candidates to be interviewed.
3. *June*—develop advertising program for all campus media.
4. *June*—review recruiting literature to insure that information is current and directed to the degrees and disciplines being sought and that it provides the best picture of your organization.
5. *July*—assign recruiters, utilizing recommendations from operating units and performance evaluations from previous year.
6. *July*—request job requirements by degree, discipline, and functional assignments from operating units.

7. *August*—review campus assignments by operating units. Make changes as necessary based on limitations imposed.
8. *August*—conduct recruiter training and orientation.
9. *September*—prepare budget for following year.
10. *September–March*—recruitment dates on campus, processing referrals, and location visits by recommended candidates.
11. *June–July*—normal report-in date for new hires. Prepare final report of year's activity.

This is a minimal chronology in a sense, but it does point out the variety of items that need attention. In addition, there are the myriad of details associated with the administration of the various supplemental programs, key-man activities, visits to operating units for problem solving, preparation of monthly reports, and so on.

Two basic factors in the planning and budgeting of any university-relations program are: (1) selecting the number and types of schools which will have a significant impact on the organization's manpower and business objectives, and (2) establishing good central control over the selection of schools, which significantly affects the economics of the recruitment process.

In selecting schools, there are a number of things that must be taken into consideration.

1. Does the school have the capability to supply qualified people when the operating units have maximum manpower requirements?
2. Are they schools where there is a productive relationship, or there is reason to believe one can be established? Remember, it takes approximately 16 months to schedule campus dates, and it often takes years to establish an "image" as a good employer.
3. What disciplines do you require? Are they limited or broad? Even if limited, they may be wide in scope when you consider the academic specialties in a particular discipline, e.g., chemists with skills in polymer, textile, physical, coating, analytical, or organic specialties.
4. What have past results been in terms of hires?
5. What is the future potential of the school as measured by its academic rating, technical/nontechnical enrollment, and degrees granted?

6. What are the economics of visiting the school in terms of man-days and travel?

All of the schools on your schedule should be analyzed continually on the basis of those six points to determine if they are truly productive and worthy of continued investment by the organization.

A second major factor in budgeting and planning in university relations is central control, which will affect the economics of the program in a positive way for a number of reasons:

1. Sharing referrals (candidates) among operating units will enhance your prospects of finding a match for the outstanding ones.
2. It becomes feasible to begin recruiting at other top-rated academic schools not previously visited under regional or local programs.
3. It provides a cross-fertilization of graduates not available under a regional or local program, i.e., you can avoid for the most part the provincial situation of hiring all Texas graduates in your Texas operations and all Virginia graduates in your Virginia operations.
4. You can strengthen your position in what is a highly competitive situation by allowing use of advertising, recruiting literature, speakers bureau, materials bureau, and other resources that would be too expensive for an individual operating unit.

Geographic Visits

Surprisingly, many organizations with fairly extensive campus-recruitment programs give little thought to the economical scheduling of their campus trips. A week of visits to schools in New England should not have to involve a team of different recruiters each day. Recruiters should be assigned geographical "swings" of three to four days and, when possible, by degree level and discipline. Once geographic swings are instituted, however, continuity of recruiters is extremely critical, because any travel cost savings may be eliminated if you have to substitute recruiters to cover part of a swing.

Assuming a half-day of travel time per campus visit, a geographic setup would allow two or three campus visits in one week (Monday, Wednesday, Friday or Tuesday and Thursday) without any great imposition, regardless of where the recruiter is based. To arrange the most effective geographic swings will take time, inasmuch as a fair amount of work is needed to coordinate dates and changes with the campus placement officer.

6.11 THE CAMPUS INTERVIEW

The most difficult task in any university-relations program is the interview. In 20 or 30 minutes, the campus recruiter must evaluate the candidate's ability, determine his personal and professional objectives, and answer questions about his own organization. Communication is so critical. The short exposure time on campus means that your recruiters must have spontaneity and enthusiasm and be thoroughly convinced that their organization is a great place in which to work. Because of the time limitations and the fact that college candidates seldom have much significant prior experience, the campus interview is thought to be the most difficult type of interview.

As is true in all interviewing, there must be some guidelines or framework established. As a matter of fact, it may be even more important here because of the time limitations imposed. There are nine critical points that should be drilled into your campus recruiters during your training sessions, and if they learn this part of their lesson well, your campus recruiting will be on the road to success.

1. What do you really need to know about the graduate? Establish a framework and be sure you need to know what you think you do.
2. Set up standards for every item in your framework. Determine beforehand what level of scholarship is acceptable, what kind of extracurricular performance is helpful, and other similar standards.
3. Know when you have obtained the information you need. Memorize your framework. You should learn to feel uncomfortable when you are in the "chit-chat" area outside of your framework.
4. Learn to probe, but not as a separate art. Probing is meaningful and effective only when it results from your dissatisfaction with what you know about the candidate.
5. Learn to predict from the graduate's past rather than from his remarks about the future.
6. Learn to recognize "cultural noise," i.e., polite talk that is essentially meaningless. Learn how to turn off "cultural noise." Turn to new area as soon as the "noise" runs down.
7. Use the interview as a source of new information. It is not a place to obtain or review materials that can be obtained in the registrar's office, the placement office, or elsewhere.

8. Face up to your biases. If you accept a man who falls below your standards or reject a man who meets them, see if you can bring yourself to write the reasons.

A Different Approach

Before getting into any further details of the campus interview, it may make sense to look at it from the other side of the desk, the interviewee's side. The interviewee knows that your presence on campus indicates that you have jobs to fill and that he has to convince you to hire him. He knows that you know more about your organization than he possibly could at this stage. He also knows that you know what kind of a person can get into and be successful in your organization. He knows that you, in a sense, have the tougher job, because you must find out what makes him tick. While you are finding out what he knows, the candidate must be trying to show you how he can fit into your environment.

The smart interviewee will realize that you will assume a lot of things about your organization (you may be too close to the forest to see the trees), and he will have read your brochure, annual report, and information sheets. So you will have to be prepared to be specific; the interviewee may also assume, and rightly so in many cases, that you won't really know that much about your organization. So even if you *have* to assign some inexperienced recruiters to a campus, be sure that they are positive and motivated, which can be a substitute for knowledge.

The interviewee has a pretty good idea (particularly after he has had several interviews) about what you will ask and will be reasonably well prepared with facts about himself, his activities, and his likes and dislikes. He knows that you will probably overemphasize grades and underemphasize work experience (the old credentials game).

He knows that you are looking for people with high potential, and he probably will have read more articles about how to be an interviewee than you have. He knows the interview is a negative role-playing process and that he must pass muster with you, because you are the organization at this point.

All of this means that the average campus candidate is smarter, more mature, and has different desires and motivations than his counterparts of two, five, or ten years ago. Thus, campus recruiters must not take anything for granted and must be on their toes and well oriented to their organization if they hope to get and maintain an edge on the competition.

Measuring Potential

Because there is little past history on which to judge the average campus candidate's future potential, probing into five basic areas should provide the best indicators during this limited interview.

1. *Grades.* But don't overemphasize; they can be an indicator of interests, but by themselves are not a particularly good predictor of success.
2. *Accomplishments.* What did the candidate do (e.g., school activities, jobs, sports), that made him different from the other students?
3. *Attitude.* Why is he in school? How does he feel about industry, jobs, and the world in general?
4. *Self-Evaluation.* How does the candidate view his strengths, weaknesses, and motivations?
5. *Future.* How does the candidate view his own potential in terms of overall objectives, job goals, and desires?

Conducting the Interview

It is important to establish rapport quickly so that the discussion can turn to the nuts and bolts of the interview. Open the interview with a first-name introduction and a brief chat about some neutral subject of general interest. Quickly create an environment in which the candidate wants to respond to your questions. Explain the purpose of the interview, emphasizing its brevity and necessity for the candidate to do most of the talking.

There will not be time for idle conversation, and it becomes quite difficult to maintain the right level of rapport and yet be extremely businesslike in gathering the necessary data. How you ask your questions and maintain control will be the major criteria for success or failure. To keep within the time frame and be businesslike without being rude or too abrupt, the four guidelines that follow should be helpful.

1. Don't ask questions that may be answered with a yes or no answer.
2. Don't ask questions that give away the answer you are expecting, i.e., "You have enjoyed your engineering courses, haven't you?"
3. Your phraseology shouldn't give the appearance of being an interrogation. Continued use of *what*, *when*, *where*, and *why* can give this impression. Introductory phrases such as "Tell me more about. . ." or

"I would be interested in hearing about. . ." create an easier atmosphere.

4. If the conversation drifts into unrelated topics, you can redirect the interview by stating, "That's interesting, but I would like to get back to the topic we were just discussing."

Once you have the facts you need about the student, use your time to match up his interests and plans with the organization's requirements. Describe the openings in the organization which seem to fit his ambitions, and determine any potential problems about geography. When a candidate indicates a specific preference for a given operating unit or job, be sure to note this clearly on the interview form to avoid any multiple referral.

In most cases, it is recommended that candidates not be rejected verbally unless there is a *clear mismatch* between your requirements and the candidate's objectives. The best approach is to thank the candidate for his time and interest and tell him that he will hear from the central office within a specified period of time. That time period must be realistic, because he will expect to hear, and an inordinate delay may cause your organization to lose some credibility on that campus.

Faculty Recommendations

A necessary and important adjunct to your successful campus interviews (those candidates whom you will refer) are the opinions of the faculty who know the candidate. The team coordinator is responsible for obtaining transcripts and written recommendations on students who are being referred. These should be enclosed with the student's resume and interview form if immediately available; if not, they can be forwarded by the school to the central office.

However, the most meaningful evaluations can be obtained from faculty members in a face-to-face situation. Group luncheons for organization representatives and faculty members are *not* conducive to obtaining faculty recommendations. It is best if a private luncheon or dinner can be arranged with selected faculty members. If this is not feasible, the campus representatives should seek out members of the faculty during breaks in the day and obtain recommendations.

6.12 REFERRAL PROCESS

In the multilocation organization, making referrals becomes a crucial step. After deciding that you have a referrable candidate, you must then decide what location is most suitable, unless there is a specific preference noted on the interview form. Where you refer the candidate is a function of two factors—what type of work the candidate desires and his geographic preference. You must recognize any geographic limitations that the candidate expresses, but have your campus recruiters stress the mobility of employees in the organization and have them talk in terms of *initial assignment* rather than a career in one operating unit.

The referral system should provide for two types of referrals—single and multiple. A *single referral* indicates that the campus recruiter and the candidate have a preference for a specific location. A *multiple referral*, on the other hand, indicates that there is no specific geographic or work preference, and the candidate should be invited to more than one operating unit. Generally speaking, multiple referrals will fall in one of two categories.

1. Although the candidate would like to live in Georgia, the work he wants to do is available only in New York. This indicates that the candidate has a conflict between personal preference and professional objectives. Therefore, it usually makes sense to try to accommodate both, since it will be difficult to predict which will override the other.
2. The candidate has not really resolved the questions he has about his functional interests, e.g., research v. marketing. Without a valid justification, it does not make sense to utilize multiple referrals. The organization must understand what has to be done to make multiple referrals economically and efficiently.

Multiple referrals require a good deal of coordination between the interested operating units. Central control pays dividends here by providing the needed coordination and a point of arbitration to ensure that the new employee is placed in the operation that will provide the opportunity for the most productive overall efforts for the organization. To remove as much self-interest by the operating units as possible, the central office should coordinate multiple visits and determine the salary to be offered (operating units cannot be allowed to compete with each other on dollars).

Finally, the central office should extend the offer, with follow-up details provided by the offering operating units.

6.13 CANDIDATE'S INTERVIEW TRIP

The basic steps involved in the "interview day" are spelled out in Chapter 7; the confirming letter, in Chapter 8.1. However, there are some details involved with a candidate's "in-plant" interview that require specific attention here.

1. Visit dates will necessarily be limited by the candidate's schedule of classes. Usually, the best dates for the campus candidate are during breaks, e.g., Christmas vacation, spring vacation, or between semesters. This clustering of dates can pose some real problems for organizations, because if the university-relations program is sizeable, it will mean an influx of candidates during a relatively short period of time, with concurrent interruptions in work routine.
2. A system of providing for prepaid transportation and on-site reimbursement of other travel expenses should be developed. Not too many college candidates are affluent enough to handle several trips in a short period of time.
3. Particular attention should be given to the community tour with respect to lower-cost housing, graduate educational facilities, and job potential for the candidate's spouse.
4. The interview schedule should be structured to allow some time for the candidate to chat with recent graduates in the organization. Also, if the candidate brings his wife on this trip or subsequent trips, don't overlook the value of enlisting the recent graduate's wife to help sell the area.

Your concern about the candidate's reaction to the visit is important because he goes back to campus and will talk about his experiences with your organization. Thus, it's up to you to make him a good salesman for your organization.

6.14 MINORITY/FEMALE RECRUITING

Although the broadest aspects of this subject were well delineated in Chapter 5, there are a number of factors that relate to campus recruiting and should be mentioned here. The predominantly minority campuses have been at a real disadvantage over the years, because lack of broad job opportunities precluded these schools, in many cases, from establishing curricula that prepared students to meet current and future needs. This has proved to be a two-edged sword by not preparing students for this changing world where there are more real opportunities opening up every day, and by forcing those students who wished to pursue some of the closed disciplines, e.g., engineering, to matriculate to predominantly white campuses. This, of course, has had a negative reaction on the minority campus, because it was unable to obtain funds to attract or retain a staff that would allow it to compete with other schools. The predominantly female campus has also suffered from the same general type of historical generalizations that have limited job opportunities for women.

It is reasonable to assume that many organizations are developing a better understanding of the problems of employing both the minority and female candidates, but all those who are concerned in any way whatsoever with university relations should be aware that a number of the classical problems still remain. Those problems are really related to lack of exposure by both parties and can be overcome to a great degree by government enforcement of antidiscrimination legislation. In addition, organizations can use their supplemental programs in a more concentrated manner than may be their practice on predominantly white campuses. Meanwhile, these problems will continue to plague both the schools and the recruiters.

1. General lack of knowledge about industry and its organization
2. The credibility (believability) gap between campus and industry
3. Nontechnical curricula
4. Predominance of female students on minority campuses, which may affect types of courses taught
5. General lack of exposure to the employment process, which compounds the credentials problem (credentials to get the job will override credentials to do the job).

Because there is such a tremendous and relatively untapped source of manpower available from predominantly minority and female campuses, it behooves all organizations that are concerned about their future to begin to emphasize support to these schools.

6.15 THE FUTURE

Even if an organization does everything right in its university-relations program, it will continue to be successful only if it stays tuned in to tomorrow. There are so many changes taking place in the business world and on campus and there will be so many more that are unforeseen at the moment, that unless an organization makes a conscious, concerted effort to stay in touch, it will not be able to compete for its share of manpower.

If the pattern holds true, by 1980 one in every six people in the work force will have a degree, as compared with only one in twelve in the mid-1960s. The value of that degree in terms of quality of knowledge diminishes each year. Unless organizations are willing to provide more help in bringing a practical approach to education that trend will continue. The campus has not and cannot under present circumstances keep up with all of the changes that are taking place in the business world. There is an extremely urgent need to bring the needs of society to the attention of the educators, with particular reference to "what" they are producing. Many educators have been insulated too long, and with some exceptions, organizations have made too little effort to have any really significant effect on the problem.

The government has not been a particularly helpful force in all of this. Rather, the government has perpetuated the necessity of a college education to the point where 14 times as much federal money is spent on that as is spent on vocational education, for example. Industry and government must work together to bring about changes in the educational system to better serve the total population.

It is extremely difficult to predict what the next decade or two might bring in the way of technological and educational change. We might assume, however, that it will be more dramatic than the past decade or two. What needs to be done now to prepare for the future on our campuses that will be instrumental in ensuring a supply of the right candidates for everyone's jobs?

1. There is an almost desperate need for more guidance and counseling through the joint efforts of organizations and campuses. Actually, this should extend down into the high schools. This must be directed primarily at the skills and motivations of the individual in a practical way.
2. Organizations will have to be more realistic about their job requirements and structure. Not every new hire is a potential replacement

for the president! How much schooling is really required? What are the factors that make people successful in a given organization?

3. Organizations need to provide students more exposure to them, to lessen the credibility (believability) gap, and to provide practical experience through more summer jobs, for example.
4. There must be more involvement in community and junior colleges. Enrollment in these schools is skyrocketing, and their quality will be greatly influenced by how much assistance is available. This should be given much more consideration in terms of aid to education.
5. A greater effort must be made at predominantly minority and female campuses, because they are an increasingly large and lucrative source of manpower. They are not being utilized effectively, and they are not getting their proper share of supplemental programs. Yet an increasing number of minority high school graduates are going to college, and some 44% of the bachelor's degrees awarded in 1972 went to women.

6.16 SUMMARY

In summary, then, the concept of university relations is a particularly appropriate approach for those organizations that are concerned with the "future." On the other hand, the employment function will have to take the initiative in selling the concept and overcoming the immediate short-term objections that will undoubtedly be raised. The forward-thinking organizations, however, will move in this direction because it is concerned about both its future *and* current manpower needs.

7
Selection and placement

7.1 INTRODUCTION

The selection and placement of people represents a problem for organizations that will continue to prove somewhat of a mystery as long as one human being has to evaluate another. The primary tool used in the processes of selection and placement is the interview. This is the way we determine what an individual's skills and abilities are and how well they will allow him to perform a particular job within the environment of an organization. Organizations are much like people; since each one is different, success or failure in one organization is not the only criterion for success or failure in another. In other words, good performance in one organization *does not* necessarily guarantee the same in another organization.

For you, the interviewer, to determine to the best of your abilities how successful a particular individual may be in your organization, you need to have controlled (directed) conversations (interviews) in order to explore what has been accomplished by the individual in the past so that you can try to predict future accomplishments. By virtue of their normal make-up, people play different roles in different situations, so you as the interviewer have the problem of sorting out the facts to find the "real" person. The emphasis in most interviews seems to be directed to "Can the individual do the job?" and yet equally or more important is "Will the individual do the job?" So, at best, interviewing for selection and placement is difficult because every person is different, and the interviewer has to figure out not only the level of skills and knowledge a person has, but also what motivates him.

Purpose of Interview

Interviewing, especially employment interviewing, should be conceived of as *basically a social situation providing a free exchange of information between two people predicated on a desire to find the person best suited for a particular job.* To effectively plan a selection process, all those involved in interviewing must realize that in selecting people, the primary concern must be centered on their competency to "perform the job" and their "willingness to do the job." To judge this potential competency, one must look at and evaluate the candidate's formal training, education, experience, progress in previous positions, references, and, if appropriate, results on tests.

Testing

Many organizations use testing in the selection process, and it can be a valuable input if the results are used to provide a point of departure and not taken as the criterion for the final decision. In other words, tests can pinpoint the candidate's areas of potential weakness, and the interviewer may want to use test results to probe a little deeper. However, everyone involved in the selection process should understand and agree on the role and value of testing as it pertains to their organization. The key question must be "How important is the information garnered from the test results to performance of the job in question?" Although we will not discuss the pros and cons of testing here, any organization that uses tests should become familiar with the Equal Employment Opportunity Commission's guidelines on testing and be prepared to prove the validity of its tests.

Job Requirements

Obviously, to make any critical judgments about the candidate's skills and abilities, there must first be a clear understanding of what actually is necessary to meet the demands of the job. This means that an interviewer *must* know in advance:

1. What skills, abilities, and experience are needed to do the job.
2. What job responsibilities or functions are involved.
3. What degree of education, mobility, and adaptability is necessary to do the job.

4. What the pressures are to which the man must respond.
5. For whom and with whom he will work.

Understanding those and other relevant details will greatly facilitate the interviewing process. Too often, the current job responsibilities of the position are not clearly understood, and the interviewer merely trusts that the information he obtains will be helpful in determining a candidate's suitability for the job. When this occurs, it is difficult to screen out candidates with marginal qualifications and experience. It also makes it extremely difficult for the candidate to make his judgments about the job.

Need To Improve

Interviewing, like all other aspects of business, is changing because people's motivations, desires, challenges, and goals are changing. Many of the difficulties in interviewing arise from the generally haphazard methods used and a lack of appreciation for the complexity of the problem, particularly in terms of what a bad selection/placement decision can mean to an organization. In far too many organizations, little thought is given and little time is expended in trying to improve this process. Although a reasonable businessman would never approve the purchase of an expensive piece of equipment without making a thorough evaluation of its construction, cost, durability, and ability to perform the task for which it was intended, the same businessman will often hire a person for an important job without any really thorough evaluation of his cost, durability, or ability to perform the job. Very often, such a decision will be made after 20 or 30 minutes of conversation, during which the "hirer" generally dominates the conversation, thereby minimizing the exchange of facts. As a result, the decision whether or not to hire is based primarily on surface impressions—the candidate's appearance, general manner, and apparent relevance of experience and training.

Almost everyone with any supervisory responsibility in an organization becomes involved in employment interviewing at some point. Interviewing would obviously be a much more meaningful process if all who have this responsibility could have some professional training. In lieu of that, there are several relatively simple techniques that if utilized objectively, will prove to be a real help in improving your skills and consequently the overall selection process in your organization.

1. With the candidate's understanding and agreement, tape your next interview. You can then play it back later and hear for yourself how well you do.
2. Time the interview to determine how long you, the interviewer, are talking as opposed to the interviewee. Use a stop watch; if you are talking more than 20% of the time, you aren't doing the job. You can't gather much data if you are doing all the talking.
3. With the interviewee's understanding and agreement, have a third person sit in on the interview and evaluate your style and technique.

Those relatively simple techniques can give you a keen insight into your interviewing skills and techniques.

No one should ever take his interviewing skill for granted as measured by the number of people he has interviewed. You must always keep in mind that your job as an interviewer is to find the right man for the job. To accomplish that successfully, you cannot afford to rest on your laurels; rather, you must approach each new interview with a plan (framework) and objectives.

The interview should not be thought of as the final step in the selection process. Rather, it is a supplement to the other factors—reference checks, information provided on the application form, and testing, if appropriate, in the total process. This chapter is intended to present an overview of interviewing, with special emphasis on the mechanics and the administration of the process rather than on techniques which are readily available elsewhere.[1]

Problem of Urgency

In interviewing, perhaps one of the most real problems is *urgency*. The job must be filled; fill it! Employment in its entirety is a risky business, so a thorough and thoughtful approach will minimize the risks. The employ-

[1]R.A. Fear, *The Evaluation Interview*, New York: McGraw Hill, 1958; Felix Lopez, Jr., *Personnel Interviewing—Theory and Practice*, New York: McGraw Hill, 1965; Milton M. Mandell, *The Selection Process*, New York: American Management Association, 1964; Lawerance L. Steinmetz, *Interviewing Skills for Supervisory Personnel*, Reading, Mass.: Addison Wesley, 1971.

ment job is not done when the personnel requisition form is completed and signed any more than it is when the job is filled. It is *done only* when the individual hired performs well and progresses in the organization.

What we are really talking about, then, is a long-range investment. Although time is of the essence in filling a job, the feeling of urgency that so often accompanies a personnel requisition is usually evidence of poor planning and may be extremely costly in the long run in terms of high turnover and high employment costs. The line manager, in particular, must be aware of the dangers in not allowing sufficient time to do the job right. The employment function must get him to realize what is involved from the initiation of a requisition to the candidate's acceptance of an offer, and then it will be apparent to him that only so much expediting can be done. The candidate *has to be recruited* and *invited in* for interviews (possibly several times). References have to be checked. An offer has to be *extended*. The offer has to be *accepted. Relocation*, if necessary, must take place. This may very easily cover a period of one to three months.

Too often, the employment process gets to be a "hurry up and wait" situation. The line manager pressures the employment function to stir up some candidates and then is too busy to interview on the day the candidate is available. Or, decisions on candidates interviewed are interminably delayed because of the rush of other business. Once candidates are identified, the line manager should be as involved as is felt necessary by the employment function.

7.2 THE SELECTION PROCESS

Four Key Points of Selection

There are four critical things that the employment function, in particular, must know and understand in order to select the right person for the job. Although these points are also important for the line manager, the employment function usually is responsible for making the initial contact and screening most of the potential candidates.

1. *Ability to do the job* should be the determining factor in selection and not the ability to get the job. Too often, the candidate's credentials for getting the job overshadow his ability for doing the job.

2. *Avoid being an amateur psychologist.* You are paid to ask questions that will elicit factual data to help you determine the candidate's ability to do the job and function in your organization.
3. *Know your organization and its people.* This is really the best way for you to be the effective assessor and salesman you must be.
4. *Know your industry.* Know the salaries, job aspects, and people in the competition.

Interviewing Dangers

It is not really too difficult to state the methodology of interviewing; it is in the implementation of the methodology that the dangers become apparent. Successful interviewing evolves from one's own personality and experience; it is not just a collection of techniques, a list of questions, or looking for desired responses. Maybe, perhaps most importantly, the good interviewer must be willing to admit to his own biases, prejudices, and weaknesses. By acknowledging his biases, he can minimize their influence on his judgement, reaction, and acceptance of the candidate's responses.

The interviewer must be willing to answer inquiries objectively and honestly, as well as to set aside his own idiosyncrasies. No list of questions, therefore, can ever supplant an interviewer's personality and experience. However, there is a long list of errors and hazards involved in interviewing, and a discussion of some of the most outstanding or frequently repeated ones follows.

1. If there is any one major problem in the interviewing, it is the inability or unwillingness of people to listen. When the interviewer doesn't listen, no meaningful data are collected, and when the interviewee doesn't listen, no meaningful data are received. In such a case it is really impossible for either person to make a sound decision.
2. When the information required on the application form is rehashed, the interviewer accomplishes little because not enough information regarding the candidate's attitudes, temperament, characteristics, ambitions, or aspirations is gained. Thus, the time of both the interviewer and the candidate has been wasted, since little knowledge has been gained by either party.
3. The interviewer should recognize his own fears. For example, he may be fearful of accepting a person who may be better qualified than he

is, or he may hesitate to admit that a person other than himself is equally or better qualified to do the job. Interviewers may also fear the "too good"; no candidate can be that good; there must be something lacking. This kind of reaction, of course, strongly suggests that the interviewer himself is not performing at his highest level of productivity and, as a consequence, is guarding his own position by his unwillingness to accept a well-qualified candidate.

4. Fear of making errors during the interview is a common mistake. Recognize that the interview is a social situation; if we observe the normal social amenities, courtesies, and skills, a great deal of apprehension will be removed. No one person, regardless of the level of his skills in interviewing, is going to be right all the time. There are just too many variables in human beings to allow for any standard of consistency.

5. Prejudice or bias on the part of the interviewer often causes a company to overlook a good candidate or to employ a person who may not be qualified for the job. Prejudice takes many forms—religious, social, racial, fraternal, scholastic, personal characteristics. In one large company, for example, a study of middle and top management revealed the startling statistic that over 50% of this group were graduated from the same school. This is an example of a "positive prejudice," but it may cause inestimable damage in the long run—too many people from the same mold may cause a real lack of innovativeness.

   We all have prejudices and biases which too often unduly influence our judgments. The key point here is to know what they are; admit them, and you are bound to do the job better. On the other hand, however, it should be pointed out that there are situations when group morale and a smoothly functioning operation can be upset by employing a person capable of performing the duties of the job but incapable of adapting to the established and accepted social standards and expectations.

   Because of the very real danger that inherent prejudice or bias may affect selection, the employment function must ensure that all who are involved in interviewing are familiar with legislative and legal regulations regarding discrimination in employment. There are legal restrictions which must be observed in the interest of the company, the interviewer, and the candidate.

6. Another real hazard is the "halo" effect, which frequently comes into play when an individual has been associated with a large, well known, and successful company. The danger is that there are many people who have reached a position of significant stature and status by mere association with successful organizations, although in reality they have done little to merit it. From the interviewer's standpoint, the tendency to generalize or to ascribe similar characteristics, traits, qualities, and assets to all members of a given group can be very misleading. In one sense, a person should be evaluated by the "company he keeps," but it must be clearly recognized that group characteristics are not necessarily those of each member.
7. The impact of physical appearance and attire unfortunately play too big a role in selection at times and there is a tendency to let these factors overly influence what is being said. For examples, studies have proved that short stature is a decided detriment for the job seeker. One of the most perceptive interviewers the author has known, was blind. His skill was based on the logic of the conversation and inflections of the candidate's voice. Since he could not judge the candidate's appearance, he proved to be generally more objective about the candidate's job abilities and skills.
8. A candidate's years of experience should never be the critical determining factor in selection. It was said a long time ago that "Ten years of experience is a lot different from one year of experience ten times." Evaluate what was accomplished!
9. Don't overemphasize educational background. Education must be evaluated as a criterion for getting rather than performing the job. Don't assume that everyone from a given school is as smart as the top student. By the same token, don't assume that a degree level is an indication of intelligence.
10. There is a unique hazard in attempting to interview several candidates in rapid succession. The interviewer may not be able to "clear his mind" from the last interview. He may carry over to the second candidate his feelings and attitudes toward the first, with resulting confusion of the two. The best method for overcoming this is to record pertinent information immediately following the termination of an interview. If necessary, apologize to the next interviewee, but take the necessary time to record your observations and comments.

If you don't do this, at the end of the day you are likely to have an extremely confused picture of all those you have interviewed. If at all possible, allow a period of time between the termination of one interview and the beginning of the next.

Briefly, these are some of the dangers present in interviewing. Often they are the result of the interviewer's method. When they exist, almost invariably the interview is nothing more than a review of the application form.

7.3 THE INTERVIEW PROCESS

Interview Facilities

The physical setting in which interviews are conducted is most significant. A special, private area should be set aside for conducting interviews. The facilities do not have to be lavish, but they must provide privacy and quiet, away from the noise and confusion of office traffic. They should convey an informal and pleasant environment.

If the interviewer's own office is used, he should get out from behind his desk, a barrier of formality which must be removed if he is to establish a truly conducive interview environment. Telephone calls or other interruptions should not be accepted, except in emergencies. A feeling of relaxation should be evident, which will signify that every consideration is being extended to the candidate.

Framework of the Interview

Almost everyone approaches and conducts interviews a little differently, using his own style and techniques. But for interviews to be really successful, a basic framework must be established to provide some direction for a meaningful conversation. Interviewers must know in some detail what it is that they need to learn about a candidate; they must be able to justify needing it; they must know the standards required for each item of information they need to obtain; and they must know when they have obtained the information. (This last is a peculiarly difficult problem for the average interviewer.)

Negative Business

A very real danger in prescreening that often makes the employment function overlook a good candidate is not really understanding the job and man requirements. If the employment function cannot focus objectively on vital information, some good candidates are bound to get away. It is also all too easy to draw general and subjective inferences about people; to some degree everyone has "hardening of the categories" such as "That's a predominantly black school, and obviously it does not measure up technically with the big 10 schools"; "I have never yet seen a good man from ABC Corporation"; "Anyone who spent 15 years with them can't be our type"; and on and on.

Remember, you are trying to find the man best qualified to do the job, so get in a *positive* frame of mind before you do any screening. Employment is basically a *negative business*—it's a screening-out process, and all too often those involved in the selection phase don't think about the positive side of the individual's qualifications, skills, and personality until it's too late. Be careful that you don't interpret statements, particularly those relating to an individual's objectives, so shortsightedly as to preclude any consideration for other current or future positions. Don't short-circuit the placement process. Realize, for example, that it is extremely difficult for the average person to write a meaningful objective on his resume, let alone write a good resume.

Interview Styles

In reality, many "styles" of interviewing provide no meaningful data. Examples of these are listed below and should be avoided if your organization hopes to have any real success in selection and placement.

1. There are still too many people who feel that they can size up a person by looking at him (the *eyeball* interview) and this is the most dangerous interview of all because it is the most superficial. "I knew he was a good man when he walked in the door and gave me that firm handshake."

2. The *standardized* interview is another faulty method. Here, the interviewer asks a series of questions in a particular standard order, usually with no variance. Many times, the candidate answers a question in the context of a previous response. The interviewer may also overlook any extension or amplification relating to questions in their order of sequence. This type of interview is too formalized and inflexible and does not permit the interviewer to really inject his own experience and personality.

3. The "*chatty conversation*" is often interpreted as an interview. Pleasantries, common experiences, and mutual acquaintances are often exchanged, but little information is gleaned by either the candidate or the interviewer.

4. The "*third degree*," or the stress interview, that basically attempts to antagonize the interviewee will frighten a candidate away. Interviews are social situations and should encompass the normal social amenities.

5. The *highly reserved and cautious* interview occurs when the interviewer sits back and conveys the impression that he must be shown, e.g., "You're the candidate; show me. What do you have to offer us?"

This leads us to the *competent interview*. This is an interview that is desired because it provides the real data needed to make the correct hiring decision.

The Competent Interview

To conduct an interview competently, you must first be convinced of the significance of each employee as a contributing member to the successful operation of the organization. You must have clearly in mind what the job responsibilities are as well as the kind of person necessary to perform them. Once you have defined and crystallized those items, you can then consider the other essentials.

Any employment interview should be viewed as a social situation, and you should look upon it as a conversation during which meaningful information will be exchanged. The interview will then become a well-planned, directed conversation, with the direction necessarily being provided by the interviewer.

Initiating the interview is a critical step and if not done correctly, you may fail to get the desired data or ever see that good candidate again. The objective here is to set the stage for possible subsequent steps. After you have introduced yourself and have established the right level of rapport, you should then explain what is going to happen. "Fred, my role in this process is to determine your interests and overall capabilities and to give you some insight into the organization. Obviously, for me to be successful, you will have to do a majority of the talking so that I may collect data." This, or some variation, gives "Fred" the general parameters of the interview. However, don't spill the beans at this point about the specifics of the job and organization because if Fred is smart, his answers will be targeted toward them.

If you set the stage correctly, you have a much better opportunity to conduct the interview properly. You will have the necessary control of the situation, i.e., you have the upper hand, because you are buying (in most cases), whereas the candidate is selling. Don't allow the situation to get out of hand so that you become the interviewee. Also remember, however, that the candidate realizes that it is a negative process and that in a sense he is being threatened. You must maintain a receptive attitude without showing negativism; you must always evaluate, but it is not your role to disapprove.

Numerous volumes have been written about various types of interviews—directive, nondirective, stress. The theory of any of these styles can be applied to the two primary interview steps in the selection/placement process—the screening interview and the actual selection interview in which the "job competency decision" is made.

Although it may be difficult at times to distinguish between the initial (screening) interview and the later interviews, technically speaking, there are four primary objectives for the "competent" employment interview.[2] Everyone involved in the selection process should know and understand these objectives, which are:

1. To afford the opportunity to judge an applicant's qualifications as a basis for sound selection and placement, i.e., to make impartial, objective judgments;
2. To give the applicant essential facts about the job and company—nature of the work, hours, benefits, opportunities for advancement—to enable him to decide intelligently about the acceptability of employment (the interview should always be two-way communications);
3. To initiate an enduring rapport—a feeling of mutual understanding and confidence—between the personnel department and the applicant who is employed (the long-range value of this initial relationship can be immeasurable);
4. To promote goodwill toward the company, whether or not the interview culminates in employment (public and community relations).

---

[2] Francis Drake, "The Personnel Man and his Job," in *The Interviewer and his Art*, ed. Robert E. Finley, New York: American Management Association, 1962, pp. 132-133.

Prescreening

Regardless of what employment sources your organization uses, the employment function will eventually be faced with the need to review the background of many candidates to determine which ones to interview on the basis of their apparent "match" to the job and man specifications that have been developed for the job in question. The more information that is available initially about a candidate, the easier it is to determine who to interview. For example, having the results of an interview by an employment agency or the personal recommendation and comments of an employee should simplify the task considerably by providing some of the basic information needed to proceed with the screening interview. For the most part, however, the employment function will be reviewing a resume, letter of application, or an application form. Although the review of an individual's background on paper may appear to be the least critical phase of the selection process, in reality it is critical because it screens out those candidates who do not meet the minimal requirements established and ensures that those who best fit your standards become involved in a face-to-face interview situation.

It is appropriate here to point out that the source of the referral has significant impact on your prescreening and the structure of the initial interview. For example, if an employment agency has referred the candidate, you can assume that the candidate has been interviewed and assessed in terms of a basic fit for your organization and that he has been given an overall view of your organization. On the other hand, if the candidate responded to an advertisement that your company ran, you may rightly assume that the response will be tailored (targeted) to the specifics of the ad, and you may have to dig harder in the initial interview to determine other details of the candidate's experience.

7.4 RESPONSIBILITIES OF THE EMPLOYMENT FUNCTION IN INTERVIEWING

In reality, the employment function plays several roles in selection and placement—as a "talent scout" to select (recruit) people to be auditioned (interviewed) and, more importantly, as a "stage manager" to guide and direct the entire production. Specifically, to provide for the greatest degree of effectiveness, the employment function should be responsible for:

1. Conducting the initial (screening) interview, eliminating those candidates who do not measure up to this first critical evaluation, and preselling the company and the job to those who do;
2. Planning for and scheduling the best combination and sequence of additional interviews for evaluation and motivation purposes;
3. Providing the administrative and logistical support for the candidates who are invited for an interview visit;
4. Briefing the team selected to interview the candidate and establishing the best climate for those interviews;
5. Consolidating the interview results into a total picture of strengths and weaknesses to identify the most promising candidate among those interviewed and providing this information to the hiring manager;
6. Keeping in touch with the candidate during and after the interview process, providing advice and encouragement as necessary;
7. Maintaining close communication with the referral source, e.g., employment agency, executive search firm, concerning the candidate's progress;
8. Providing reference information on the candidate to complete the "information package" (see Chapter 9.1);
9. "Educating" the line departments on a continuing basis concerning their role and responsibilities in the selection/placement process. This education may take many forms, but four of the most important factors are:

   a) *Plan*—prepare for the interview and be sure to allocate the necessary time. Urgency and time pressures result only in a poor decision.

   b) *Ask questions*—this is a data-gathering process and there must be an exchange of information. Ask broad, general questions to which there are no pat answers.

   c) *Recognize your own peculiarities* and hang-ups and those of your organization, e.g., hiring in your own image, hiring certain disciplines from only certain schools.

d) *Be honest*—this will be the most positive indicator to the candidate about what kind of environment really exists and be straightforward in answering questions.

These points show that appropriate planning and careful control of the interview phase of the selection process are key responsibilities of the employment function. The employment function's actions (or lack thereof) affects both the judgment by line management of the candidate and the candidate's overall impression of the organization.

Planning and Preparation

Planning is an extremely important part of the overall strategy of the selection/placement process that usually gets too little attention. Most people think they have an inherent skill for sizing up another person. In other words, too often the interviewer realizes after he has started that he is not prepared, and the interview degenerates into an aimless conversation with no exchange of data. Learn to use all the information that is available at whatever point in time you become involved in the interview process. Such information may include a resume, an application form, correspondence, reference information, and the comments of other interviewers. Hopefully, anyone in your organization who has a responsibility for interviewing is well versed on the four key points (p. 156-157) and job requirements (p. 153-154). Know what the objective of the interview is! Know when you have achieved it!

Application Form

The application form (Chapter 8.2) can be a real asset to your selection process and particularly so in the prescreening and screening interviews. However, it will be of value only if looked upon as a tool for providing information and not as "that form that Employment makes everyone fill out." A resume is helpful, but it accentuates the positive and may underemphasize important details. If at all possible, have the candidate complete the application beforehand. It doesn't add anything to the "image" of the day to spend the first half hour in the lobby completing an application form.

Employee Agreements

If everything is now positive and the person appears to be a likely candidate, there is one more immediate concern—determining what, if any, obligation the individual has to current or past employers about the disclosure of confidential or proprietary information. This is particularly relevant with technical people, who with few exceptions have some form of "patent inventions and secrecy agreements" with their current and/or past employers. Even in the absence of a written agreement, however, an employee has a very real moral and ethical obligation to his present and past employers. If it appears that there could be some degree of conflict between the candidate's past job activity and the potential assignment with your organization, the initial contact and/or interview should be structured to determine if it is feasible to even pursue further interviews, let alone extend an offer.

Initial Contact

Once you have decided that you are interested in an individual's background and there are no apparent conflicts, it is time for the initial contact. It is very important that you try to create the most favorable climate with the candidate in the initial contact, as this will form his first impression of your company, and it may be a lasting one. The following recommendations should prove helpful in making this a meaningful and productive first step:

1. Speed and timing are critical. Good candidates do not last long in the market place. A telephone call to the individual's home is highly recommended. However, avoid telegrams or letters if at all possible. Personalize this initial contact!
2. Solicit as much additional information as possible. Try to discover any special preferences the candidate may have about a new job, environment, or organization. If relocation is involved, explore any potential problems. Fill in any blank spot on the resume or application form.
3. Provide the candidate with enough additional information to stimulate his interest in the company and desire for further discussions. Avoid, however, being too specific on such variable factors as salary and possibilities for promotion.

If all goes well on the phone, don't hesitate to extend an invitation for "in-house" interviews. Indicate best date(s), pertinent instructions about travel and expenses, and confirm these details in writing.

Having established the climate in which the face-to-face interview process can begin, you are then ready for the first meeting with the candidate. The process thus far has been largely that of screening out, and it will remain negative until at some point in the interviews it is decided that the candidate is employable. Then the positive process of placement begins.

Interview Arrangements

The prescreening process has confirmed that a candidate who, at least appears to have potential for employment by your organization is available. One of the truest indications of what kind of organization you are will be reflected in the candidate's interview visit. From the moment he arrives in the parking lot, he will be forming impressions; everyone he meets will have some impact—the guard on the gate, the receptionist, and your secretary. Those impressions are important to the organization, as is the obvious planning that will be apparent to the candidate as he goes through a good selection process.

Get things organized and have a plan for the interview(s). If the candidate is coming from out of town, make the necessary arrangements and confirm them. Transportation may best be arranged by the individual once the time framework is known, but all other arrangements—motel/hotel, transportation instructions, reimbursement of expenses, and hosting—should be made by the employment function.

As soon as a mutually convenient date has been established, a schedule must be arranged and so recorded on the interview schedule form. This form, as part of the candidate package, should be in the hands of *all* interviewers at least one day prior to the candidate's visit. If there is time, the candidate should receive a confirmation of the day's schedule (see Chapter 8.1).

This interview schedule should begin and end with the employment function. If a screening interview has not been conducted, now is the time; if it has already taken place, this time may be used exclusively for orientation to the organization and the interviewers. Ending the interview day with the employment function will provide a good opportunity to explore the candidate's impressions and observations and to determine his level of interest.

If possible, as each interview on the schedule is concluded, it will be very helpful for some feedback to be made to the employment function. This will be a real assist in tying up the loose ends. The employment function may appear to be a friendly and objective sounding post after an arduous schedule of line-department interviews. This is also the time to explain expense reimbursement, follow-up process to interviews, and respond to any specific or miscellaneous questions the candidate may have.

The employment function should bear primary responsibility for ensuring maintenance of the interview schedule and for coping with unexpected delays or changes. A good technique here is to use a "host system." Have a peer of the candidate be host for the day, with a nonevaluative responsibility.

Time for Interviews

Morning interviews are often more effective than those conducted after lunch, as the average person is more alert and energetic in the morning. The actual time necessary for the interview should be predetermined to remove the feeling of urgency. An interview should never be "squeezed in" between two pressing business engagements. This is also true for the candidate. If he has a rigid schedule, the interview should be postponed to another, more suitable time. Interviews that come close to the closing hour of business should be avoided for this same reason, namely, a prevalent feeling of urgency. An interview that takes place during lunch or dinner can easily lead to indigestion for either or both parties. If you must interview over a meal, allow more than normal interview time; you can't eat and run and expect to gather meaningful data.

A short break for coffee during the interview sometimes confirms the feeling of relaxation, but it should take place in a setting in which the interview can continue. To introduce a candidate to a number of people during such a break sometimes puts him too much "on guard," and this feeling must then be removed when the interview continues. If he is to meet others in the company, he should meet them after the initial interview.

Interviewing

Now you should be ready to conduct the competent interview, and to do so you must understand that just as the interviewee plays roles, so must you. "A successful interviewer has to be a very good actor. Whether he functions as a fact finder, a counselor, or a decision maker, he is continually enacting the role of participant-observer."[3] The role of participant is to actively elicit responses to determine if the candidate can and

[3] F.M. Lopez, Jr., *Personnel Interviewing: Theory and Practice*, New York: McGraw-Hill, 1965, p. 39.

will do the job. The role of observer is to stop, look, listen, and evaluate.

The observer has two primary responsibilities, and both are difficult.

1. He must listen; he must concentrate on the candidate and not let anything he says go unheard or be misunderstood.
2. He must evaluate; he must determine objectively that what he heard furthers the candidate's employment potential.

The participant leads the interview and thus is accountable for its outcome. This involves creating an atmosphere in which the candidate feels free to express himself and to participate actively in the give and take of the interview.

Screening Interview

The screening interview should attempt to cover as much ground as possible and yet gather enough meaningful data to recommend those qualified candidates and screen out those candidates lacking the basic qualifications. In order to gather data that will be useful in your evaluation, you must remember that what the candidate tells you will be predicated on your questions and statements. Questions must be phrased so as to penetrate to the heart of the matter and yet must not give the impression of being too barbed, too direct, or too "investigative." They must be worded so as to sustain the interview as a pleasant conversation. Never ask a question without a clear purpose in mind. Have a plan. Although everyone has his own style, you should know what major areas you want to explore and you should use a chronological approach to each of them. Know what questions have to be asked to get the data required (what, when, why, and how). Know when you have sufficient information so that you can make an orderly transition to the next line of questioning.

The screening interview is not the time to "oversell," but it is important to give the candidate a good indication of the opportunities in the organization. The candidate should be given a basic understanding of the job in terms of the actual and potential areas of challenge, interest, and accomplishment afforded by the company's projects and operations. Too many times a well-qualified candidate will reject an opportunity for further interviews because the duties of the job and its potential were not outlined specifically and fully at this stage.

The interviews that follow the screening interview provide the opportunity to continue the dialogue established and to get to know the "real" candidate. This is the pivotal point of the employment process. Employment's key function is to see that the candidate is, in fact, interviewed in detail. All too often, a candidate spends the better part of his time in a series of "screening interviews," with the result that the company never gets to know the "real" person or what he can do.

It is recognized that every individual interviews in his own manner and it is not intended that this chapter describe the only satisfactory way to interview. However, by adapting your individual techniques to the broad outlines presented, it may help both the employment function and the line department to conduct interviews in a better organized, intelligent, and forthright manner.

The Real Person

In addition to the candidate's "technical" competence, you, the interviewer, must be equally concerned about the candidate's personality, especially with regard to his relationships with the people for whom and with whom he will work. This aspect of the individual is the one most often overlooked or given only minimal attention. Most interviewing on this point consists of determining whether or not the person appears to be satisfactory in terms of his ability to get along with others. However, you should really be interested in finding out what he actually is rather than what he thinks he is or what he makes himself appear to be.

Individually, people have several different "pictures" of themselves. The first, and most immediately observable, is what they want others to see. Another is the picture of what they think they are. Still another is the picture of what they would like to be—their ambitions, desires, and hopes—and this internal picture is known only to themselves and is not communicated to others.

The most significant "picture," the one that concerns us as interviewers, is the one most difficult to ascertain—the picture of *what the candidate really is*. This is a picture often obscured by an individual in an effort to hide those parts of his temperament that he does not wish to admit to either himself or others. To fulfill the obligation of finding the person best suited for the job, the applicant's true "self" must be determined as fully as possible. By so doing, the interviewer will certainly have more assurance that if the individual is selected, he will "pay dividends," in terms of not only profit, but also increased morale, contributions to the group of which he becomes a part, and to himself by being able to perform satisfactorily.

In trying to find out what the "real person" is like, there are 12 primary areas you are trying to evaluate to determine his suitability as a potential employee:

1. The candidate's intellectual ability
2. The way in which the candidate relates to and with other people
3. The candidate's past experience and the effectiveness of his performance
4. The way in which the candidate compares with others in similarly rated jobs
5. The candidate's reasons for wanting to relocate
6. The candidate's special areas of competence
7. The candidate's strengths and weaknesses
8. Other people's opinions of the candidate as both a person and an employee
9. The candidate's outlook, attitudes, and opinions of what constitutes sound employer/employee relationships
10. The candidate's view of the function for which he is being considered
11. The candidate's technical competence
12. The candidate's (and his family's) outlook on life.

You can find the answers to these questions, as well as others, if you enter into the interviewing situation with an open, inquiring, alert mind. But always remember, many risks still remain in employment, even when all the correct techniques, methods, and systems are used. You can use the interview, the application form, testing (if appropriate and valid), and reference checks in an effort to minimize the risks, but the risks will never be completely eliminated—people are too complex.

In short, the interviewer's task is to try to gather enough information to determine what and how the candidate has accomplished what he has and why that makes him a better candidate than others.

Terminating the Interview

After you, the interviewer, have decided that you have sufficient information on which to base a decision, you must then consider how to terminate the interview. The primary concern in terminating an interview, whether or not it has been positive, is to maintain good will. This, of course, can be relatively simple if you feel you have a positive situation. If you have a preplanned interview schedule, you simply move ahead as planned. If there is no preplanned schedule, you might say: "It appears that we have some mutual interests and should explore them further; we would like to have you come back on Tuesday"; "Everything appears to be positive at this point, so let me talk with the appropriate people and get back to you with a suggested date for further interviews"; or something to that effect.

Even if you have a negative situation and there is a preplanned schedule it generally will make sense to give the candidate some further exposure, if only to have others confirm your judgment and (particularly if the candidate has traveled some distance) to let the candidate feel that he got a "fair shake." If you were conducting an initial-screening interview, you could tell the candidate that "there does not appear to be a match and in the interests of both of us, let's drop it." Be sure to explain your reasons, however, so that there is no misunderstanding that could possibly result in a violation of antidiscrimination legislation. If it appears to be a particularly delicate situation and a verbal turndown may cause ill will, stall and send a rejection letter after a few days.

Whatever your decision, put a time frame on the next step and follow through. The employment function is a very critical member of the public relations team. You never know when that candidate may become a stockholder, a customer, or a spokesman in the community.

7.5 RESPONSIBILITIES OF THE LINE MANAGER

If the employment function has done an effective interviewing job and has concluded that it has an employable candidate to pass up the line for further interviews, the second most difficult part of the selection/placement process begins. This, the scheduling, coordinating aspect gets little attention in many organizations, yet as has been mentioned, from the candidate's standpoint, it may be the difference between his interest or noninterest in the organization. The candidate's impressions of how he and the total process are handled will be an indication to him of how your organization is run. Therefore, line managers must be sure that line interviews are planned, structured, and well coordinated.

In reality, the line manager's responsibilities in interviewing are not too dissimilar from those of the employment function, although he is more concerned with the actual interview than with all of the detailed administrative aspects of the process. But remember, employment is a part-time function for the line manager. He must, however, be attuned to all of the sensitivities involved in interviewing. He must never forget what it is like to be a candidate and how a candidate likes to be treated. The candidate being interviewed is a guest in your facilities and should be handled with courtesy and respect. Let the employment function be the stage manager! Once the decision is made to move ahead with line interviews, the "employment check list" is initiated and becomes the first part of the "candidate package" (see p. 176). This "package" will grow as each successive step takes place and will eventually contain all the pertinent information on the candidate—resume, reference checks, interview schedule.

When the identification of the specific manpower need was being developed with the line manager at the beginning of the employment process, some identification of other people who would be part of the interview process was also made. Don't overlook the possibility of bringing people from *other* functional areas into the act now. It may be advantageous to have the candidate get some exposure to people in unrelated functions of your organization, for it is not unreasonable to assume that the job in question will in all probability require a good deal of contact outside of its specific functional area. Therefore, giving the candidate as broad an exposure to the total environment as possible should be a plus. However, all of the people who are party to the selection process should be provided with a copy of the "candidate package."

Assuming that most organizations will give multiple interviews to a given candidate prior to a final decision, it would seem logical to structure the interviews. In other words, assign particular aspects of the candidate's background and experience to a specific interviewer for exploration. In addition, those areas in the candidate's background and experience that may need further exploration, as determined by the employment function's interview, should be discussed with the line interviewers so that each of them can gather data on those points within the structure of his interview. This will help avoid any more duplication than is necessary and should provide more factual data in the final analysis. With each interviewer playing his part well, the final compilation of comments will be much more meaningful in the final assessment of the candidate.

While the employment function and the line manager play equally important roles in the selection process, the line manager, by virtue of his responsibility for the hiring decision, is the major factor in the placement process. The placement process really begins once the line manager has determined that the candidate has the basic skills and abilities to function in his operation. He must be prepared to satisfy the candidate's motivations and desires; otherwise, all of his efforts to this point have been for naught.

Part of the thinking process about placement must take into consideration the fact that most jobs have a so-called minimum exposure time which a new employee must experience before the accuracy of the selection decision is known. This time can vary, depending on such things as the job responsibilities, technical knowledge, etc., and therefore it may be months before the wisdom of the hiring decision is known. This fact alone should verify the need for a planned, thoughtful, and thorough selection placement process.

Critical to good placement is attention to several specific details, primarily by the line manager, who is responsible for the in-depth probing of the candidate's actual work experience, skills, and abilities. The line manager, therefore, must:

1. Make sure that both he and the candidate are "talking the same language." For example, organizations may give different meanings to "R&D" or "Industrial Relations."
2. Make a concerted effort to match the job to the individual. He must be flexible in matching the candidate to the job specification. It's rare when an individual hired matches exactly the original specification for the job. Job structure is changing by necessity, and this must be understood, or your organization may suffer more and more from increased turnover and low morale (see Chapter 1.7).

Line Interview

If the normal pattern of interviews is followed, the screening interview by the employment function provides the best candidate for further interviews by the line. However, before we go any further, let's redefine selection and placement and touch on the responsibilities of the employment function and the line department. Selection, in its simplest terms, is an assessment of overall abilities and capabilities, and placement is an assessment of whether the candidate can perform a specific job in the organization. For both the employment function and the line manager to make the best judgments in selection and placement, each must conduct thorough and meaningful interviews.

The specific role of the line interview is built on the base of the employment function's screening interview. The screening interview may be the crucial item in the whole employment process to this point, because the whole process is now in balance. The employment function must communicate its evaluation of the candidate in a very precise manner and indicate what appears to be the candidate's weak areas, those that will require probing by the line. This is why structured multiple interviews are so good; they allow each interviewer to probe into a specific area of, hopefully, his personal expertise.

Whereas the employment function develops information primarily on the candidate's training, background, education, and experience and provides general information on the organization and the job, the line department assesses the candidate's technical capabilities and overall knowledge to work in a given functional area and specific job and predicts how well the candidate will fit into the particular operation. It is obvious, therefore, that the most meaningful employment decisions result from close cooperation between the employment function and the line departments.

7.6 CONTROL OF INTERVIEWS

Control of the selection/placement process is important to not only the overall economy and efficiency of any employment function, but also the interview sequence. The need for a planned, orderly approach in all communications between the employment function and the line manager is an absolute necessity. This problem can be minimized by the utilization of five basic forms (see Chapter 8.2).

1. Application Form
2. Interview Comments Form
3. Interview Schedule Form
4. Employment Check List Form
5. Reference Check Form.

Unfortunately, the basic documents of employment—the application form and/or resume—often become all things to all people. The notes, dates, and times indiscriminately scribbled on the application or resume become an illegible, confusing, and useless combination of interview comments, interview schedule, and employment check list form.

"Packaging the candidate" in an individual folder that includes all relevant information (the five forms plus a resume) on him at a given point in time will bring an orderliness and discipline to the process that in turn will be instrumental in providing control. When the line manager receives the candidate package, he will feel more confident about his role in the selection/placement process.

There should be some central point of control for each activity with a candidate from the date of his original inquiry to his reporting on board as a new employee. This control is so necessary if the process is to be efficient and economical in providing the right people for job openings. The "candidate package" will be supplemented by verbal evaluations of the candidate's strengths and weaknesses as gleaned from the line-department interviews.

There is another "package" that has a definite role in the process, the pre- and post-interview candidate package. The pre-interview package might contain a copy of the organizations annual report, any pertinent recruiting literature (college brochure, discipline booklets, e.g., "What a Mechanical Engineer Does at XYZ Corporation"), interview schedule and, if feasible, brief biographies of interviewers. The postinterview package might contain literature on the organization's benefits programs, a copy of the job description, and a handout sheet on relocation policy. These are only examples; depending on the circumstances, you might want to use more or less information.

7.7 INTERNATIONAL ASPECT

The interview process for an international candidate should follow the same basic pattern as for any other candidate. However, there are some details that are necessarily unique because of differences in the job environment.

1. An essential factor is the attitude of the organization, which must be attuned to the concept that international assignments are meaningful in career pathing. "Expatriate" (which Webster defines as: to banish, withdraw, separate, abandon), which has such a negative connotation, should be removed from an organization's vocabulary.
2. What are the special requirements of the job over and above the job description, e.g., language facility, social demands, working conditions, teaching ability. Each of these points must be covered in some

detail; therefore, it is almost imperative that interviewers be people who have "been there."

3. Candidates' motivation is extremely important. What is his real, inner motivation for wanting the job? You should be sure it isn't just the extra dollars or the desire to get away from some problem(s) that is the incentive.
4. The evaluation must also emphasize the longer-range prospects. There must be some plan for the individual when he returns—re-entry from an international assignment should not have to be as traumatic as it generally is.
5. The social and cultural aspects of the international job assignment must be discussed in detail. This will be particularly critical with a foreign national relocating to the United States, for example.
6. Many international organizations devote a fair amount of time to "orienting" an employee's wife, so it may be quite appropriate in some instances to interview her, as well as her husband. It will be particularly helpful to know what her feelings and motivations are; she may be a critical factor in the success or failure of her husband's assignment.

7.8 SUMMARY

In summary, let's look at some of the very practical but often overlooked facts about interviewing. These are examples of the common-sense aspects of interviewing that anyone who has a degree of responsibility in this area should review and reflect on.

1. You need exposure and practice to improve your skills; interviewing, like driving a car, cannot be learned by reading a book.
2. An interviewer has two jobs: to gather data and to evaluate data.
3. Since predicting the future is so difficult, you must evaluate the past.
4. The interview should not be used to collect routine data (the application form and resume should provide that), but rather to gather new information.
5. To gather and evaluate data properly, the interviewer must first know himself so that he can accomplish his task objectively.

6. The interviewer must listen and guide and never forget that people like to talk about themselves.
7. Remember, you can learn a lot by being involved in interviewing, so be receptive.

The basics of interviewing don't really vary very much in terms of the level of the person being interviewed or the number of interviewers involved. The amount of detail and depth of questioning will vary, however. There is more to explore, for example, with the experienced man than with the recent college graduate. The same basic approach to interviewing, can be used for members of minority groups, female candidates, and the campus interviewees. However, there are aspects to interviewing individuals in those categories that do require a certain, special awareness, and these were discussed in Chapters 5 and 6.

Interviewing is a challenge, and no one ever reaches perfection. You can continue to improve, however, if you keep an open mind and evaluate your own techniques after each interview. Remember, you must never take as a measure of your skill the number of people you have interviewed.

8

Correspondence, forms, records, and reports

These items, the paperwork, are viewed as the "routine" of most functions and usually get fairly pedestrian treatment. The employment function's paperwork is no exception. As routine as these things may seem to be, however, they truly will be a reflection of a good or bad employment function. Data, so critical to the success of employment, by no stretch of the imagination should ever become the reason for the employment function's existence; rather, data can help accomplish the process more efficiently and economically.

The most dramatic changes that have occurred in the paperwork aspect of employment have resulted directly from antidiscrimination (see Chapter 5.1) and other legislation relating to such things as preferential hiring (Executive Order 11598—Listing of Job Vacancies with the Federal State Employment Service System) and reference information (Fair Credit Reporting Act Public Law 91.508). There have been some half-humorous references in recent years concerning the need for the personnel man to be a legal expert. However, this becomes more and more of a possibility every day; if there is anyone in the personnel spectrum who is under the gun on a daily basis in terms of understanding and complying with this myriad of laws and regulations, it is the employment function. The employment function, which deals with many people in a given period of time who are not part of its organization, is more vulnerable to general criticism and official complaint. Although new laws and legislation have had dramatic impact on the paperwork aspect of employment, let's not overlook the on-going necessity to do these things well, because they are so instrumental in making the function work.

8.1 CORRESPONDENCE

Although you should always try to personalize the employment process in every conceivable manner, there will always be circumstances for which letters are necessary. The offer letter is the prime example of the importance of correspondence in the process. This letter becomes a legal contract in essence and must be detailed, thorough, and above all, accurate.

Correspondence is a major part of the employment function's clerical workload, and it is also a particularly sensitive area because it may be the first, or in many cases the only, contact an individual or some other organization has with your organization. That first letter will be "your" organization to an individual, and remember, first impressions are lasting. For that reason alone, your letters must embody professionalism, honesty, and courtesy.

There can be, and are, any number of styles of letters utilized in an employment function, but probably the most critical and most often used are the interview-invitation letter, the offer letter, the rejection letter, the reference letter, and an equal opportunity employer letter to your employment sources.

The Interview-Invitation Letter

Even strong advocates of personalizing the invitation for interview would agree that there is value in confirming the details of the invitation to *all* of the people who will be involved. The primary thrust of this letter is to present the "plan for the day" and to spell out as many specifics as possible to avoid any misunderstanding. The format on p. 182 illustrates the major points that need to be covered.

This type of letter spells out the critical details for the candidate, the interested department manager, and the source (in this case an employment agency), as follows:

1. Source of original contact, which should preclude any confusion in obligation if the person is hired
2. General idea of who he will meet with for interviews (if you can be specific by name, so much the better)
3. Travel information, including a comment on class of travel, accommodations, and the amount of time that will be required
4. Reimbursement of expenses

Date

Dear Mr. Jones:

I wanted to confirm your interview visit that we discussed by phone on Tuesday evening, June 26.

<u>or</u>

We received your resume from Jones Associates of Chicago, Illinois, and would like to have you visit our offices here in Richmond on Wednesday, July 6.

Our plans are to have you interview with four staff members of the Industrial Engineering Department. It would be best if you flew in (tourist class) the night prior to your interview. We will make guaranteed reservations for you at the Ajax Motel at 133 West Central Avenue, and they will confirm to you. Upon your arrival, take a taxi from the airport to the motel. I will meet you for breakfast at 7:30 A.M. on Wednesday morning, July 6, and we will proceed from there to our offices. It is planned that your interview schedule will run until 3 P.M., so you might plan your return accordingly (allow one hour to reach the airport). Upon submission of your expenses, we will reimburse you after completion of your visit.

We are looking forward to your visit. If you have any questions, please call me (collect) at (214) 666-7777.

Very truly yours,

cc: Jones Associates
W. Jones (Industrial Engineering
Dept. Mgr.)

5. Carbon copies to the source of the referral and to the interested department manager so that all involved know the candidate's interview schedule.

The Rejection Letter

There are two primary uses for this letter: first, as a response to the unsolicited inquiries that all organizations receive in varying volume; and second, in response to actual interviews. Because you are dealing with human feelings and emotions, it is most important that you don't overlook the public-relations aspect in spelling out the facts for rejection.

It is a good business practice to answer all inquiries, solicited or unsolicited. This will definitely be a factor in your reputation as an employer. Antidiscrimination legislation has brought additional sensitivities and pressures to bear in this area, with emphasis on age, race, and sex. The progressive organization, however, should always approach this task honestly. In most instances, a straightforward reply will make friends of those people you reject.

There are two formats (shown on pp. 184 and 185.) that meet these criteria. The first format tells the individual you have never met that:

1. You received and reviewed his inquiry
2. You have verified what he probably knew, i.e., that you have openings in marketing. You also have told him that he lacks the *specific* experience you require.
3. You have left the door open for the future by indicating your procedure for retaining inquiries of interest.

Points 2 and 3 in particular should leave the person in a positive frame of mind about your organization, because most organizations just don't bother or send very routine form letters.

The second type of rejection letter is applicable when the man has been in for interviews, but did not measure up to the job requirements or to the other candidates for the job. This letter, which is in many ways the most difficult to write, should accomplish the following:

1. Indicated that it was not a waste of time for XYZ Corporation ("interesting and informative day," "enjoyed the opportunity to talk with you about mutual problems")

Date

Dear Mr. Brown:

Your inquiry of Thursday, 3 May 1972 to Mr. Green, our Vice-President of Marketing, was directed to me for review and reply.

<u>or</u>

The additional information I requested was received, and we appreciate your promptness.

I have reviewed your letter and resumé with appropriate members of the staff in both of the divisions that currently have marketing needs. Unfortunately, there does not appear to be a mutually beneficial situation at this point in time. This is due primarily to our strong emphasis on specific consumer goods and marketing experience rather than a reflection on your fine background.

We make it a practice to retain employment inquiries of people whose backgrounds are of general interest, even though not immediately applicable. Therefore, we will retain your file and will feel free to contact you should our situation change.

Thank you for your interest and cooperation, and we wish you every success in your job search.

Very truly yours,

J. D. White
Director of Employment

Date

Dear Fred:

It certainly was a pleasure to meet you on Wednesday, and I hope you found it an interesting and informative day. Messrs. Smith, Rogers, and Black enjoyed the opportunity to talk with you about mutual problems and are very appreciative of your time and interest in XYZ Corporation.

Unfortunately, our collective opinion is that your exposure to the types of analytical problems we experience here is not sufficient to allow you to make the immediate contribution that we feel is necessary. This in no way should be interpreted as a reflection on your very excellent background, but rather on the peculiar nature of this phase of our business. From your discussions with Bill Rogers, I am sure you realize the importance of this phase of our operations and the need for specific know-how.

I received and have processed your trip expenses, and you should receive a check within the next week. Again, thank you for your cooperation and patience, and if I can ever be of service, please don't hesitate to contact me.

Very truly yours,

D. J. White
Director of Employment

cc: Acme Associates
W. Rogers (Dept.)

2. Told him that it was a group judgment that his experience did not measure up and asked him to understand this decision as a fellow professional ("you realize from your discussions with Bill Rogers")
3. Acknowledged receipt of his expenses and your plan for reimbursement
4. Ended the situation on a positive note ("if I can be of service, please don't hesitate to contact me")
5. Informed the appropriate people (by carbon copies) that the individual is no longer being considered.

The Offer Letter

This is the most important piece of correspondence in the employment process. It is essentially a legal document spelling out the obligations of the organization in terms of salary and benefits. Whenever possible, it is advantageous to extend the offer verbally (in person, whenever feasible) and confirm it by letter (see Chapter 9.1). The offer-letter format on pp. 188-189 should cover most aspects of any employment offer quite thoroughly and should be adaptable to most organizations.

This letter presents enough detail to confirm the verbal offer and also spells out enough specifics. It is important that the details be clarified, because they become an important part of the base for making a very critical decision. Also, some of these details are not heard or are forgotten by the candidate when the salary offer is extended verbally; people hear only what they want to hear or what they think is most important. So, it pays to re-affirm the details to avoid any misunderstanding when the person becomes an employee.

These are the primary letters to be used with candidates, and they can be adapted as the situation requires. To repeat, all your correspondence with candidates should reflect your professionalism, honesty, and courtesy. Another important aspect is timeliness, because *all* parties involved in the employment process should know as soon as possible the status of a given situation so that they can get about their other business.

Source Letter (EEO)

All organizations that are equal-opportunity employers as designated by law are required to send a letter to all sources from which they request referrals (colleges, employment agencies, executive-search firms) stating that they are an equal-opportunity employer. The letter must also specify that they expect referrals in keeping with that commitment. A sample letter is shown on p. 190.

This type of letter must be sent to all solicited sources. It indicates the organization's compliance with its responsibility by stating that as an equal-opportunity employer:

1. The organization does not discriminate in its employment practices
2. The relationship will continue only if the source adheres to nondiscriminatory practices
3. The relationship will be terminated if the source feels it cannot comply.

Copies of these letters must be retained in your files for review as requested by the appropriate compliance agency.

Reference Letters

Although reference checking is much more meaningful when done verbally (by phone or in person), there may be occasions when that is impossible and a letter will have to be used. Also, the verification of employment dates and salary information or the gathering of routine factual information on a recent graduate may be accomplished most efficiently by letter.

If the situation requires that a letter be used for an in-depth reference, bear in mind that there are shortcomings, not the least of which are: getting no answer at all or misunderstanding the terminology used by the respondee, which may affect your evaluation of the candidate. The use of a letter will almost certainly guarantee only a positive response, because you lose the extemporaneousness of the verbal contact. However, try to develop your letters along factual lines so that the responses are as meaningful as possible.

These letters gather and/or verify certain facts provided by the candidate. This reference information, although helpful in your total assessment of the candidate, must be considered in terms of how it was developed and should not carry the same weight that a good in-person or telephone reference check would.

PERSONAL AND CONFIDENTIAL

Date

Dear ______________:

This letter will confirm the terms of our offer of employment for the position of ___________________, XYZ Corporation, reporting to___________________.

We are pleased to offer you this position at a salary of $______ per month. As we discussed with you, this position makes you eligible for incentive income (bonus). Inasmuch as you will not be an employee for the full year, your bonus for this year will be prorated from the time you report for work.

This offer is contingent upon your satisfactory completion of a medical examination, which we can arrange for you. Or, you may go to your personal physician. If you choose the latter course, have your physician forward the results and his bill to Dr. J. Jonas, our medical director, at this address.

Listed below are the benefits coverage applicable to you or listed below are the benefits and allowances as specified under our expatriation policy.

1. Insurance
   You will be eligible for $00000 term life insurance, which carries over at retirement in the amount of $0000. This insurance is paid for by the company, but there is an imputed value of insurance coverage above $50,000, which must be considered as part of your gross income, on which you must pay your normal tax rate. This income will approximate $0000 per year. There is no waiting period involved to become eligible for this insurance coverage, which includes normal hospitalization. Major medical is an optional plan in which you may enroll with no waiting period. This is a contributory group program, and you and your dependents are covered for a premium of $000 per month. Your long-term disability coverage will cost you $00 per month. The amount of benefits payable under this plan is $0000 per month. In addition, you will be covered by an accidental death and dismemberment policy in the amount of $0000 and

a business-travel accident policy in the amount of $0000. Both of these are noncontributory plans.

2. Retirement
The Retirement Income Plan is a noncontributory final pay-type plan. You will be eligible to participate after two years of service.

3. Stock Option
This position entitles you to a stock option, subject to approval by a committee of the Board of Directors. This will be recommended to the committee as soon as possible after you report for work. The initial offering will be for X shares. Option price is based on 100% of market prices on date of grant.

4. Vacation
You are eligible for X weeks' vacation.

5. You will receive a comprehensive annual physical examination. This is voluntary and at no cost to you.

6. We are scheduled on a 40-hour week, and the work day is from 8 A.M. to 5 P.M., with an hour for lunch.

7. We are paid bimonthly, on the 15th and 30th.

8. As we discussed, we will pay the cost of your relocation from Chicago to Richmond, Virginia, within the guidelines spelled out in the enclosed procedure.

We are pleased that you will be visiting the weekend of July 7-8, and should you have any problems or questions, please call me at home (412) 377-2121.

Further details of the various benefits programs are outlined in the enclosed booklet. If you have any questions about these or any other aspect of your employment, we will be glad to clarify them for you. Needless to say, all of us who have been involved in discussions with you are extremely anxious for you to join us and are looking forward to it.

Very truly yours,

cc: Jones Assoc.
C. R. Bryan (Manufacturing Dept.)

Date

Gentlemen:

As an equal-opportunity employer, we request and encourage your assistance in the positive support of equal-opportunity legislation. In particular, we have a long-standing policy of nondiscrimination in employment, and we do not discriminate against any employee or applicant for employment because of his age, sex, race, creed, color, or national origin.

Inasmuch as we are committed to these responsibilities as an equal-opportunity employer, our continued dealings with any employment agency, executive-search consultant, or campus placement service is based on its understanding and adherence to this policy.

Therefore, we expect your referrals to us to include qualified minority group and female applicants for those positions we list with you. We assume that unless we hear otherwise from you, we can expect your continued cooperation.

Sincerely,

CC: File

Letter for an in-depth reference from an individual

Date

Dear _______________:

Mr./Ms. ____________ has applied for employment with us as __________ and has given your name as a reference, with authorization to comment with respect to work habits, ability, etc. All information that you provide will be considered confidential. Inasmuch as we would like to resolve ____________ candidacy, we would appreciate receiving your frank and objective answers as soon as possible. A self-addressed stamped envelope is enclosed for your convenience.

1. How long have you known Mr. /Ms. ____________?

2. How would you rate his/her ability in the following:

   a) Knowledge of job
   b) Cooperation with others
   c) Quality and quantity of work
   d) Initiative and ingenuity

3. What are the candidate's strong points?

4. What are the candidate's weak points?

5. Why did he/she leave?

6. Would you re-employ the candidate?

7. Are there any additional points of information that you feel would be helpful to us in making our determination?

Thank you very much for your cooperation and assistance.

Very truly yours,

D. J. White
Director of Employment

Letter to the Personnel Department

Date

Dear Sir:

Mr./Ms.____________________has applied for employment with us as____________________, and we wanted to verify several facts.

1. Dates employed by you:__________to__________.
   If not correct:__________to__________.
2. Position title:____________________.
3. Salary:____________________per year.
4. Reason for leaving:____________________.
5. Would you re-employ:____________________?
   If no, why not:____________________
   ____________________?
6. Any additional information or comments that you feel might be helpful to us in making the best placement for Mr./Ms.:____________________
   ____
   ____________________.

Your replies will be held in confidence, and we appreciate your courtesy in responding as soon as possible. A self-addressed stamped envelope is enclosed for your use. Thank you for your assistance.

Very truly yours,

D. K. White
Director of Employment

Letter to the college or university

Date

Dear Sir:

Mr./Ms.__________________________has applied for a position with us, and we wished to verify several facts.

1. Are dates of attendance correct?

   From______________________to___________________________.

   If not, what are correct dates?

   __________________________to___________________________.

2. Degree received?____.

3. Major concentration?____________________________________.

4. Honors conferred?______________________________________.

5. Any additional information?_____________________________.

   ____.

Your cooperation is appreciated, and we look forward to your early reply. A self-addressed stamped envelope is enclosed for your convenience.

Very truly yours,

D. K. White
Director of Employment

Because there can be so many routine letters in the employment process, organizations should approach the problem of correspondence realistically, taking those steps that will make it as efficient and economical as possible. For example, don't overlook the use of form letters, which, thanks to the variety of automated typewriters available today, don't have to look like form letters. Don't hesitate to consider "contracting out" the more routine letters to typing services. You may be pleasantly surprised to find the cost dramatically less than what you may have anticipated. Telegrams, although a much less personal approach, may be the answer in certain volume situations.

Above all, be certain that your correspondence is factual, businesslike, and as personalized as possible. Remember, it is "the organization" to the recipient.

8.2 FORMS

Forms usually trigger an immediate negative reaction in most people, and unfortunately, it is particularly true with the forms needed in the employment process. For example, there is a certain disdain which the request for completion of a job requisition or employment application form generates.

Forms, in a sense, require a frame of mind similar to that needed for budgeting. People must understand the *need* for forms. In a very practical sense, there is no choice about the use of some forms, which are required by the government. Aside from that, however, it would be extremely difficult for employment or any other function in an organization to operate successfully without using some forms for communicating certain information. Such forms serve five basic purposes:

1. To save you work by not creating more—a properly designed Employment Application Form can shorten your interviewing time
2. To serve as a record—the Employment Application Form becomes the basis for the individual's personnel record
3. To combine or consolidate information—the Employment Check List is an up-to-the-minute status of all aspects of the individual candidate's progress through the employment process
4. To "merchandise" the employment function—the Interview Schedule Form reflects your careful planning and provides the control necessary to ensure best results.

5. To provide a method for facilitating your decisions—the Interview Report Form is a record of both specific responses and timeliness.

Forms can also be a reflection of the experience gained over a period of time by all the people involved in the employment process. This experience will lead to revisions, development of new forms, or elimination of forms not really needed.

The number of employment forms utilized by an organization will in all probability depend on its overall employment philosophy and specific needs. However, most employment functions will need nine basic forms, even though organizations may have very different needs for data and varying ability to gather and report data. No attempt has been made here to suggest a "program" or system for these forms, because each organization will have to approach the problem of forms within the context of its data capabilities. For example, organizations with a computer-based personnel system may find some or all of the information on these forms "programmable." The intent here is merely to show the information required by an efficient employment function rather than a specified format.

1. Employment Application Form—the basic employment form, which is one of the four major inputs in the selection process and which complements interviews, tests, and reference checks. Because it covers such a broad spectrum of information, this form must be reviewed on a regular basis to make sure it reflects compliance with all applicable legislation. (See pp. 197-202)
2. Candidate Referral Form—for use in referring a candidate's resume, application, or file to a line department or an operating unit. This form is used primarily to ensure that there is a timely follow-up so that the candidate and the source may be informed about the status of his application. This form is shown on p. 203.
3. Interview Report Forms—two forms should be used for recording interview comments: one is for the experienced candidate; the other for the campus candidate. A separate form is needed for the campus candidate because this type of interview requires so many different bits of data and the time for interviewing is so limited. The Interview Report Form for the experienced candidate allows for a more narrative write-up of the interview, which reflects the greater time spent on the interview and a more structured schedule. These forms are shown on pp. 204 and 205-206.

4. The Employment Check List—a status report which indicates what steps in the employment process have been completed at a given point in time. This form is shown on pp. 207-208.
5. Telephone Reference Check Form—provides both the guidelines for conducting an in-depth reference check and an easy format in which to present the results. This form is shown on pp. 209-210.
6. Interview Schedule Form—spells out the parameters of the "interview day" and any pertinent instructions or comments needed to alert the interviewers. This form is shown on p. 211.
7. Personnel Requisition Forms—two forms (long and short) are recommended here because of the complexity of more senior jobs in an organization and the variance of opinion about the "real" qualifications. Therefore, the long form is set up to provide greater detail and appropriate approval to ensure maximum guidance in initiating the employment process. These forms are shown on pp. 212-214.
8. Campus Trip Report—a potpourri of information about a given campus visit, the information requested ranges from faculty members who are helpful to recommended restaurants and motels. This is the Bible for planning future trips and as an on-campus guide for campus recruiters. This form is shown on pp. 215-216.
9. Medical Report Form—used to provide evidence of general medical fitness of the candidate to indicate approval to hire or not. (The detailed medical report on any individual should be confidential information and should therefore be retained by the appropriate medical department.) This form is shown on p. 217.

8.3 RECORDS AND REPORTS

Every day, more and more information is requested or required by your organization for its own internal purposes or by local, state, or federal government. This need for data can become a major problem if you try to do everything for everybody and also maintain a desired level of efficiency. A certain amount of data is quite critical to the efficient administration of the employment function, but the specific amount depends on the needs and requirements imposed by your organization or the particular government or compliance agency. Basically, then, we are talking about recording and reporting the data necessary to evaluate the

XYZ CORPORATION

Employment Application Form
Professional/Technical Positions

In order that your application may be properly evaluated, it is essential that all of the following questions be answered as carefully and completely as possible. If you are hired, your application becomes part of your permanent records; otherwise, it is kept on file for future reference.

The Age Discrimination and Employment Act of 1967 prohibits discrimination on the basis of age with respect to individuals who are at least 40 but less than 65 years of age.

Any items on this form which you feel tend to violate Federal or State civil rights or F.E.P.C. legislation need not be completed.

XYZ IS AN EQUAL OPPORTUNITY EMPLOYER M/F

PERSONAL

Please Print

NAME (Last) (First) (Middle)	Date form completed
Present Address (street, city, state, zip code)	Area code & Telephone No.
Permanent Address, if different (street, city, state, zip code)	Area code & Telephone No.

Date of Birth	Sex	Height	Weight	Date available for employment

Marital Status Single ☐ Married ☐	Social Security No.
Are you a U.S. Citizen? Yes ☐ No ☐	Type of work desired Full-time ☐ Summer ☐

Willing to Relocate

☐ Yes ☐ No ☐ U.S. ☐ Foreign

Do you have travel restrictions? ☐ Yes ☐ No Restrictions? ____________

What prompted this application? ____________

____

Have you previously applied to XYZ? ______ Where ________ When ________

Interests

Describe briefly type of work desired. State reason for preference

____

____

Education

List in chronological order names of High Schools and Colleges attended	From Mo. & Yr.	To Mo. & Yr.	Graduate Mo. & Yr.	Degree	Academic Major	Grade-point Average (Ex: 2.8/4.0)

List publications, thesis, etc., and major professor

____

____

Rank in graduating class (e.g. top 1/3, middle 1/3, bottom 1/3):
High School ______ College ______

What was your average in your major subject? A B+ B B- C+ C ______________________

Highest grades in ____

Scholastic honors, scholarships, assistantships, etc. ______________________________

Met college expenses: Working ____%, G.I. bill ____%, Parents ____%, Scholarships ____%,
Other ____

Attending school now? ______ Where? ______________________________
Studying? ____

Foreign languages: Speak ______________________________________

Read ______________________________________

Write ______________________________________

____

Activities (excluding religious and political groups)

High school activities

____

____

Campus activities and offices held ______________________________

To what professional organizations do you belong? List offices held:

____

____

What hobbies do you have at present? ______________________________

____

What books, magazines, journals, etc., do you read frequently?

____

____

Employment History (give last position first)

1. Name of company ______ Address ______
   Type of business ______
   Dates of employment Mo.____Yr.____to Mo.____Yr.____
   Reason for leaving ______
   Salary: Start ______ Now ______
   Title of jobs and duties ______

   Name and addresss of supervisor (include title) to contact concerning work ability

2. Name of company ______ Address ______
   Type of business ______
   Dates of employment Mo.____Yr.____to Mo.____Yr.____
   Reason for leaving ______
   Salary: Start ______ Now ______
   Title of jobs and duties ______

   Name and address of supervisor (include title) to contact concerning work ability

3. Name of company ______ Address ______
   Type of business ______
   Dates of employment Mo.____Yr.____ to Mo.____Yr.____
   Reason for leaving ______
   Salary: Start ______ Final ______
   Title of jobs and duties ______

   Name and address of supervisor (include title) to contact concerning work ability

U.S. Military Service

Selective Service Status | Selective Service No. | Present Military Status

Branch Rate or Rank In Out Type of Discharge
Honorable ☐ Other ☐

References

List three references who are not relatives or previous supervisors:

Name Address Occupation Years known

Name Address Occupation Years known

Name Address Occupation Years known

In case of emergency, notify: __________________________

Name Address Phone number

Additional Data

Have you ever been convicted or are you presently under charges for violating any law (excluding minor traffic regulations)? Yes ________ No ________. If your answer is yes, give complete details. __________________________

Use space below and additional sheets to give any other information you desire concerning work experience, education, accomplishments, etc. __________________________

"In accordance with ¶ 606 of Title VI of the Consumer Credit Protection Act, you are hereby advised that XYZ Inc. may procure or cause to be prepared an investigative consumer report, including information as to your character, general reputation, personal characteristics and mode of living, whichever are applicable; and you are further advised of your right, within a reasonable time of this notice, to make written request of XYZ Inc. for a complete and accurate disclosure of the nature and scope of the investigation requested."

I hereby affirm that all statements made herein are true and correct. I authorize this Company to conduct whatever investigation it deems necessary to confirm statements submitted on this application. If investigation determines any untrue statement was made, I accept this as sufficient ground for dismissal.

I also authorize this Company to obtain and also authorize and request each former employer and person, firm or corporation, given as reference, to answer any and all questions that may be asked, and to give any and all information that may be sought in connection with this application or concerning me or my work, habits, character or skill or my actions in any transaction, except where my written statement upon this form requests that no investigation be made.

I agree to submit myself, upon request, for physical examination by the Company's physician and understand that failing to pass said examination, I will not be employed.

The use of this application form does not indicate that there are any positions available, and in no way obligates the Company.

Date Write usual signature

CANDIDATE REFERRAL

To: ____________________ Date __________

From: ____________________

Applicant ____________________

Position considered for ____________________

Status

Resume received from ____________________

Inquiry answered on __________ by __________

☐ Candidate interviewed (file attached) ____________________

Action Requested

☐ Handle as appropriate (*no reply required*)

☐ *Reply directly* to candidate

☐ *Clear* interest with ____________________
before contacting

☐ Return to originator (use comments)

Comments

INTERVIEW REPORT

Candidate ______________________________

Position considered for ______________________________

Knowledge (is he technically qualified? Does he know enough to get the job done? Considering such factors as his education, prior experience, and record of achievement to date, should he be able to function in this assignment?)

Check one: Comments:

☐ Adequate

☐ Particularly strong

☐ Doesn't meet minimum requirements

Skills (Will he be able to successfully apply his know-how? Considering such factors as intellectual and problem-solving ability, communication skills, social awareness, etc., does he have enough developed capability to function in this environment?)

Check one: Comments:

☐ Adequate

☐ Particularly strong

☐ Doesn't meet minimum requirements

Attitudes (What is his personal style—is he, for example, confident? Considering such factors as his initiative, willingness to work, aspirations, flexibility, self-insight, and sensitivity to people, how is he likely to respond to the demands and rewards of the job—how is he likely to behave in this environment?)

Check one: Comments:

☐ Adequate

☐ Particularly well-suited

☐ Not well-suited

Summary comments and recommendations (Please express any other thoughts you have about this candidate's employability and future prospects with XYZ.)

Would you employ this candidate?

☐ Yes ☐ No

Interviewer	Date

CAMPUS INTERVIEW REPORT

NAME (Last)	(First)	(Middle)	College (Use std. abbrev.)
College address	Zip code	Telephone No.	Type of employment: ☐ Permanent ☐ Summer ☐ Part-time
Home address	Zip code	Telephone No.	

Degree level	Discipline	Degree	Date(s)	Military (U.S.)

U.S. citizen ☐ Visa	Marital Status ☐ Single ☐ Married

Month available	Grade average	Class rank	Faculty adviser

Faculty rating (circle one)

1. Well above average 2. Above average 3. Average 4. Below average

Work experience (circle one)

2 years plus 1 year plus less than 1 year 2 summers plus 1 summer none

Rating	Outstanding	Well above average	Above average	Average	Below average
Appearance/initial impression					
Maturity					
Intelligence					
Self-expression					
Initiative and enthusiasm					
Technical potential					
Supervisory potential					

Additional comments:

Faculty comments:

Job interests:

Geographic preference

Referral
(Location—Dept./Contact) ____________________
Alternate ____________________

Special instructions (tickle next year, hold for summer, etc.)

Reject (special instructions)

Application form in mail

Date(s) available for interview

Date must reach decision

Recruiter	Location	Date

EMPLOYMENT CHECK LIST

Candidate

Position considered for

Interviews

By	On	By	On
By	On	By	On
By	On	By	On
By	On	By	On

Test and Assessment

Tested on	Assessed on
Results	

References

Number conducted	Results

Contract Clearance (if any)

By	On	Results

Employment Offer

Base salary	Bonus	Option

Comments

Approved by	On
Verbal offer by	On
Written offer by	On

Medical

Result	Cleared by	On

Placement

Personnel Department notified by	On	File

TELEPHONE REFERENCE CHECK FORM

Name of candidate ________________________________

Position considered for ________________________________

Organization name ________________________________

Date ________________________________

Name and title of individual contacted ________________________________

(Relationship to candidate) ________________________________

____

Identify yourself by name, title, and organization and explain purpose of call. The following basic questions should be asked; however, the most valuable information may be developed from extemporaneous questions.

____

1. Dates employed: From ______________ to ______________

2. Last position held: Title/nature of job/span of control, etc.

   ____

   ____

   ____

   ____

3. Previous position(s): ________________________________

   ____

   ____

4. Salary: Beginning ______________ Present ______________

5. Evaluation of performance: (In comparison to others and based on his skills and abilities)

____

____

____

6. Greatest strengths?: _______________

____

____

7. Greatest weakness?: _______________

____

____

8. Underwhat circumstances is he leaving? _______________

____

____

9. Would you rehire? __________ If no, why not? _______________

____

____

10. Additional comments: _______________

____

____

Thank the "reference" and assure him that the information is private and confidential.

Name _______________ Date _______________

INTERVIEW SCHEDULE

Candidate	Date of visit

Position considered for

Here is the schedule which has been established for this candidate. He will be presented to you in person by the individual preceding you on the schedule. Please take him to the individual following you on the schedule.

Time		Interviewer
A.M.	P.M.	

Special arrangements:

Please complete and return the attached interview report as soon as possible upon completion of the interview.

By Date

PERSONNEL REQUISITION

Education, Knowledge, Experience, and Personal Characteristics Required for the Position

Qualification categories	**Absolutely necessary** Those qualifications which constitute minimum requirements for the position *without which no candidate* may be considered.	**Desirable** Those qualifications which improve ability to do the job and which indicate a preferred candidate.
Education: Course of study, special programs, degree as necessary, e.g.: B.S., M.S., graduate courses in marketing, courses in operations research, etc.		
Knowledge: Necessary general job knowledge, knowledge of factual data, method and process, theoretical knowledge such as competitive market operations, technical products, government accounting requirements		
Experience: Specific on-the-job experience necessary, such as development of major contract proposals, directing product research projects, negotiating labor agreements		

Special Requirements: Special aptitudes and abilities necessary or desirable such as writing ability, freedom to travel extensively, specialized outside contacts.		
Personal Characteristics: Special requirements such as unusual social skills and poise, unusual ability to withstand pressure and frustration, mature appearance, etc.		

Approval

By ______________________________ Date ______________

By ______________________________ Date ______________

By ______________________________ Date ______________

PERSONNEL REQUISITION

____

Date

Position title	Reports to (title)			
Hiring range (monthly)	Dept./Location	Date required		
Replacement for	Promotion	Transfer	Termination	Addition budgeted

Major responsibilities: ______________________________

____

Work experience (number of years, nature, etc.): ____________________

Personal attributes: ____________________

Other requirements (language facility, travel %, etc.): ____________________

Requested by: ____________________ Date ____________

Approved by: ____________________ Date ____________

Requisition No. ______________ Position No. ______________

Date received ______________ Date filled ______________

Source ____________________

Name: ____________________ Reports ______________

Promotion __________ Transfer __________ New __________

CAMPUS TRIP REPORT

School Representative Date

Name	Title or dept.	Contacted this year?	Should be advised of next visit		
			Yes/No	By repres.	By corp.

Recruitment

List suggestions for continued improvement of future recruiting trips here (Include additional comments concerning your contacts; unusual aspects of recruitment at this school; additional information (references, transcripts, etc.) that can be obtained or requested by recruiters, etc.)

Describe fully how company visits are publicized by the school

Does this school permit prescreening of resumes prior to visit? When and with whom is this arranged?

Which departments provide list of students?	Must these be requested each year?	From whom?

Approximate number of graduates at present in following categories

Type	Engineering	Business	Accounting	Other
BS				
MS				
Ph.D.				

Miscellaneous

Recommended dates next year	Did you request	Confirm	Should discontinue recruiting here
Fall:	☐ Yes ☐ No	☐ Yes ☐ No	
Spring:	☐ Yes ☐ No	☐ Yes ☐ No	☐

Which candidates, if hired, could assist our future efforts here?

Information re: competitive salary offers (Include degree level, discipline, source.)

Recommended motel/hotel ______________________________

Recommended restaurants ______________________________

Recommended transportation ☐ Public ☐ Car Rental

Other ______________________________

MEDICAL REPORT

Candidate ______________________________

Position considered for ______________________________

Operating unit and location ______________________________

Examining physician ______________________ Date __________

Date report anticipated __________ Communicate results to __________

Medical Classification

☐ Approved for hire ☐ Disapproved for hire

By	Date

performance of the employment function and the organization in meeting some required standards.

One problem with reports is that many are prepared merely out of habit. If allowed to continue, this problem can result in an information explosion and wasted money. One solution to the problem is to have managers evaluate periodically the usefulness of their reports in terms of costs to both sender and recipient.[1]

Records, as well as reports, need to be continually evaluated in terms of costs and their contribution to the operation of the organization. Exceptions to this, obviously, are those records and reports required by law. However, even here, there may be a better way of collecting the required data, and that is really the crux of the problem—*not* the physical record or report.

If your organization has a systems group, they may be able to provide some valuable assistance. If your organization does not have this capability, the employment function should assume the responsibility for continually seeking ways to provide the necessary data in the most efficient and economical manner. Regardless of who is responsible, however, the on-going objective must be to determine "What is really needed?"

Organizations that already have computerized personnel records will have a real advantage in keeping track of a diversity of information. However, a little ingenuity in adapting some of the ideas that follow will allow any organization to maintain whatever information is required. Regardless of the type of data system, however, the organization's employment philosophy will dictate what information to track and what information to keep, (over and above that required by law). The basic data ingredient in any employment process is the potential or active job candidate, and all the data necessarily revolve around them.

Organization Records and Reports

In order to develop effective measurements of the efficiency and economy of its employment efforts, an organization will need to record and report, at a minimum, the types of information outlined below. Suggested formats for presenting it are also shown, and these formats can be easily adapted to an organization's particular needs. These formats are shown on pp. 222-227.

[1]Reprinted by permission from "Management in Action," *Management*, July 1972, pp. 38-39.

1. *Number of candidates* for a given job (Employment Status Report)
    a) The number of candidates can be a very critical measure of how well the job is defined and should be a prime indicator of how well the selection process is working, i.e., an unusually high number of candidates may be indicative of a misunderstanding of job requirements and/or bad communication between the parties involved in the process. The total number of candidates considered may be a legal requirement (see Item 3).
2. *Number of Applications by race and sex* (number of applications received)
3. *Number of candidate interviews on specific jobs* and the total for a given period of time (Employment Status Report)
    a) This may be an indication of both the symptoms described in item 1 a) and a possible need for review of sources. Are the ones being utilized capable of finding the type and caliber of people needed?
4. *Source of all candidates* (Candidate Status Record)
    a) This is a key factor in determining the effectiveness of various sources and a good measure of the economics of the employment function. For example, what is the ratio of advertising expenditures to useable responses?
5. *The number of offers made* (Employment Status Report)
    a) This is the truest measure of the value of your sources—which ones are turning up candidates you want to hire, e.g., the employment agency that sends you candidates who receive offers is doing its job. However, the candidate's acceptance or rejection of your offer is a measure of the effectiveness of your employment process rather than that of the referring source.
6. *The number of acceptances* (Professional/Technical Hire Report and Employment Status Report)
    a) This is the ultimate measure of success of the employment process—if the individuals accepting are within the parameters of the job specifications and salary ranges and are of the caliber needed to help the organization achieve its objectives.
7. *The number of offers pending* (Employment Status Report)

a) This form indicates the level of continuing effort that may be required to meet the manpower goals. (Historical data should provide a good definition of the need for the level of employment activity that will be necessary to recruit "X" number of candidates, receive "X" number of offers, and receive "X" number of acceptances.)

8. *The number of declinations* (Employment Status Report)

   a) This form gives an obvious indication of some of the problems about interview, offer, acceptance, and pending statistics. It also shows a possible warning sign (when confined to some specific area) that that segment of the organization may not be doing its job and therefore probably needs some help.

9. *The number of hires that are replacements and additions* (Professional/Technical Hire Report)

   a) A good requisition system should assist by providing controls (through approval) to maintain the desired or required headcount. This statistic will provide a "hard" figure of what has actually transpired.

10. *The job title and salary level* (Professional/Technical Hire Report)

    a) This also provides "hard" figures and an indication that job classification and salary administration policy/procedures are being observed.

11. *The status of a given candidate at a given time in the employment process* (Candidate Status Record and Employment Check List)

    a) This form (see Chapter 8.2) provides status information on any active candidate. It is important to know the status and some basic information on all candidates for future reference and for such mundane requests as knowing "what happened to the President's next door neighbors' son."

12. *Status of key candidates* (Key Candidate Report)

    a) This form informs those with a "need to know" what activity is is taking place on higher-level jobs.

13. *The dollar expenditures in the various employment budget classifications* (Monthly Accounting Summary Report)

    a) This form provides the key control on the economy of the employment process; by considering all of the foregoing data, you can determine whether the job is getting done realistically for the dollars expended.

Government Records and Reports

The law requires that specific employment information be maintained and reported. Should your organization be under the auspices of a compliance agency, you may have to meet specific employment objectives set by the agency, and this will in all probability require additional records and reports. Organizations that are government contractors, have 50 or more employees, and have a contract of $50,000 or more (as specified by Executive Order 11246) must do the following:

1. Establish a system to identify all employees by race and sex. The easiest method may be to utilize the payroll data base.
2. Retain completed application forms for six months.
3. Submit the Employer Information Report EEO-1 to the federal government annually. This report is a compilation of an organization's work force by job category, total employment, and numbers of minority employees by group (see pp. 228-229).
4. Be able to furnish a current report of all applications received by race and sex.
5. Annually develop a written Affirmative Action Plan in compliance with Revised Order 4 (Executive Order 11246); the organization may also be required to submit a copy of its Affirmative Action Plan for review.
6. Be prepared to submit upon request certain documents and records pertaining to the use, validation, and results of any paper-and-pencil or performance measure used as a basis for *any* employment decision; an organization with a disparate rejection rate among one race or sex as a whole must validate its tests. The *Federal Register*, vol. 35, no. 149—Sat. August 1, 1970, Title 29—Labor Part 1607—Guidelines on Employee Selection Procedures and *Federal Register* vol. 36, no. 192—Sat. October 2, 1971, Title 41—Public Contracts and Property Management Part 60-3 Employee Testing and Other Selection Procedures spell out the requirements of testing and validation in some detail.
7. Be prepared to report regularly to the compliance agency on the total number of candidates interviewed for each job opening by race and sex.

EMPLOYMENT STATUS REPORT

Location

Period ending

Job Title	Job Level	Source	Number of Candidates	Number of Interviews	Number of Offers	Number of Acceptances	Number Pending	Number of Declinations

APPLICATIONS RECEIVED RECORD

Location	Week ending

Male

Occupations	White	Negro	Oriental	American Indian	Spanish American	Total
Officials and managers						
Professionals						
Technicians						
Office and clerical						
Craftsmen						
Operatives						
Total						

Female

Occupations	White	Negro	Oriental	American Indian	Spanish American	Total
Officials and managers						
Professionals						
Technicians						
Office and clerical						
Craftsmen						
Operatives						
Total						
Grand total						

CANDIDATE STATUS RECORD

Name (last, first, middle initial)	Business telephone
Address	Home telephone

Date of inquiry:	**Source:** ☐ Agency ☐ College ☐ Adv. ☐ Search ☐ Direct ☐ Empl. ref.
Action	**Status**
Date ________ ________________	Date ________ ________________
________________	________________
________________	________________
Date ________ ________________	Date ________ ________________
________________	________________
________________	________________
Date ________ ________________	Date ________ ________________
________________	________________
________________	________________
Date ________ ________________	Date ________ ________________
________________	________________
________________	________________

Comments:

File retained:

(CONFIDENTIAL)

PROFESSIONAL/TECHNICAL HIRE REPORT

Name ______________________ Date ______________

Location ______________________ Date employed ______________

Job title ______________________ Salary ______________

Soc. Sec. No. ______________________ Classification ______________

Source: Direct ☐ Adv. ☐ Empl. agency ☐
College ☐ Search ☐ Emp. ref. ☐

Replacement __________ Name of individual replaced ______________

New position __________ Authorized by (Pers. Req. No.) __________

Race: Negro ☐ Cauc. ☐ Span.—surname Amer. ☐ Amer. Ind. ☐ Oriental ☐

Age ______ Sex M ☐ F ☐ Number of candidates ______ Number of minority candidates ______

Additional comments:

cc: Corporate Employment

By ______________________

MONTHLY ACCOUNTING SUMMARY REPORT

Month of ____________________

Department ______________ Unit ________________

Account Title/No.	Budget	Amount exp. to date last year	Amount exp. this month last year	Amount exp. to date	Amount exp. this month	Over Under
Total						

KEY CANDIDATE REPORT

Total	Hiring executive	Date Initiated	No. of candidates seen	Responsible person/firm	Candidates	Status

Standard Form 100 (Revised)
January 1970
Approved BOB-124-R0002
100-207

EQUAL EMPLOYMENT OPPORTUNITY

EMPLOYER INFORMATION REPORT EEO-1

Joint Reporting Committee

- Equal Employment Opportunity Commission
- Office of Federal Contract Compliance

Section A - TYPE OF REPORT

Refer to instructions for number and types of reports to be filed.

1. Indicate by marking in the appropriate box the type of reporting unit for which this copy of the form is submitted (MARK ONLY ONE BOX).

(1) ☐ Single-establishment Employer Report

Multi-establishment Employer:
(2) ☐ Consolidated Report
(3) ☐ Headquarters Unit Report
(4) ☐ Individual Establishment Report (submit one for each establishment with 25 or more employees)
(5) ☐ Special Report

2. Total number of reports being filed by this Company (Answer on Consolidated Report only)

Section B - COMPANY IDENTIFICATION *(To be answered by all employers)* — OFFICE USE ONLY

1. Name of Company which owns or controls the establishment for which this report is filed (if same as label, skip to item 2, this section) — a.

Address (Number and street)	City or town	County	State	ZIP code	b.

b. Employer Identification No. ☐☐☐☐☐☐☐☐☐

2. Establishment for which this report is filed.

a. Name of establishment — c.

Address (Number and street)	City or town	County	State	ZIP Code	d.

b. Employer Identification No. ☐☐☐☐☐☐☐☐☐ (If same as label, skip.)

3. Parent of affiliated company (Multi-establishment Employers: Answer on Consolidated Report only)

a. Name of parent or affiliated company — b. Employer Identification No ☐☐☐☐☐☐☐☐☐

Address (Number and street)	City or town	County	State	ZIP code

Section C - EMPLOYERS WHO ARE REQUIRED TO FILE *(To be answered by all employers)*

☐ Yes ☐ No 1. Does the entire company have at least 100 employees in the payroll period for which you are reporting?

☐ Yes ☐ No 2. Is your company affiliated through common ownership and/or centralized management with other entities in an enterprise with a total employment of 100 or more?

NOTE: If the answer is NO to BOTH questions, skip to Section G; otherwise complete ENTIRE form.

☐ Yes ☐ No 3. Does the company or any of its establishments (a) have a prime contract with any agency of the Federal Government, a Federally-assisted construction contract, or a subcontract at any tier under any prime Government contract, amounting to more than $10,000; or (b) serve as a depository of Federal Government funds; or (c) serve as an issuing and paying agent of U.S. Savings Bonds and Notes; or (d) hold a Federal Government bill of lading in any amount?

Section D - EMPLOYMENT DATA

Employment at this establishment—Report all permanent, temporary, or part-time employees including apprentices and on-the-job trainees unless specifically excluded as set forth in the instructions. Enter the appropriate figures on all lines and in all columns. Blank spaces will be considered as zeros. *In columns 1, 2, and 3, include ALL employees in the establishment including those in minority groups.*

Job Categories (See Appendix (4) for definitions)	TOTAL EMPLOYEES IN ESTABLISHMENT			MINORITY GROUP EMPLOYEES (See Appendix (5) for definitions)							
				MALE				FEMALE			
	Total Employees Including Minorities (1)	Total Male Including Minorities (2)	Total Female Including Minorities (3)	Negro (4)	Oriental (5)	American Indian * (6)	Spanish Surnamed American (7)	Negro (8)	Oriental (9)	American Indian * (10)	Spanish Surnamed American (11)
Officials and managers											
Professionals											
Technicians											
Sales workers											
Office and clerical											
Craftsmen (Skilled)											
Operatives (Semi-skilled)											
Laborers (Unskilled)											
Service workers											
TOTAL →											
Total employment reported in previous EEO-1 report											

(The trainees below should also be included in the figures for the appropriate occupational categories above)

Formal On-the-job trainees		(1)	(2)	(3)	(4)	(5)	(6)	(7)	(8)	(9)	(10)	(11)
	White collar											
	Production											

*In Alaska include Eskimos and Aleuts with American Indians

NOTE: On consolidated report, skip questions 2-5 and Section E.
How was information as to race or ethnic group in Section D obtained?

1 ☐ Visual Survey 3 ☐ Other - Specify ....
2 ☐ Employment Record

3. Dates of payroll period used -

4. Pay period of last report submitted for this establishment

5. Does this establishment employ apprentices?
This year? 1 ☐ Yes 2 ☐ No
Last year? 1 ☐ Yes 2 ☐ No

Section E - ESTABLISHMENT INFORMATION

1. Is the location of the establishment the same as that reported last year?
1 ☐ Yes 2 ☐ No 3 ☐ Did not report last year 4 ☐ Reported on combined basis

2. Is the major business activity at this establishment the same as that reported last year?
1 ☐ Yes 2 ☐ No 3 ☐ No report last year 4 ☐ Reported on combined basis

OFFICE USE ONLY

3. What is the major activity of this establishment? (Be specific, i.e., manufacturing steel castings, retail grocer, wholesale plumbing supplies, title insurance, etc. Include the specific type of product or type of service provided, as well as the principal business or industrial activity.

e.

Section F - REMARKS

Use this item to give any identification data appearing on last report which differs from that given above, explain major changes in composition or reporting units, and other pertinent information.

Section G - CERTIFICATION (See Instructions G)

Check one
1. ☐ All reports are accurate and were prepared in accordance with the instructions (check on consolidated only)
2. ☐ This report is accurate and was prepared in accordance with the instructions.

Name of Authorized Official	Title	Signature		Date	
Name of person to contact regarding this report (Type or print)	Address (Number and street)				
Title	City and State	ZIP code	Telephone Area Code	Number	Extension

All reports and information obtained from individual reports will be kept confidential as required by Section 709 (e) of Title VII
WILLFULLY FALSE STATEMENTS ON THIS REPORT ARE PUNISHABLE BY LAW. U.S. CODE. TITLE 18 SECTION 1001

OMB No. 44-R1460

QUARTERLY REPORT OF NEW HIRES

(To be completed by Federal contractors and subcontractors subject to Executive Order 11598)

	NUMBER OF HIRES
1. TOTAL NEW HIRES	
2. VIETNAM-ERA VETERANS HIRED	
Quarter Ending	Date Submitted ....

These report forms are being supplied as a convenience to Federal contractors and subcontractors to meet their reporting requirements on hires in accordance with Federal regulations (41 CFR 50-250) implementing Executive Order 11598. Contractors should reproduce copies of this form as required.

Instructions for Submittal of Report

Line 1 - Enter the total number of new hires, including Vietnam-era veterans, during the period covered.

Line 2 - Enter the number of Vietnam-era veterans hired during the period covered.

This report should be submitted to the local employment service office serving the area by the 7th of the month following the calendar quarter to which data pertain. A contractor or subcontractor with more than one establishment in a State may submit the quarterly reports for all such establishments to the State office of the __________ State Employment Service.

Definitions

(1) New Hires are temporary or permanent additions to the employment roll of (a) anyone who has never been employed by the organization, or (b) former employees who were not called back by the employer or are not returning from military leave.

(2) Vietnam Era Veteran. A veteran separated on or after August 5, 1964, and who has received other than a dishonorable discharge.

Any questions regarding this matter should be referred to the nearest office of the __________ State Employment Service.

SUBMITTED BY:	
Name of Firm	Signature
Street Address	
City, State and ZIP Code	Title

In addition, Executive Order 11598—Hiring of Vietnam-Era Veterans requires the filing of a quarterly report (OMB No. 44-R1460, see p. 230) of new hires with the appropriate state employment office of the United States Employment Service (USES).

Those requirements for record keeping and reporting make it mandatory that you keep your line managers well informed, because their understanding of all the problems about reports *required by the government* may well save the organization time and anguish in the final analysis by helping avoid government audits and/or reviews. Such an audit or review gives the government access to your personnel and employment records and reports, so it behooves all employment functions to maintain accurate and up-to-date information

There may be a need for additional records and reports, but those discussed here answer the most critical questions about the activities of the employment process. The government records and reports speak for themselves, and when, for whatever reason, they are thought to be inadequate, we can assume that new ones will be forthcoming.

The rapid increase in the number and detail of both federal and state legislation pertaining to employment practices and procedures makes it imperative that all organizations institute a continuing review of all their employment forms. The employment function must necessarily take the lead in insuring that the organization stays alert. All the people in an organization who are part of or party to the employment process must be kept informed of all changes and requirements as they are effected.

9
Hiring, relocation, and orientation

9.1 HIRING

All of the efforts, time, and money invested in the candidate are rapidly reaching a climax at this point. Hopefully, you have done all the things necessary to be sure that the candidate you have selected is the right person for the job and that he has shown interest in being hired by you. At this stage, the only things that remain to be done before making an offer to the candidate are reference checks and a physical examination.

References are usually listed on the application form, but you may want to supplement this information by asking for additional references that may provide more spontaneous information. You will already have some knowledge of the candidate's physical condition from the information available on the application form.

Reference Checks

Reference checks can be either an extremely valuable input or a complete waste of time and energy. Surprisingly, this phase of the employment process is often neglected and even completely disregarded in many organizations, although a properly conducted reference check can save untold dollars by forestalling wrong hiring decisions. (This should not imply, however, that references are the major criterion in the hire/not hire decision; rather, they are one, albeit critical, part of the total decision-making process.)

Some organizations prefer to check references prior to interviews; some, after an initial interview. A majority, however, wait until interviews have been completed and a definite mutuality of interest has been established. This seems to be a much more realistic approach, because by then you know enough about the candidate to be able to ask intelligent, penetrating questions rather than to attempt to verify your own good judgment, which may be the biggest danger in reference-checking. As indicated in Chapter 8, there are two basic ways to gather reference information—by letter and by phone. The most meaningful information is that given spontaneously—over the telephone.

The employment function's role is to establish the company's professional credentials as an employer and insure that the candidate understands the need for a thorough investigation of his background. Identify key people in his job environment and community who will be able to make constructive comments about his capabilities, performance, adjustment, stability, strengths, and development needs. The candidate should be assured that the company makes every effort to protect his interests. You are not checking on the truthfulness of his statements, but rather you are attempting to make sure that you have as complete a picture as possible.

Thorough reference-checking by a skilled person provides a perspective of the candidate not obtainable by the use of any other technique. In interviewing, we are concerned primarily with answering the question "How does the candidate see himself?" Background investigation reveals how he is seen by other people who are now or have been related to him in one or more of several environments.

The real problem, of course, is to get direct and honest responses from people who have, in most cases, been prepared for your inquiry. It is always possible to identify people other than the standard references presented, but you must exercise extreme discretion under these circumstances. You cannot afford to be responsible for the candidate's losing his job, for example. Indeed, lawsuits have been instituted because of overzealous reference-checkers who may also run into problems with the Fair Credit Reporting Act. It makes a lot more sense to put your ingenuity to work getting your questions answered objectively by the standard references.

Good interviewers usually make good reference-checkers because the technique and motivation are really the same—to get meaningful inputs about the candidate. Reference should give you a broader perspective of the candidate, because these people will be providing information from a variety of views in a different environment than your interviews did. Like interviewers, each person involved in obtaining references develops his own techniques and lines of questioning. There are, however, several key questions that can be asked in exploring critical areas. You must always assume that the people given as references will attempt to speak positively about the candidate. It thus becomes the responsibility of the reference checker to ask the questions that will provide the most meaningful information.

Theoretically, there are two phases in conducting a background investigation: (1) routine verification and (2) the in-depth probe. The verification check simply confirms the facts presented by the candidate—type of schooling and degree, dates of employment, job title and responsibilities, salary, etc. When a candidate has been properly interviewed and tested, there are very few cases in which verification checks show up significant discrepancies.

The more important phase is the in-depth probe—discussions with people who have been closely associated with the candidate and who are both able and willing to comment candidly about his assets and liabilities. Through such discussions, the reference checker is able to view the candidate through the eyes of his instructors, past and present supervisors and associates, as well as his business and social acquaintances. This composite view of the candidate—his reputation and future prospects—supplements the other data developed about him and establishes this technique as an integral part of the selection and placement process.

You must also assume that any "reference," like anyone else, will have some personal hang-ups. If these can be identified, you may be able to exploit them and use them as a factor in your final analysis of the candidate. For example, an objective view of a man's ability to perform a given technical job may be colored by a reference source who does not believe that a technician who completes a degree at night school can ever be a competent performer.

The steps involved in a thorough in-depth probe are as follows:

1. Clear the procedure with the candidate. Assure him that the organization is making every effort to evaluate his potential for success and will protect the confidentiality of the situation.
2. Try to talk with the candidate's boss, his boss (if applicable), a co-worker (peer), a former boss (if applicable), and someone in another functional area who had a significant level of contact with the candidate.

3. Preplan the telephone contacts. Determine which references will probably offer the most balanced view of the candidate and who, within the organization, is likely to get the most reliable information from the reference. Decide from the data developed about the candidate to date and from the nature of the position for which he is being considered which factors in his background require the most thorough investigation.
4. With younger candidates, academic references are appropriate and may well be the only ones. Bear in mind that the reference criteria they use may just be grades, which are usually an extremely poor indication of the candidate's job abilities.
5. Once you have made contact with a reference, be sure that he has the time and inclination to talk. Generally speaking, avoid Monday mornings and the middle and end of the work day.
6. Introduce yourself by title and indicate the purpose of your call. However, do not volunteer any more than the minimum information at this stage. (Briefly explain the position for which the candidate is being considered, but make *no* comments about the interview results.)
7. Establish concretely what connection the reference has had with the candidate—what organization, length of time, and at what location.
8. Verify the basic data—whether the candidate did hold the position claimed, for the period claimed, performed the duties claimed, and earned the salary claimed.
9. Begin with factual questions. What did the candidate's job entail? What did he actually do? What were his specific responsibilities?
10. Get the reference to do the talking; do not ask questions that elicit yes or no responses.
11. Be very precise about the candidate's specific skills, abilities, and business sense. Is he innovative? Give me an example. What are the standards of success in your organization? How extensive is his knowledge of the field? How broad are his interests? Examples? Is he a team man? How does he get along with co-workers? Is he aggressive? Examples!
12. With discretion, find out something about his family relationships and activities in his community. This should never come across as

being nosy, but rather as expressing your interest in the candidate as a stable, responsible person.

13. If you have difficulty pinning down specifics, you may want to throw out some loaded questions to attempt to turn the reference's thinking to a different tack. For example, "If you were going to invest all of "your" money in a venture, what reservations would you have about the candidate's being the general manager?" You will have to place great emphasis on your ability to interpret not only the words but also the inflection and context in which the answers are put. Be objective and again, *do not* volunteer any more information than you have to until you feel confident with the data you have gathered.
14. For your higher-level candidates, it is always useful to try to talk with the controller of the candidate's organization. Controllers generally tend to take a more pragmatic view of an operation and the individuals in it.

The results of each reference should be recapped and compared, since each reference re-establishes the context in which the next reference will take place. This is particularly important when more than one individual is making reference calls. When all reference comments have been obtained, they should be consolidated and summarized in order to present the most reliable, comprehensive picture of how a select few of the candidate's associates see his strengths and weaknesses.

Hopefully, your efforts will have solicited meaningful information, and you must now interpret it in a completely factual, objective way and present it to the hiring manager as part of the total evaluation package for making the final hire/not hire decision.

Although the preceding reference-checking approach was slanted toward the telephone check, do not overlook the "in-person" reference check. Although not too often feasible, the face-to-face talk with a reference is especially important when the candidate is being considered for a top-management position. At this point, it may be well worth your while to invest a few additional dollars in order to get really definitive information.

In summary, reference checking, as a selection and placement tool, is only as reliable as the employment function's use of it. No single technique can provide "the answer," but misuse of any technique can influence the selection process negatively.

Physical Examination

The employment function must see to it that the prospective employee undergoes a physical examination before he accepts the position and resigns from his current job. An approved, organization-sponsored physical should be a firm condition of employment.

Too often this step in the employment process is an "afterthought"; occasionally, it is completely overlooked and does not take place until the man has started employment with the organization. Obviously, it is imperative that the prospective employee be physically able to perform his immediate assignment and any projected future assignments. The organization owes him this protection before he commits himself. Neither the company nor the prospective employee needs the problems and liabilities that can arise if a serious health problem is discovered during a postemployment physical examination. This examination will be looked on favorably by the candidate as insurance before he leaves the umbrella of benefits he has with his present employer.

Depending on the policy of the organization, the physical may be given by a physician designated by the organization, by a medical clinic, or by the prospective employee's personal physician. In theory, it should precede an offer; in practice, however, the offer is often made contingent upon the candidate's successful completion of a physical examination.

The Offer

All the pieces are in place now—interviews, references, physical exam—and the line manager has access to all the inputs and makes a positive decision. You are now ready to make the offer.

The offer (including all aspects of the initial compensation package) is mutually agreed upon by the line manager and the personnel department. The starting salary depends on the candidate's experience and potential, the market value of his skills, and the relationship of the new employee's salary to others in the department. This is a much more critical step in the employment process than is realized, and the way in which it is handled may be the difference between the candidate's acceptance or declination of the offer, regardless of how well things have gone to this point or the degree of emphasis the candidate has attached to salary.

Timing must be realistic. The employment function must listen carefully to determine when the candidate will be most receptive to an offer. This involves knowing the candidate's other interview commitments, when relocation will be feasible, how soon he will be mentally and emotionally prepared to break the ties with his current employer, and why he is ranking his job alternatives in a given order. Nothing annoys a prospective candidate more than an excessive waiting period between final interviews and the employment decision. This may well be an indication to the candidate that the organization is slow to make decisions. Delaying the final offer results in the loss of good candidates. You must move quickly to capitalize on recruiting and selection efforts, but *only* when you sense that the climate is right for a positive decision, and not so quickly as to destroy the feeling of professionalism which the candidate has sensed up to that point. The candidate must feel that he has been judged worthy of joining the team, and he must sense that professional people have made every effort to evaluate his credentials and potential for success in the organization.

This should be as personalized as any other step in the total employment process. You should also consider involving the wife at this point; she will be particularly important now that the final decision is down to the wire. She will be the one to bear the brunt of the relocation problem and any problems with the family. She will, in all probability, have questions that the candidate would never think of or might never ask. Whether or not any candidate will admit it, his wife plays an extremely important part in the final decision and should be involved.

The offer should never be extended at the end of a hectic series of interviews. Rather, it should be extended in person or at least verbally by phone and then confirmed by letter (see Chapter 8.1). This will be another indication of your interest in the candidate as an individual and will also provide a good opportunity to clarify any details. When extending an offer to a more senior candidate, it almost always will pay dividends to do it face to face. This provides an ideal opportunity to work out any critical details that may force you to stretch your policies or set some precedents.

In arranging for the "offer discussion," indicate that you would like to know about any of the wife's or family's concerns or inputs. Emphasize this, because most candidates will be reluctant to discuss these points, feeling that to do so would indicate their lack of decisiveness or authority. Yet the worst thing that can happen is to have the candidate accept and prove to be a disappointment in the job merely because he had some hang-up about the move. Do your best to alleviate any problems before they happen.

In making the offer, you should utilize the reasons for the prospective employee's interest in a new position as selling points. Among the most frequent reasons professional people change jobs are:

- Opportunity to broaden experience and responsibility
- Changes within the current organization
- Need for more professional recognition
- Personal factors involving their families
- Improvement in compensation.

The specifics of the offer must all be worked out prior to this discussion. This is not the time to bargain or negotiate. You should be precise and indicate that the salary is a measure of the value of the job rather than a percentage increase over his current salary. Although there may be situations in which you will have to negotiate, presenting the offer in a very positive manner will overcome some of the candidate's normal tendency to bargain.

If there is some additional type of compensation involved, be sure and explain it thoroughly, e.g., "You are eligible for this additional income, but it is predicated on performance–yours and/or the organization's." This will help avoid any misunderstandings in a lean year. You should also indicate when employees are paid. If, for example, you pay once a month, it may be a shock to the person who is budgeting on a semimonthly basis. The offer letter should express salary only in per-month terms, even though you express it verbally in annual terms. Such things as stock options or investment plans should be covered in some detail with reference to restrictions, vesting rights, or other aspects.

To reiterate, be specific in extending the offer: the new employee's superior, the parameters of the job, and the physical location. Detail your benefits program (insurance, medical, vacation) step by step, and indicate that you will spell out details in the offer letter. (If you have a booklet outlining your benefits, this is a good time to pass it along. This can be the first step in orientation.)

Your relocation policy should also be spelled out with particular reference to any limitations or restrictions (weight, movement of frozen foods, automobiles, boats, etc.) and tax liability. If you recommend a mover, be explicit about instructions for arranging the move. Be sure that the candidate's wife has all the information she needs; if she is not present, make all of these points in a positive manner. "We want to be sure that your wife understands this move, so if she has any questions, regardless of how trivial, we want to know so that the move can be accomplished with the least disruption to her and the family." This may prompt the question about the collection of 300 antique coffee cups that have to be packed individually in styrofoam. Better to know now than later!

Follow up the verbal offer as soon as possible with your offer letter. A word of caution, however; don't pressure the candidate for an immediate decision or a reporting date. There are always some loose ends to clean up when someone leaves a job. You must be positive but reasonable, bearing in mind that two to four weeks' notice is not unusual and that a yes or no on the offer does require thought and discussion by the candidate. The candidate should have a week to ten days in which to make a decision, but never put a deadline on it. Discuss it frankly, and it will be brought to a mutually satisfactory solution.

If an employment agency or executive-search firm has been involved, it should be informed as to the specifics of the offer *before* it is made. The referral source is usually in close communication with the prospective employee and can "presell," feed back possible areas of concern expressed by the candidate, and provide postoffer encouragement.

9.2 RELOCATION

The actual relocation can be a traumatic experience, no matter how often the new employee has had to do it. Since relocation is one of your major cost-per-hire expenses, you should make every effort to expedite the move and ease the burden on the new employee. As was stated earlier, your relocation procedure need not try "to cover every nickle of expense," but rather to facilitate the move and have a new, productive employee as soon as possible. Flexibility is important here and whether we admit it or not, that special individual or that new V.P. will get some breaks in his move. In the normal situation, you may want to provide a copy of your relocation policy/procedure or prepare a handout summary to guide the new employee. Be sure that the more confusing points are covered, e.g., who pays for carpet installation, appliance servicing, and realtors' fees, the amount of special relocation allowances, and when and to whom the new employee should submit expenses.

Information about the local community will be a major factor in relocation, and the new employee will undoubtedly have innumerable questions about schools, shopping, transportation, food prices, and on and on. An approach here, although not the total answer, is to have the wife visit the community either during a house-hunting trip or, better yet, at the point when a firm decision is to be made. There are several relatively inexpensive things you might consider to prepare for this trip more efficiently.

1. Favored realtors can provide some pretrip orientation to the market via letter or phone. This should not be done, however, without the new employee's agreement.
2. Arrange for a subscription to the local paper that carries most of the real estate and shopping ads.
3. Arrange to have the Chamber of Commerce and other local civic and religious organizations send information on the community and activities. For your new minority employees, don't overlook local fair-housing groups, the Urban League, or other civic-action groups.

These things may prove to be among the most positive steps in this whole process. They certainly should put the family in a more positive frame of mind about the "new job."

International Aspect

When filling an international job, the whole process of the offer and relocation becomes more detailed. The benefits and compensation are in reality structured to overcome some of the inconvenience of being overseas and to provide for the same standard of living. The offer must detail such things as the following:

1. Any overseas premium (percentage of base salary), which in reality is a compensation for family inconvenience
2. Special relocation allowance, used primarily to offset variations in living costs
3. Housing allowance, to ensure housing as equivalent as possible to American standards
4. Hardship allowance, a compensation for living in particularly difficult locations
5. Education allowance, to ensure adequate schooling for the new employee's children
6. Car allowance, given to equalize cost with American standards
7. Tax allowance, to ensure that employee pays no more tax than he would pay in the United States.

In order to communicate all the details clearly, it becomes very important to try to do it face to face. The wife now becomes a very critical factor and should be party to these discussions.

It will also be very helpful to provide a written summary of all these points over and above the statements in the offer letter. This summary can also be supplemented by a country summary which will be most valuable if the new employee did not have a "country visit" prior to acceptance. The whole idea is to provide as many insights as possible into all the nitty-gritty details, because in all probability the new employee will be faced with major adjustments to working conditions and social customs. Finally, since relocation costs are high and the organization must make a substantial investment before the individual ever gets on the job, it becomes imperative that you avoid any possible misunderstandings or disillusionments by providing *all* the information.

Hiring is a very personalized part of the employment process whether you are developing reference information or telling the candidate's wife about the price of beef in the local supermarket. Know your facts, present them in a positive manner, and try to understand what the other party is going through as the final decision is being made; try to put yourself of in their shoes, but be businesslike and understanding. Your chances of success will be greatly enhanced if you put all of these thoughts to work.

A final thought on relocation. After the new employee has moved, be sure to contact him to see how things went. Was the mover efficient and neat? Was the realtor helpful? Has the family encountered any unusual problems? This type of information will be invaluable not only for future relocations, but also to help you solve any immediate crises before they become disrupting problems.

9.3 ORIENTATION

It is interesting and a bit of an enigma that organizations that are willing to invest so much money and time in finding employees assume the job is done once their offer is accepted. The new employee is too often left to fend for himself during the first, very crucial days or weeks on the job. Almost regardless of how well handled the employment process has been to this point, you should insure that the "introductory process" is handled as well, or you may undo a lot of good work. Common sense dictates the degree of attention that should be given to the orientation process. With a comprehensive orientation program, however, the new employee will not have to spend as much time "on his own" adjusting to a new situation and will therefore be impacting more quickly on the economics and efficiency of the organization.

When the offer has been accepted, the reporting date finalized, and the various forms officially placing the employee on the payroll have been prepared, there is an unfortunate tendency to "let down." The new employee, on the other hand, has probably not really had the opportunity to get a real insight into the realities of working for XYZ Corporation. Most of the dialogue to this point has been concentrated on determining his skills and abilities and selling the virtues of the organization. So, there is still the very important matter of arranging and facilitating the new employee's reception into the organization. This will involve coordination with other departments and probably, when relocation is involved, outside agencies or services. Orientation may be handled on an individual or group basis, depending on such circumstances as coincidence of reporting dates, similar backgrounds, etc.

Although orientation procedures may vary in different parts of the organization, you should always see to it that the new employee is introduced and is processed into the company in a thoughtful, professional manner. Neither party can assume that the level of the new hire precludes him from the orientation process. It is not unreasonable to organize separate orientation programs for different levels of new employees. Many times the higher-level employees are reluctant to ask some of the more "routine" questions during the offer negotiations and then don't get a chance to do so in a group orientation session. There are also differences in benefit coverages for various levels or categories of personnel, and it is difficult to discuss these exceptions within a group.

It is therefore best if the orientation is conducted on an individual or at least a peer-group basis. In reality, individual orientation begins during the interview process, and this is an area that can be expanded to provide "prehire orientation" information. The emphasis on individual or peer orientation is to insure the best possible understanding of the organization and its policies. From a functional viewpoint, more and more organizations make it a practice to have the "benefits" and "services" specialists provide individualized information to new employees.

Prior to the new employee's arrival, you should confirm details of the assignment and reporting date with the appropriate department head, arrange or assist in finding office space and equipment, establish a telephone listing, and preplan the sequence and content of the actual orientation program.

Normally, the personnel department provides the first part of the employee's orientation. A good orientation program generally has two phases: one given by the personnel department, and the other given by the line department. Both departments must play very specific roles if the orientation program is to be really meaningful. The personnel department should have primary responsibility for the following:

1. Explaining the benefits and how to complete the necessary forms
2. Explaining the patents and inventions agreement (or whatever type of agreement or contract you utilize)
3. Explaining how to fill out other "personnel" forms, e.g., income tax forms and personnel inventories
4. Explaining performance-review procedures and salary-administration practices
5. Explaining the organization's general rules about working hours, breaks, vacations, pay days, etc.
6. Describing procedures and method for reimbursement of expenses
7. Outlining procedures for obtaining medical assistance and necessary emergency assistance
8. Explaining how to obtain office supplies, petty cash, etc.
9. Explaining procedures for making travel arrangements
10. Issuing applicable ID and credit cards
11. Answering any questions the new employee may have.

The line department should have primary responsibility for:

1. Insuring that both internal and external (as appropriate) appointment announcements are made
2. Discussing departmental and organizational structure (some organizations now use pictures of, at least, the key management people)
3. Explaining in more detail the philosophy and objectives of the organ-

ization and how the department's goals and objectives contribute to the overall corporate goals

4. Introducing the new employee to as many people as possible; this will also be a major factor in quickly establishing meaningful communication channels
5. Explaining pertinent accounting and administrative procedures
6. Explaining to the new employee that this "initial period" is a two-way street, i.e., the new employee must make the effort to orient himself to the environment and all that that entails.

Many organizations are making their orientation more meaningful by not trying to cover everything on that first Monday morning. First, have the new employee complete essential forms, e.g., W-4 and invention agreements, and tell him about the organization's basic rules and procedures. After the new employee has had some time to acclimate himself to the new job (a week to ten days), have a follow-up orientation session. This will provide a more meaningful interchange, because the new employee will now have something concrete to relate to.

Many organizations find that an employee handbook is a most effective tool and present it to the new employee along with the booklets about specific benefits. In addition to detailed information about matters covered in the interview, the employee handbook describes company policy about such things as vacations and holidays, medical examinations, and payroll information. This handbook may be given to the new employee before he officially joins your organization, if you feel it will help "sell" the candidate on your organization.

The employee's personnel record (containing all pertinent data on the new employee) should now be established, and a date for a follow-up interview within 30 to 60 days should be set up to determine if there are any problems and to see if the employee has become acclimated to the new environment.

In summary, employment's primary functions with regard to the mechanics of orientation and placement are to adequately plan for the new employee's arrival and coordinate the orientation program in such a way as to reinforce the employee's decision to join the organization and to insure his immediate contribution.

Additional orientation efforts should be made in international operations. Both the new employee and his wife should have an orientation to the community (schools, shopping, laws, and customs), and language-training facilities should be made available if feasible, so that the family can make a quicker adjustment to the new environment.

10 Out-placement

10.1 INTRODUCTION

This newest responsibility for the employment function evolved somewhat by accident in most organizations. Although ushering in tremendous new challenges and potential for American business, the 1970s also posed new and large-scale manpower problems. These problems centered on rising labor, material, and transportation costs and were compounded by foreign competition. It was becoming readily apparent that many organizations had not really devoted much effort or thought to their manpower problems (either planning or utilization). During the previous years of rapid growth, a great deal of staffing had been done with little thought or planning. As a result, in many instances hiring standards and selection criteria were diluted to get people on the payroll. Many organizations hired not only too many people, but also those with the narrow skills or knowledge needed to solve a particular problem at a particular time; these people were then retained long after their skills or knowledge were needed.

As the economic picture became darker in 1970 and 1971, many organizations had to reduce the costs of doing business, and they found that one of the simplest ways was to reduce the payroll. This is not quite as simple as it sounds, however. The impact of such action is enormous, yet many organizations cannot fathom this because they don't understand what obligations they assume when they hire people.

This chapter has been adapted by permission from D.H. Sweet, "Something New in Personnel—Out-Placement," *Personnel Journal*, July 1971, pp. 559-564.

Whatever it's called—reduction in force, layoff, termination without cause, or discharge—it is always a traumatic experience for all the people involved. When faced with this problem, it is not enough to just "pay the guy off and get him out." There is a more involved and significant obligation between employee and employer. The employer is obliged to help his new hires become successful employees and real contributors to the organization. Conversely, and equally important, the employee has an obligation to make every effort to contribute to the success of the organization.

This obligation actually takes many shapes and forms when employees are the victims of a "reduction," and a primary one is for the employer to provide the tools and guidance to assist them in relocating where their skills and abilities may be more fully utilized. Thus, the obligation really transcends just the individual; it encompasses the stockholders, the industry, and the economy. One of the greatest impacts is that felt on the campuses, in the community, within the organization itself, and in professional organizations such as IEEE and AICHE. How companies handle their "reduction" will also have significant impact on both the internal morale of the organization and the community when recruiting efforts are resumed.

The severity of these problems and impacts can be lessened when out-placement is handled in a truly professional and businesslike manner and with sensitivity for the terminees' problems. This chapter outlines an approach to out-placement that has been utilized successfully and should be adaptable to any organization that wants to do a meaningful job for its displaced people. Although *directed primarily* at a "reduction in force," the techniques and procedures can also be used to help the individual employee whose performance, for legitimate reasons, isn't up to par. This is a very real obligation—to appraise employees and to help them relocate if there is not a mutually beneficial relationship. *In other words, out-placement should be an on-going program rather than one utilized only when there is a reduction in force.* Indeed, this may be the most significant point for the future. Chapter 1.1 discussed increasing turnover, and the day is coming when organizations will foster turnover to improve their operations—they will make their personnel systems (appraisals, stewardship) work.[1] Once they understand that this makes sense, they will of necessity develop a process similar to that outlined in this chapter because

---

[1] Richard T. Kimball makes a strong argument for this approach in his article "Planned Professional Manpower Mobility," *Conference Board Record,* September 1972, pp. 54-58.

it will be an accepted responsibility to help employees out of their organization and into another where their skills and talents may be better utilized.

10.2 PAY THEM OFF AND GET THEM OUT

When faced with the need to release an employee or group of employees, most organizations do take the classical approach, i.e., "pay them off and get them out." The "payoff" is important in terms of keeping the employee reasonably solvent until he can find something else. But, and this is the catch, the average man has no real expertise in finding another job. Most job-hunters go about this so poorly that if they used the same methods to try to market a new product, they would be fired for incompetence. However, this incompetence is also logical, because most people go through the job-hunting experience only two or three times in their careers. Thus, the "pay off" must be supplemented with out-placement counseling and assistance, or the organization is doing only half the job.

Thus, the naivete of both the individual and the company is what poses the problem and is the motivating force behind this new function—out-placement. We will not be talking about the employee who is "fired" for cause, but rather about the employee who is the victim of a "reduction in force" or someone who has not "made it" in terms of performance; he is the man you want to help.

As has been stated, the approach the average person takes to job hunting is crudely conceived because of their mistaken assumption that is is an easy task that does not require much planning, thought, concentration or effort. This lack of planning and thought is also affected by the employee's hurt ego, and his emotional reaction may range from complete irrationality to "I accept it as a practical business decision." No organization should ever overlook the fact, however, that there will almost always be some degree of animosity toward them. For any organization, the problem initially comes down to dollars and cents. However the situation is handled, it will be costly, so it makes sense to do it right and even spend a few more dollars to insure the greatest possible positive reaction under the circumstances.

10.3 IT'S A PEOPLE PROBLEM

The 1970s also ushered in an era in which the white-collar professional became a major, unprecedented part of the nation's unemployment statistics. When employees were terminated in the past, it was assumed that they were poor performers, and they therefore carried the stigma of "being fired." There has been so much publicity in recent years about reductions in force in scores of organizations that the "stigma" of being out of work is not the albatross it once was. It is generally assumed nowadays that economic factors rather than the individual's performance is the reason for his termination.

What can your organization do to ease the total impact when faced with this problem? The most critical thing is to recognize the problem for what it is: a people problem and *not* just a dollars-and-cents problem. Once this is understood, plans can be developed that will help ease the problem considerably. To provide a focal point for such a plan, let's assume that the employment function has been doing its job and that it knows the organization, the people, and their problems well enough to provide the competent counseling and guidance that will be required. If the employment function has been successful over the years in achieving its hiring objectives, it should have achieved a rapport with all levels of management and can thus move very comfortably into this new role of out-placement.

Credibility

A particularly important aspect of any cost-reduction program is determining the best way to maintain the organization's credibility with those who remain. Depending on the severity of the reduction, organizations must plan on increased turnover due to the adverse reaction of some of those people not affected. The soundest approach is to insure the dissemination of accurate information about the extent of and reason for the reduction. All employees not terminated in the reduction should be informed as soon as possible what has transpired; otherwise, you may cause irreparable harm to employee relations and morale. This is the time to reassure people and *is not* the time to institute other cost-reduction efforts that affect them directly. The organization's credibility in the community will be enhanced by publicizing the assistance that is given to employees being let go, but this effort will succeed *only if you have a meaningful program.*

10.4 THE PLAN

In putting an out-placement plan together, you must first determine how much effort you *want* or can *afford* to make. You must therefore consider the following questions.

1. Will out-placement be done in-house, or will you utilize an outside firm? There are a number of firms that have developed a real expertise in out-placement, and your contacts in other organizations that have undergone reductions in force should be able to provide information on them. The best approach, though, if the employment function has been doing its job, is to make it responsible. Since relationships with employees and knowledge of the organization will be a major determinant in the success of this type of program, the employment function should be able to perform this task better than an outside firm. But be realistic on this point; an out-placement program of any magnitude may tie up a number of people for an extended period of time when you consider that on an *average*, it will take up to three months to get an experienced professional employee relocated to a new job.

2. Will *all* people affected receive assistance? Ultimately, this decision must rest with the terminees. However, don't underestimate the response to this offer of assistance; if relationships in the organization are good, most of your terminees will, in the final analysis, want help.

3. Will secretarial, phone, and office service be provided and if so, where? If these things can be done, there is no question that they are a big plus for you as well as for your displaced people and certainly provides them with a tremendous psychological boost. However, these services should be predicated on this basis:

    a) Facilities will not be in the terminated employees' regular work area.

    b) Facilities will be available to all terminees and should not be considered as anyone's private domain. (You may want to make exceptions here, possibly based on the level or seniority of the terminee.)

    c) There will be some time limitation on the availability of these facilities.

Once the degree or amount of assistance you wish to provide has been determined, the operational details of the plan can be worked out. Because of the differences *in* and *within* organizations, it would make sense to have all of the people who will be involved in administering the plan get together and to let them make the basic decisions about the details; this will ensure unanimity to the approach.

The size of the organization will obviously have real impact on how detailed the plan is and how much effort may be expended, but it should at least take into consideration the following:

1. The corporate employment function should be the focal point for the out-placement program.
2. All announcements and initial meetings with people to be terminated should be handled by line managers.
3. Each operating unit (plant, lab, and division) should designate an individual as out-placement representative.
4. The corporate employment function should, as deemed necessary, conduct seminars on job-hunting for any *group* of individuals in any part of the organization.
5. "Problem individuals" as designated by operating units could be directed specifically to the corporate employment function for counseling and assistance. ("Problem" is generally defined as the more senior people, those with attitude problems, or simply those who line management feels would benefit by this exposure.)
6. Out-placement representatives should coordinate their activities with the corporate employment function.
7. The corporate employment function should also be responsible for:
   a) Developing and distributing some kind of a guide to job-hunting—a simple brochure covering the basic points as outlined in this chapter. There is a real value in being able to hand the terminee something that will help provide him with a point of reference, and may be the first concrete indication of the organization's sincerity.
   b) Developing a new type of relationship with select third parties (employment agencies and executive-search firms) to enlist their support in working with your employees who are being terminated.
   c) Providing listings of appropriate contacts in other organizations for mail campaigns.
   d) Developing lists of job openings in other organizations for dissemination to out-placement representatives.
   e) Developing an "accounting report" to provide regular up-to-date status reports of terminees.

A Painful Task

Terminating anyone is a painful and emotional chore, especially when it is a termination "without cause." In formulating your plan for out-placement, there are a number of things that can be done to make the task easier:

1. The employee who is responsible for "giving the word" must be direct and explicit with the employee affected and must give the details of why it happened. This is not really the time for tact, because you must be sure that there is no misunderstanding about what has happened. The terminee needs all of the facts so that he can begin to plan a job search.
2. Timing is important. If at all possible, don't terminate employees until the end of the day. This will allow them a little face-saving with their peers, i.e., by going home, they won't have to face co-workers immediately.
3. If the person being released gets angry, *don't* lower yourself to the same level. You must be the professional.
4. It may make sense to delay a detailed discussion of severance package—salary, vacation, benefits—until the person has had a chance to digest what has happened. But when these are explained, be sure to go into some detail and be sure you are "heard." This discussion should be supplemented by a written summary for the individual.
5. Severance pay is better than notice for a number of reasons, not the least of which is that it gets the individual out into the job market and busy immediately. This should also help prevent any undue disruptions with his former co-workers who remain.
6. Make sure that the individual understands that he was not "fired" (remove that word from your vocabulary), but that he was a victim of circumstance. Some people stay, some people go in a cost reduction.
   a) Unless you have a number of poor performers, it is extremely difficult to select those to be terminated. Seven criteria may be helpful, however:
      1) The employee's discipline
      2) Program on which the employee works
      3) Performance appraisal

4) Potential appraisal
5) Specific expertise
6) Experience in general
7) Overall capability.[2]

10.5 THE ENCOUNTER WITH THE BOSS

Now that the basic decisions have been made and a plan has been developed, the face-to-face encounters begin. The first of these is the discussion with the "boss," which is hardly ever satisfactory because he is uncomfortable and wants to get it over with, and the employee is upset and hears only that he doesn't have a job any longer. But facts are facts, and they must be accepted because these decisions are seldom irrevocable. The facts are: a business decision has been made and it really isn't a question of whether anyone likes it or not; the employee is a victim of circumstance and must realize the situation; people lose jobs every day, so it's not a unique situation. At this time, the displaced employee should be informed of the assistance that is available from the employment function and of the necessity to talk with the personnel function about the details of the severance package, if applicable. This should also relieve some of the pressure on the "boss" by providing a positive aspect to the conversation.

10.6 THE SELF-EVALUATION PHASE

The role of the out-placement representatives starts now, in this first encounter with the individual since he has been officially told that he is being terminated. The remainder of this chapter is directed to that end—the employment function's role *in guiding the "terminee"* in the job hunt.

The first task is to get the terminee to develop an objective, realistic approach—"a change of environment may be the best thing that ever happened." The employee terminated will have to do some self-evaluation in terms of job goals, motivations, type of organization, the industry that they feel most compatible with, and so on. He must understand that this self-evaluation has to be a continuing process as he passes through each phase of his job search; it can't be a one-time thing. He must also under-

[2]Madeline Pollinger, "Companies Aim to Soften Layoff Blow," *Chemical and Engineering News*, July 26, 1971, pp. 12-15.

stand that *he* has to do this; he is the only one who can make the necessary decisions.

Because all human beings are different, it is difficult to spell out the specifics of how best to do this self-evaluation, but the following ideas should provide a good point of departure for you in guiding them.

1. *Get them in the right frame of mind about the organization and their ex-boss.* Regardless of how they feel about what's happened, it's happened, and they have *no* choice but to be positive about it if they hope to find a job in a reasonable period of time. Remind them that when they start interviewing, most interviewers can spot "sour grapes" quite easily from a tone of voice or a facial expression. Any degree of negativism about a past employer is not taken favorably. It is just another negative factor in a negative process. Because the most recent work experience is generally the most important to the prospective employer, it must be portrayed as a positive situation. If anyone is negative about an organization, he is in a sense demeaning his experience there. Get them to think in terms of "the job was always considered a base for a bigger, better job, and this merely accelerated the time schedule."
2. *Get them in the right frame of mind about themselves.* Their frame of mind will only be as good as their reflectiveness. Get them to think! What really has happened? They must look for a new job just as positively as if they were happy and secure in the job and were approached by a third party to explore another opportunity. Don't let them consider any compromise; get them to think positive! "I know I'm good, and I know what I'm worth; I can sell that!" To help them gain a better perspective of themselves, have them think through the following; it may be the first time they have considered these factors objectively.
   a) *Where should I be heading?*
      1) Should I stay in the same industry?
      2) Should I look into new fields?
      3) What kind of an organization do I really like?
      4) Where do I think I want to be five or ten years from now?
      5) What do I want in a job? Security, less pressures, *or* a fast track and tough competition?

6) What really is my goal?

7) Has my previous experience helped develop the tools to achieve those goals?

8) What does my family want? What do they see as the goal in all this? (Don't let them underestimate the wife's input; she may be in a better position to see the "forest," while they see only the trees.)

3. *Get them to take a long, hard look at themselves.*

   a) You know you're good, but what do other people think?

   b) Were you cooperative? Sensitive?

   c) Were you known as a "hard-nose"?

   d) Are you a big company man, or would you be better in a smaller, less structured organization?

   e) What makes you run? What turns you off, and what turns you on?

   f) Did the ends always justify the means?

   g) What are your strengths and weaknesses?

4. *Get them to take stock of their finances*:

   a) to help adjust the family to what is in all probability a new situation for them

   b) to determine what flexibility they have in job-hunting in terms of time so they can set realistic objectives without panic

   c) to better prepare for negotiating when they develop an interesting job situation.

Finances are not a subject that most people wish to discuss with someone else, but it may be worthwhile to pass along some helpful suggestions. First, don't hesitate to register for unemployment compensation. Granted, this is not going to provide a great amount of income, but it will help. Second, bills and mortgages may be the most immediate problems; however, a direct approach with creditors usually results in a reasonable compromise. Most creditors will be amenable to working out some type of partial payment plan if the individual takes the initiative. Third, don't let them neglect their health and life insurance. If your organization's plan provides coverage for a specified number of days, fine, but then be sure that they have continuing coverage on their own.

As they do this self-evaluative thinking, get them to begin to condition themselves to one level higher than their usual aggressiveness. They will probably have more competition in this "job hunting" than in any job they have ever had, and they must do it better than any job they have ever had. Get them into an aggressive frame of mind.

To most effectively accomplish this very critical self-evaluation, suggest to them that they take a few hours in a quiet place and really think all of these points through thoroughly, honestly, and objectively. This may very well prove to be some of the most productive time they have spent in years. Once they feel confident that they have a realistic evaluation of themselves, they are ready for the initial step of the actual job hunt—references.

10.7 REFERENCES

This is a particularly crucial step in any job hunt. In the final analysis it may make the difference in wrapping up that offer, but so often it is a neglected step, one that seems to be taken for granted. Before you let your terminees do anything else, be sure that they:

1. Decide who their references ought to be. Obviously, these must be people who know not only their *job* capabilities, but also the "compleat" person.
   a) Their ex-boss *has* to be one, regardless of the circumstances.
   b) The higher the level of the references, the better, e.g., a vice-president rather than a department head.
2. Have them ask each of these people if they would be willing to serve as a reference, and establish with them the "party line" (in essence, why they are looking).
3. To provide as much continuity as possible, be sure that each reference knows who the other references are.

Once their interviews begin, and in some instances prior to interviews, they may be asked for their references. (References should not be listed on a resume, and caution them to always try to avoid allowing any contact to be made until some obvious, mutual interest has been established between them and a potential employer.) When asked, they should give the name, title, and business phone number of each reference. Impress on them that once they have identified their references to a potential employer, there is a real advantage in getting back in touch with each reference and letting him know that he will be contacted. Now the terminated employee should tell the reference why the potential employer is of interest to him and the aspects of his background that the potential employer seems to want to pursue further. This accomplishes several things not the least of which is that it helps insure that the reference will give spontaneous and meaningful answers to the questions posed by the person checking references.

In short, there are four key points to tell terminated employees about references:

1. Don't list references on resume
2. When asked, give *name*, *title*, and business phone of each reference
3. Keep references informed of important developments
4. *Be sure* to let them know when you get placed.

10.8 THE RESUME

Developing a resume is a difficult task, primarily because the writer does not really understand *its purpose*. Unfortunately, most people feel that they have real expertise when it comes to writing one, yet how many times does anyone prepare a resume during his career? Nobody is really that expert at preparing a resume, but understanding what it is supposed to do will help you help your terminees prepare a better one than their competition.

The resume has to presell; personality and "chemistry" play no role until the individual gets in the door. Until that point, the prospective employer doesn't know whether the individual is dumb or smart, fat or thin, etc. Thus, the resume becomes an extremely critical piece of paper, one that must have all the "right" information on it so that it will prompt the recipient to want to meet the writer.

Before they begin preparing a resume, have your terminees ask themselves a few questions: What turns you on when you read a resume? What turns you off when you read a resume? What do you look for in a resume? How long a resume do you like?

Before getting into specifics about the format and content of a resume, let's make one point absolutely clear: *the employment process is a negative process*—it's a screening-out process. Although any meaningful selection process provides for an evaluation of both the strengths and weaknesses of an individual, it is human nature for people to start their evaluation of other people in a negative vein. "Why is he looking," "What's wrong with him," is the classical approach to the interview, and even though most people like to think they are completely objective in evaluating other people, they are in reality looking harder for knockouts than they are for the pluses. Don't give "them" any obvious knockouts before there is a chance to sell, and that can only be done face to face.

There are lots of rules about developing a resume, but the basic ones are outlined below and are included in the sample resume format on pp. 262-263.

1. *No* resume needs to be longer than two pages. Realistically, the odds that it will get read in its entirety diminish with each extra page. It just won't be read as objectively if too lengthy.
2. The information included on a resume should be precise and logical. The reader has to be able to form a mental picture of the writer from what is said.
3. The resume should be tailored to highlight particular accomplishments, goals, and desires. Many people prefer to develop several styles of resumes, i.e., a simple biographical sketch, a functional or results-oriented resume, or as shown in the sample resume, a combination of these. If the writer develops several styles, he should set some objectives—determine the purpose of each style. The number of resume styles or variations will be predicated on how specialized the individual's background and experience are.
4. The resume writer should say what needs to be said, but no more. The writer should always be honest and straightforward, but he should *not* volunteer information that could preclude his getting to the face-to-face situation.
5. Unless a logical, meaningful objective can be developed, the writer shouldn't bother; the organization might not be looking for "one of you today," even though other jobs might be available. In other words a statement of objective that is too specific may preclude the individual's consideration for other jobs within the organization.
6. Job descriptions should be built on strengths and accomplishments. A mere *job title* will not sell; moreover it may have an entirely different connotation in another organization. Therefore, the job

responsibilities should be spelled out, particularly supervisory and budgetary responsibility, accomplishments, and results. By emphasizing the unique and innovative aspects of his previous job, the resume writer tells the potential employer what makes him better than the next candidate.

7. The don'ts of resume writing are:
   a) Don't use a picture
   b) Don't state salary
   c) Don't try to explain each job change
   d) Don't state race
   e) Don't put birthdate on unless under 40 years of age.

There are probably many more, but these are the most crucial. Remember, *employment is a negative process*!

The sample resume that follows incorporates all of these thoughts. Use the resume as a point of departure, but remember, resumes are very personal things, and it is very difficult for one person to correctly characterize another, particularly about accomplishments. Before you read the sample resume, however, one more caution: *don't* let anyone try to write his finished resume on the first draft. Have him write it out in long hand, with no concern about length; just get all the details down so that nothing is overlooked. Then review it with him and condense it to a maximum of two pages.

10.9 SOURCES

Hopefully, you have by now helped the terminee develop a positive frame of mind: he knows what he wants to do, he has his references in order, and his resume is complete. Your task now is to get him to organize his potential job sources. To do this intelligently, he must understand each source; he must forget the generalizations and prejudices that he may have developed over the years about blind ads, employment agencies, or whatever. If he is to be successful in any reasonable period of time, he will have to utilize *all* the sources available to him *at least initially*, until he can determine where his best results are coming from. At that point, he can begin to set priorities and better pinpoint his efforts, but *not* until they have all been tried. Since sources were covered in some detail in Chapter

4, the discussion here will be centered on the terminee's use of sources. The cardinal rule here is that anything that can possibly be productive should be utilized by the terminee.

In discussing sources with the terminee, be sure and indicate that there is no particular order of priority for productivity. Every job hunter's situation is unique, and job leads can come at any time, from any source.

Friends and Associates

A job hunter's friends and associates, one of the prime sources available to him, are rarely utilized properly. A major obstacle to the effective "use" of friends and associates is the individual's ego; no one really likes to admit to someone else that he is looking for a job involuntarily. This, of course, is ridiculous, because almost without exception, everyone he contacts will be sympathetic and responsive and will try to be helpful.

As the first step, get your terminee to sit down and make a list of his friends and associates who can possibly be helpful (these should, obviously, be people whom he knows well professionally and with whom he has a reasonable level of rapport). These might be people in the organization, people in other organizations, people met at business meetings, people known at school. This list will grow as the terminee gets further along in his job search, so he must keep thinking every day, "Who do I know who can be helpful?"

One can't be hesitant or bashful with this source. Each person on the list must be contacted and told "I've got a problem." And even though these contacts don't have anything specific to offer at that precise moment, at least they have now been alerted to the problem. This source, more than any other, will tend to snowball; the terminee tells them, they tell someone else, and on and on. "*Use them*," e.g., "We don't have anything here, Charlie, but I hear from Fred Green over at ABC Corporation that they are very actively looking for accountants." The terminee should not let it stop there; he should not let him off the hook. He should ask him if he will make the contact with Fred Green at ABC; this will open the door more quickly because it will constitute an endorsement in Fred's eyes. If Charlie can't make the call, he may be willing to let the terminee use his name, which is also a form of endorsement.

The initiative for follow-up obviously rests with the job hunter, who must understand that once a contact is initiated, it is *his problem* to make the most of it. He mustn't sit back and wait for good old Bill to do what

PERSONAL

Donald J. Green	Married, 3 children
42 Wildwood Way	Excellent health
Charlotte, North Carolina	Born March 8, 1932
Home Phone: 702-333-1279	Office Phone: 702-231-0422

EDUCATION

U. of Maryland, College Park, Md.	-	BS Marketing 1956
U. of No. Carolina, Charlotte, N.C.	-	30 hours towards MBA
IBM Corporation, White Plains, N.Y.	-	7-week course in EDP

OBJECTIVE

To achieve a more responsible position in the marketing organization of a major company, with the potential to move into general management.

LOCATION

No restrictions

WORK EXPERIENCE

1966 to Present - Coleon Plastics Corporation, Charlotte, N.C.

May 1968 to Present - Corporate Marketing Manager

Responsible for marketing efforts of this engineering plastics manufacturer, including market research, product planning, advertising and sales promotion, field sales, and product service. Report to VP Marketing and supervise 25 people, most of whom are technically trained. The business has grown 25% during this period (12 to 16 million) while maintaining an operating budget of 1.2 million. 44% of total sales were from products four years old or less. Developed unique system for IBM 360 to analyze market research and planning data.

February 1966 to May 1968 - Regional Sales Manager, Baltimore, Md.

Responsible for sales of highly technical line of engineering plastic products for vibration and noise control. Recruited, trained, and supervised six Sales Engineers in six-state region. Personally sold the power lawn mower industry on the concept of "Quiet Mower Motors."

1963 to 1966 - ABC Textile Company, Bowie, Md.

January 1964 to February 1966 - Sales Manager, Shelby, N.C.

Responsible for sales in North and South Carolina for this diversified textile firm. Doubled sales in this new territory during the first year and doubled again in second year (gross sales last 12 months, 2.5 million). Supervised 2 salesmen.

January 1963 to January 1964 - Market Research Analyst, Bowie, Md.

Performed necessary market research to set up sales territories for expanding sales organization.

1960 to 1963 - Jones and Brown Textiles, Washington, D.C.

Various jobs in manufacturing and production control. Ultimately responsible for material control, production scheduling, planning, and time analysis for 950-man textile plant.

MILITARY SERVICE

U.S. Navy - August 1956 to June 1960 - Gunnery Officer on destroyer (U.S.S. Evans). No reserve obligation.

OUTSIDE ACTIVITIES

Program Committee - SPE
Member - Chemical Specialties Manufacturing Association
Director - Charlotte Chamber of Commerce

PUBLICATIONS

"The Future for Engineering Plastics in 2 Cycle Engines," Plastic World, April 1966

"A New Approach to Market Analysis," Harvard Business Review, November 1967

References furnished upon request.

he said he would; he must bug him in a nice way until he does something. If Bill just won't cooperate, he should be crossed off of the terminee's list of "useful" friends and associates.

Organizations of Interest

Just as he made his list of friends and associates, now have the terminee make a list of organizations that, for one reason or another, are of interest to him. When this list is completed, have him review it against the friends and associates being contacted to be sure that any possible personal contact in the list of organizations is not being overlooked.

The odds are, however, that there will be a number of organizations that he will have to approach on a direct contact basis (the "cold contact"). The cold contact should be by letter, although some people would disagree and recommend using the phone as the primary contact. That approach would seem to leave something to be desired; its possible that the terminee's call may come at an inconvenient time, and even if he is able to get through to the right person at the right time, he will almost invariably be asked to forward a resume. So to avoid any immediate negative reaction, the terminee should be encouraged to write! Be sure to get the point across to your terminees that there is a frightening sameness to this type of letter. Since this is a key method for opening the door, it certainly deserves as much attention as any other business letter would. They should be told to avoid the "form letter," e.g., "Dear Sir, I am an accountant, and I know how to add and subtract and keep the books. I am looking for a job. . ."

Your terminees can gain an important competitive edge by considering three points before writing to any organization.

1. Why are they really interested in the organization? This will be the key in determining what they say. Then, they must tailor their words and slant their skills and accomplishments to the *specific* problem or needs of the organization insofar as they can be identified.
2. Identify the key functional person in the organization as related to interests and background. The terminee should write to him, being sure to use his correct title. Regardless of what the terminee may have heard, he should not write to the presidents of big organizations, who are not paid to read employment inquiries. (Source information on organizations and individuals in them is available in a miscellany of publications, e.g., *Standard and Poors*, *Dun and Bradstreet Million*

Dollar Directory, Reference Book of Corporate Management, American Men of Science, Who's Who, Moody's, etc.) More detailed information on letters is given on p. 269.

3. The terminee should be sure that all letters are individually typed, a professional touch that the competition usually overlooks. Nothing is quite so unprofessional as a mimeographed letter with a long-hand salutation. The terminee may even want to consider the possibility of utilizing a professional typing service: it may be well worth the cost.

Advertising

To properly utilize this source, people have to "unlearn" any misconceptions they may have about ads and media. They should be prepared to answer any ad that is of interest and is in line with their experience and background. Blind ads should pose no problem now; they are looking for a job, so all the stops are out. They should follow all the appropriate media for their industry and/or functional area, e.g., *Chemical and Engineering News*; *Electronic News*; *Machine Design*. Absolute *musts* are the Sunday *New York Times* ("Business and Finance" as well as "Classified" sections) and the *Wall Street Journal*. Obviously, they should follow any media that covers a particular geographic area of interest to them (basically, out-of-town newspapers, which allow up-to-date access to even remote labor markets). As in every other aspect of job hunting, there are some tricks of the trade to gaining the fullest utilization from this source, so have your terminees give some consideration to the following suggestions before they respond to an advertisement:

1. *Read the ad several times.* Try to figure out what the organization placing the ad is really looking for. Ads are run to find someone to solve a problem, so before responding to the ad, try to identify the organization's problem. Read past the title and salary that headline the ad.
2. *Follow instructions* in the ad; if it says to include salary history, include salary history; use address exactly as stated in ad. (Don't try to bypass the personnel function here. If it says to reply to Mr. J. Brown, Employment Manager, follow the instructions.)
3. Don't necessarily feel that a response must be mailed on the day the ad is run. It is usually better to avoid having your response arrive with everyone else's. No job gets filled that fast, and once the crush is over, your response may get a much more objective screening.

Employment Agencies and Executive-Search Firms

"Third parties" are invaluable to the job hunter if he understands how to use them correctly. The employment function can play a critical role here by supplying the contacts and exerting some leverage with these firms. The problem is that most people know a dozen or so of these firms or have a friend who has a handy-dandy list of several hundred firms that they will suggest the terminee write to. Logically, however, this tactic doesn't make sense because there are good firms and bad firms; some firms handle jobs only in certain salary ranges; and some handle only certain disciplines. The problem is to sift out the ones that potentially can be helpful and get maximum mileage out of them.

Chapter 4, "Manpower Sources," explored the whys and wherefores of third parties in some detail, so here we will say only that the real key to understanding third parties is to understand how they are paid for their services. An employment agency does not get any money until it places a candidate in a job; the agency works on contingency. In *almost* all cases, the agency's fee is paid by the hiring company; however, most states have laws stipulating that applicants sign a contract agreeing to pay the fee if the hiring organization does not. If the terminee does not wish to pay a fee, he must make it perfectly clear to the agency at the outset that unless there are unusual extenuating circumstances, only "fee paid" jobs are acceptable. Within reason, no one should have to pay anyone any money to help him find a job. This is a particularly important point in light of the proliferation of the so-called job or career counselors. These firms charge a fee for doing what nearly any individual can do just as well and in most cases, better, utilizing the thoughts in this chapter and some common sense.

Because it works on *contingency*, the employment agency will make only as much effort for an individual as it sees fit—in other words, based on its feeling about what the potential payoff might be for those efforts. As with other job sources, the most effective utilization of this one is an introduction (endorsement) that will open the door and also give the agency the confidence that investing its time will be worthwhile. As your people should do in all other phases of their job hunt, be sure that they play it "straight and above board" with these agency contacts. They must level with them and keep them informed. Don't allow them to play any games that will compromise you in your other dealings with the agency. Even though your efforts may be primarily in out-placing now, the day will come when you will again need these agencies as a source for new hires.

If the employment agency is misunderstood by the job hunter, the *executive-search firm* is probably even more so. True executive-search firms work only as consultants (get paid for their time which is spent on specific assignments). *They do not do contingency work.* This can be a good source for the individual making over $25,000 a year, but generally speaking, it is of little value for people below that level. Also, this source can be of value only if approached correctly; because these firms work only on assignment, they are generally reluctant to spend time with just anyone who wanders in. The odds are slim that a person just happening along will be a "fit" on a current assignment.

Even though the search firms generally don't like to be tagged with a specialty, many of them, either because of the nature of their on-going clients or the general type of work they do, become specialized. So, to effectively use this source, the terminee must sort out these firms to avoid approaching those that would have no interest in his specialty. As a general rule, the active job seeker is a little suspect to them anyway, because their efforts are geared to identifying the person who is happily employed—the attractive candidate. So taking those things into consideration, the terminee must have an entree—an introduction (endorsement). Also, any of these firms that have done or are doing business with your organization will usually not talk with anyone about leaving without first getting clearance. This will make an introduction by the employment function almost mandatory.

Even though the odds are slim that the timing is right for a particular background to fit a specific search that may be in progress, it never hurts to try to get your terminee's face and resume before some of these firms for future reference or for any ideas they may have about his job-hunting campaign. This may even strengthen your working relationship with the firm.

Banks, Consultants, Public-Accounting Firms, and Construction Firms

These are all productive sources, but they are often overlooked. Banks with their innumerable business contacts, are usually responsive to most aspects of a potential or current customer's business needs which, in many cases, means people. They will be aware of potential job situations and are more than willing to make a referral to help a customer. The consulting firms, such as McKinsey, Arthur D. Little, etc., (as distinguished from the executive-search consultants) are involved with a variety of clients at any given time. Although they generally do not get paid to refer people, it is obviously advantageous to them to be able to refer good ones as the situation arises in line with whatever they are doing for the client.

Some of the public-accounting firms have gone into the "people" business and are therefore a logical source to tap. Regardless of that, these firms are a good source because they are also very client-oriented.

Last, and seldom thought of, are engineering construction or industrial construction firms, which also have a strong client/customer orientation as well as an "ear to the ground" in terms of where the action is. All four of these sources are most productive when an introduction is made—use your personal contacts.

Miscellaneous Sources

There are other potential job sources that need to be mentioned, but they generally do not prove as productive as the ones discussed previously. They can, for the most part, be utilized with very little effort and should be, at least initially.

Position-Wanted Ads

These ads can be found in the appropriate trade publications or newspapers, e.g., the *Wall Street Journal.* A typical ad might state: "Engineer with outstanding skills in technical sales has proven record for getting results, experience in recruiting and training technical salesmen, budgets, forecasting, etc. For detailed resume, write Box #499." This will cost the job seeker some money, but the ad can provide some good exposure that other sources might not.

Alumni-Placement Offices

A number of schools now have active programs. These offices function basically as a clearing house for matching job-seeking alumni to the needs of interested organizations. Although most alumni-placement offices are not well supported either financially or with staff, the terminee should not overlook this source. It only costs a postage stamp and a copy of his resume.

Technical Society Placement Services

Almost all technical societies now have some type of employment register with no usage charge for members. One of the best known is the American Chemical Society (ACS) clearing house, which operates via regular mailings to organizations, ads in society publications, or arranging interviews at society meetings. The purpose of this service is to assist members in making job contacts. Ther terminee should be encouraged to invest a postage stamp and a copy of his resume.

Job Banks

In recent years, a number of these systems have been developed and have received wide publicity. In return for a small fee ranging from roughly $5 to $50, an individual may have his credentials entered into a computerized job bank for a specified period of time (usually one year). The job-bank then contracts with client organizations to utilize the inputs in the bank for the purpose of matching their individuals to job requirements.

These are the major, and probably the most productive, sources available to the job hunter. It would be difficult to establish a rank order, not only because each individual's situation is different, but also because time can be so critical in terms of both the individual's needs and the utilization of some of these sources. So, use them all, and let initial results be the determining factor in setting priorities.

10.10 LETTERS

A variety of letters will be needed as the job hunt progresses, the critical one being the "cold" letter to a specific organization or in response to an advertisement. These letters, by necessity, should always be highly individualized and personal, as well as professional and businesslike—a tall order. Don't let your terminees be satisfied with any letter that wouldn't meet their own business standards. These letters should be a topical, condensed version of the individual, whereas his resume is chronological and in some detail.

To repeat, the terminee's primary consideration must be to tailor the letter to the specifics of the situation; if responding to an ad, he should read the ad thoroughly and highlight that phase of his experience and skills that would best appear to solve the problem posed. When writing an organization, he should find out something about it. What are its product lines? What problems do they have? What are their new businesses? The job hunter should use source books, annual reports, and stockbrokers, to determine some of these specifics, then tailor his response to these specifics and highlight his background and experience in relation to them. In other words, he has to say in his own style, "Here I am; I am interested in you and can help you for this specific reason(s). If you are interested in me, let me know." That sounds simple, but there is a very fine line between a good and bad "employment inquiry" letter, and the competition usually will not take the time or thought necessary to write a good letter. In preparing better letters than the competition's, the job hunter should keep in mind some particularly pertinent do's and don'ts.

1. Keep it *concise yet factual*—not more than two-thirds of a page long. Refer to the resume which will be enclosed. (This is a controversial point, but if you don't provide a resume, the burden is on the organization to come back and ask for one; remember, it's a negative process.)
2. When writing, the terminee should *put himself in the organization's shoes* and write accordingly. What does he think the organization would like to know about him?
3. This letter *should not repeat what's in the resume*; the letter should be used to make the recipient want to read the resume. But nonetheless, the letter should stress accomplishments and results.
4. The salary question may be posed in an advertisement, but the applicant *should not be any more specific* than he has to. Until some mutuality of interest is established, this is a difficult point and may cause a knockout before any face-to-face meeting takes place. The applicant might say, "I am currently making $21,000 plus bonus, but my requirements are open"; "My current income is in the low 20's, and my requirements are flexible"; "My salary requirements are in the $25-30,000 range."
5. If there is any specific contact information, it should be spelled out here, e.g., times available, phone numbers, alternate addresses.
6. The letter should be addressed to a specific person by name and title.
7. Too often, this type of letter only tells the potential employer just what he already assumes. "You are an accountant and thus can add and subtract and keep the books." What the job hunter must tell him is what he *doesn't assume*. What makes this person better than the next accountant who inquires?

In this letter campaign, initially anyway, the job seeker should not hesitate to "overdo it"; he should send out a number of letters. Although this is not necessarily the best source, some broad coverage here may have some of the snowball effect that the job seeker's personal contacts do. However, this should still be done on a reasonably selective basis, and there must be a reason for writing the letters—what, based on his accomplishments, can the job hunter do for the organization?

The job seeker should not try to be cute. He should sell, but he should not oversell. He should make his point and stop. He is only presenting some cold facts. The selling takes place after the door is opened.

10.11 INTERVIEW AND FOLLOW-UP

As various contacts are made, impress on your terminees that they must follow up aggressively—they have to take the initiative! When Acme Recruiting Associates responds to their initial inquiry with the "we don't have an open position with one of our clients" letter, be sure that they check back with Acme in a couple of weeks. Job orders can change overnight, as can the job picture in any organization. Be sure and have them follow up any and all concrete leads and invitations to talk, even though they may not have a great deal of initial interest, for example, in the geography of a particular situation. Until it has been explored, who knows how interesting it may or may not be. Every interview that is suggested at the beginning of the job hunt should be taken, because this is an opportunity for the job hunter to learn by exposure and practice, and this will pay dividends later even if they are all of no interest. This point is particularly pertinent in terms of the executive-search firms and employment agencies; if they want to talk with your people, be sure they do it. They can help your people a lot better and may provide worthwhile counsel, but only if they get face to face. Remember, you have the people with the problem; they are looking for a job!

Before your terminees get involved in the interview process, there are many things for them to think about. A particular danger here may well be that because they have interviewed people in their previous positions, they will assume that they know how to be an interviewee. Nothing could be farther from the truth, because they should never forget that the interviewer is in command; they may have to learn all over how to be the "respondee." Some of the more critical aspects of being the interviewee are outlined below and should be passed along to your terminees. These are not necessarily all of the things that should be considered by your terminees, but they should provide a point of departure.

1. Job hunters must remember that they are going through a negative process. The interviewer is going to try to find out what's wrong—reasons not to hire. They must be straightforward and honest (if they tell the truth, they don't have to remember what they said). If

they don't know the answer to a question, they should admit it rather than trying to fake it.

2. They should try to put themselves in the interviewer's shoes—what will he want to know? How will he try to get the information?
3. They have to get the best fix on what kind of person is trying to hire them. Is he conservative? Is he sensitive? How does he match their personality? How does he compare with previous bosses?
4. Is the job a meaningful one? Will it allow them to really do the things they want, and will they be able to get the support to do it?
5. Who are some of the other people they will be working with? In all probability, they will have more contact with them than they might have with their boss.
    a) They should be sure to meet those people—not just the person they would work for, but also people above, people at peer level and those who work in other functions.
6. Salary discussions, which are always a very individual thing, unfortunately in most cases enter into the interview structure before any mutuality of interest has been established.
    a) The job seeker should try to generalize as much as possible if questioned before mutual interest has been established, e.g., "I'm thinking in terms of $23,000, but I'm flexible, and when you get a better fix on me and I get a better fix on the job, we can get more specific."
    b) They must let the interviewer know they are flexible in terms of the job geography and compensation, but they should not consider a lateral move or less money unless there are unusual extenuating circumstances.
7. *They must be sure to ask questions.* They need to check out the potential employer through acquaintances, *Dun & Bradstreet*, etc., as thoroughly as they are being checked through interviews and references. The job seeker should *always remember* that a "good boss" would not hire someone who didn't want to know as much about him as he does about the applicant.
8. They should be prepared for the classical questions about their:
    a) Strengths and weaknesses

b) Objectives for the next five to ten years

c) Motivations

d) Reasons for leaving their present job

e) Ability to assimilate rapidly so as to become a contributor to the new employer

f) Qualifications for doing the job

g) Management ability and examples to support their claims.

Remember, the job seeker is not just looking for a job; he wants to find the right one. Your responsibility is to help him figure out what he has to offer and how it can be applied to help both himself and his prospective employer.

Have them do a critique after finishing any interview. Sit down with them and think it through—question by question and response by response. What didn't they handle well? Where could they have elaborated more? What did they learn that will help in the next one? Did they ask good (pertinent) questions? This can be a most valuable exercise, and they can count on the fact that the interviewing organization having done this kind of an evaluation and being prepared to zero in on any apparent weak areas if there are further interviews.

If they felt the interview went well have them drop a note to the key interviewer, a courtesy that most people ignore. For example, "I appreciated the opportunity to explore the possibility of a situation with you (or be more specific if feasible). I was impressed with what I saw and heard and am interested in exploring it further if you are..."

Remember, the interview is the culmination of all their efforts and your help to this point, so be sure they do it right. Make sure they are being themselves, being honest, and maintaining a positive frame of mind. If at all feasible, discuss each interview with them afterwards and provide appropriate constructive criticism and guidance.

10.12 RECORDS

Be sure that your people keep records of everything they do—contacts, dates, ads answered, copies of letters. As their contacts begin to develop, they will have to know exactly where they stand at any given point in each specific situation. They will have to know what needs to be done and when to follow up. A simple way for them to do this is to set up a looseleaf binder with a section for each source and all the pertinent information relating to it, e.g., employment agencies—name, phone number, address, name of contact, and leads generated (by company name, date interviewed, name of interviewers, results). In addition, they might keep a separate section on interviews, by company name, date, and status as a quick reference point (see pp. 276-277 for sample forms).

The reason for this emphasis on records is important inasmuch as the average job hunter will generate an unforseen amount of activity over a given period of time, and he cannot afford to duplicate his efforts or run the risk of not following up. Good records will allow him to keep things in order and will help ensure full utilization of his most valuable commodity—*time*. Records will also be helpful when he gets located and wants to let *all* of the people who helped him know where he is now located. As the "counselor," these records will be extremely valuable in terms of your evaluating and directing the job hunter's activity.

10.13 THE TIMETABLE

The job-hunting process can be illustrated by showing each of the critical steps to be taken and providing a space for objectives to be set, i.e., dates to accomplish each step (Fig. 10.1). The value of this is that it will make

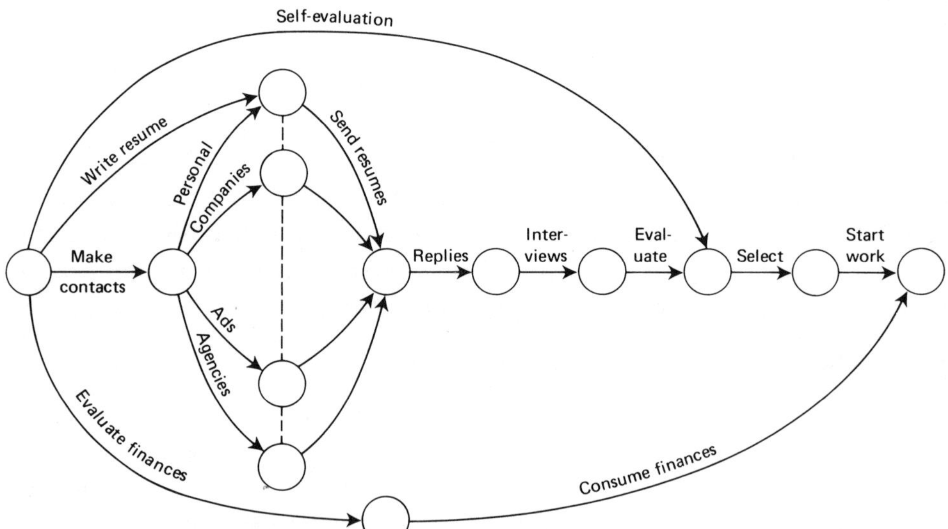

Fig. 10.1. Timetable for job-hunting activities.

your terminees plan and set objectives and keep their total thinking process working. This will also help as they evaluate and re-evaluate each step throughout the process, because new ideas will become apparent every day. This process will also help them remember that job hunting is a full-time job and that they have to work at it as hard and with as much professionalism as they have in any job they have ever had. This is not the time to go off a 40-hour week; there is always something to do! Before you do anything else, be sure to cover all of the points in this chapter with them; then have them set their objectives with this timetable as their guide.

The Job-Hunting Curve

The various phases of job hunting can be illustrated as shown in Fig. 10.2. This figure shows the phases that all job hunters go through, regardless of the level of their job, their salary, or their age. The "job-hunting curve" is simply an inverted bell curve with *A* representing the individual's beginning point in the job hunt. *B* represents the period when he is making contacts and generating leads. *C* represents the time he spends awaiting the results of his activity during phase *B*. *D* is the critical point, because now it will seem that all of his efforts are at a standstill and that he will never find a job. At this low point, the job seeker will begin to think of compromise—less salary, less responsible job, and he now really needs someone to talk to and lean on. (Ideally, this should be you or a friend who has been through a job hunt recently.) *E* represents the beginning of response (interviews) to the activity generated at *B*. *F* is the culmination of all the efforts of *A*, *B*, *C*, *D*, and *E*—job offers and a final decision on the new job.

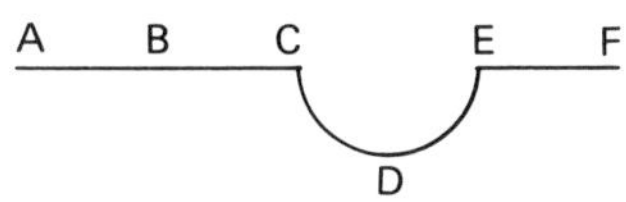

Fig. 10.2. The job-hunting curve.

Everyone who looks for a job must understand that regardless of their personal situation or the circumstances involved, their job hunt will follow this pattern—only the time will vary. They must understand that they will experience many frustrations and disappointments before they are successful, but they must also remember that they are *not* unique by being in this situation, and above all, they must maintain a positive attitude. Job hunting is a lonely and demanding task.

INTERVIEW RECORD

Company Name	Date	Interviewers	Status
ABC 200 Park Ave. N.Y., N.Y.	7/14/72	F. Johnson, Director of Employment E. Thomas, V.P. of Marketing	Indicates definite interest. Have two other people to interview. Will be back to me by 7/25/72.

SOURCE RECORD

Name/contact	Date	Action	Follow-up
Action Personnel Agency, 272 Fifth Ave., N.Y., N.Y. 212-687-0020, Sam Jones	7/10/72	Interviewed by Jones. He will refer resume to ITT and ABC—thinks there is a fit.	To call him on 7/16/72 if I have not heard back.
		Example: Personal Contact	
F.D. Smith, Director of Marketing, WACO Chemical 2 Park Ave., N.Y., N.Y.	7/2/72	Phoned Smith at suggestion of Bernie. He will contact Cyanamid for me—used to be Manager of Marketing, Agricultural Chem.	To call him 7/7/72

10.14 MORE TO TERMINATION THAN MONEY

It should be obvious by now that your organization's acceptance of this type of counseling and assistance is predicated on a number of factors which, unfortunately, cannot always be controlled. However, the two primary factors that will make for success are a belief by the organization that there is more to termination than money and having the expertise in the employment function that will insure acceptance by those being released, regardless of level. There is no question that if an organization is willing to invest the time and money, it can ease the individual's burden when he is terminated. By so doing, the organization will retain a good image on the campus, in the general business community, and in the community at large.

Out-placement should, and will, become an accepted function because even those organizations that do not understand their obligation in this respect will learn that helping people "out" will be particularly critical to their image in today's rapidly changing and more conscience-oriented society. The time and money invested in out-placement will provide, even though it may appear intangible, the greatest return on investment any company could have.

Index